Over & Above

To Mitch

Heartfelt thanks for the eloquent foreword and more than forty years of friendship and inspiration.

Hamish!

Signed: Jack Kelly.

To my wife, Jan.

This book has been very carefully prepared, but no responsibility is taken for the correctness of the information it contains. Neither the author nor the publisher can assume liability for any damages or injuries resulting from information contained in this book.

Jack Kelly

OVER & ABOVE

TRAMPOLINE GYMNASTICS
TOWARDS WORLD CLASS PERFORMANCE

Meyer & Meyer Sport

British Library Cataloguing in Publication Data

A catalogue record for this book is available from the British Library

Over & Above

Maidenhead: Meyer & Meyer Sport (UK) Ltd., 2014

ISBN: 978-1-78255-034-1

All rights reserved, especially the right to copy and distribute, including the translation rights. No part of this work may be reproduced—including by photocopy, microfilm or any other means— processed, stored electronically, copied or distributed in any form whatsoever without the written permission of the publisher.

© 2014 by Meyer & Meyer Sport (UK) Ltd.

Aachen, Auckland, Beirut, Budapest, Cairo, Cape Town, Dubai, Hägendorf,

Indianapolis, Singapore, Sydney, Tehran, Wien

Member of the World Sport Publishers' Association (WSPA)

Printed by: B.O.S.S Druck und Medien GmbH, Germany

ISBN: 978-1-78255-034-1

E-Mail: info@m-m-sports.com

www.m-m-sports.com

CONTENTS

FOREWORD 8

HOW TO USE THIS BOOK 10

SECTION ONE: SERVING THE APPRENTICESHIP 13

Chapter 1: READ BETWEEN THE LINES 13

Chapter 2: TRAMPOLINING … WHAT'S THAT? 17

Chapter 3: BITTEN BY THE BUG 23

Chapter 4: A REALITY CHECK! 35

Chapter 5: RADICAL RE-THINK 41

Chapter 6: MAKING IT HAPPEN 49

Chapter 7: GETTING MY ACT TOGETHER 57

Chapter 8: SEEING THE BIGGER PICTURE 61

Chapter 9: NEW CHALLENGE 67

Chapter 10: STARTING THE PROCESS 71

SECTION TWO: TECHNICAL CONCEPTS 75

Chapter 11: THE TECHNIQUE/EQUIPMENT RELATIONSHIP 75

Chapter 12: TRAMPOLINING IS TOO EASY! 83

Over & Above

Chapter 13: WHEN IS 'THE TAKE-OFF' NOT 'THE TAKE-OFF'? 87

Chapter 14: EVERY TAKE-OFF IS SIMPLY A MODIFIED STRAIGHT JUMP 93

SECTION THREE: TECHNICAL APPLICATION 99

Chapter 15: THE STRAIGHT JUMP 99

Chapter 16: THE PERFORMANCE CHIMNEY 119

Chapter 17: TUNE IN TO TEMPO 133

Chapter 18: ARM SETTING 141

Chapter 19: THINKING ABOUT LINKING 149

Chapter 20: TRAINING TO INCREASE TIME OF FLIGHT 165

Chapter 21: THE TWIST IS THE EASY BIT! 171

Chapter 22: DEVELOPING A TRAINING "GPS" TO IMPROVE COMPETITION PERFORMANCE 183

Contents

SECTION FOUR: MAXIMIZING POTENTIAL 191

Chapter 23: GETTING THE BIGGEST BANG FOR YOUR BUCK! 191

Chapter 24: THE TRAMPOLINE "TALENT PACKAGE" 205

Chapter 25: PRINCIPLES OF FITNESS TRAINING FOR TRAMPOLINE 215

Chapter 26: COACH LIKE A COACH, NOT LIKE A JUDGE 233

Chapter 27: READINESS 239

Chapter 28: PREPARING TO COMPETE 245

Chapter 29: USING SWOT ANALYSIS AS A PLANNING TOOL 255

Chapter 30: INTRODUCING DAVE ROSS 261

Chapter 31: LOST AND FOUND! 267

Chapter 32: THE THIRTY ESSENTIAL PRINCIPLES 285

Chapter 33: CONCLUSION 297

REFERENCES 298

ACKNOWLEDGEMENTS 299

CREDITS 301

Over & Above

FOREWORD

In passing on the fruits of a lifetime career in his sport, Jack Kelly has made a gift of *his* gift – the ability to translate astute clinical observation into clear practical messages. His is a rare quality indeed; the capacity to elevate the science of coaching into an art form by blending technical knowledge with effective and compassionate delivery. Jack is a true exponent of the "Craft of Coaching," and his credentials are impeccable.

When I first met Jack, his love affair with trampolining had hardly begun. He cut an imposing figure amongst a motley array of enthusiastic kids and aspiring coaches, all looking to him for guidance and inspiration – and all unaware, as far as I know, that he was only a pace or two in front of them in terms of exact technical knowledge. Jack's honesty regarding this is disarming and typical of him. However, given his own impressive sporting pedigree and determination to find something more reliable than the "chuck it and see" mentality that prevailed in some quarters, it was obvious to anyone who encountered him in those days that here was a potential innovator, a pioneer who would leave an indelible mark on his chosen sport. It would just be a matter of time. Jack set about the task of learning his trade, visiting the established citadels of the sport and objectively sifting through the advice and information gleaned – some rejected, some retained, but all of it weighed. What set him apart even in the early days – and I suspect it is so even now – was a willingness to listen and learn. During those formative years, I watched as he built a system that laid foundations for inevitable success, based upon sound fundamentals and a tireless attention to preparation and detail.

Our technical collaboration came from a joint appreciation of the importance of physical conditioning and the acquisition of transferrable gymnastic skills – areas that broke new ground in the discipline of trampolining. This was the Apex-Harlow period, which helped us develop an approach to coaching that would last a lifetime. The methodology was grounded in profound trust in biomechanical truths and the value of physical readiness, alongside the analysis of sequential movement, and the isolation and perfection of the essential components of a particular skill.

Foreword

Nearly fifty years later, Jack's energy has not waned in the slightest. He is as keen as ever to pass on his knowledge and experience to today's and tomorrow's coaches. I am certain those who read the pages that follow will have their appetites whetted to join the ranks of his many followers. Jack Kelly could without a doubt have made his mark as a coach in any number of sports, and it is to our lasting benefit that he chose trampolining.

I am immensely honored to have been afforded this opportunity to preface Jack's long awaited literary legacy, a work that not only addresses technical and methodological issues but reveals more than a hint of his remarkable insight. A man who has produced world champions and who has earned the respect of the world's most successful coaches — someone I am proud to call a friend.

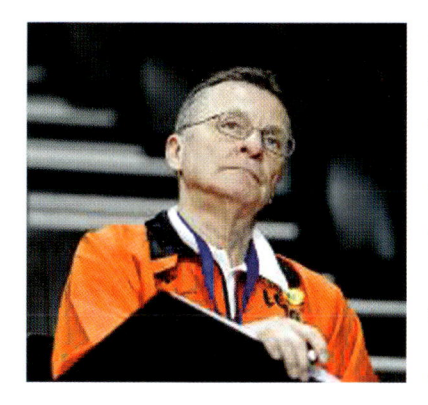

Mitch Fenner
British Gymnastics Honorary National Coach
& Master Coach

Head Coach and Director of Elite Coaching
KNGU (Netherlands) Male Artistic Gymnastics

Gymnastics Commentator for BBC and FIG.

Mitch Fenner

Over & Above

HOW TO USE THIS BOOK

The author working with development coaches in the Netherlands.

In order to obtain the full benefits from this book, it is best to progress logically through the chapters as I have written them. I have, however, set out the information in such a way as to enable the reader to dip in and find useful advice and practice drills relating to the many underlying technical requirements of trampoline gymnastics. It should be borne in mind, however, that some of the advice and recommendations within this volume will be dependent upon the logically argued cases in previous chapters.

The examples of drills, practices and worksheets are just that – examples, and my aim has been to stimulate coaches' imaginations and creativity to develop their own personal variations.

The illustrative drawings are deliberately gender neutral, simplistic and diagrammatic to support the principles outlined in the text. They do not attempt to express the wide range of individual variations. Each individual frame in an illustrated sequence should be seen as part of process rather than a fixed position. Where possible, illustrations are in a vertical format with ascending and descending arrows rather than the often-misleading horizontal style that fails to represent the true directional nature of trampoline gymnastics.

The action photographs of World Class trampoline gymnasts are intended to be inspirational rather than instructional. I have, however, taken the opportunity to associate each one with a key technical principle which is fully described in the text.

How to Use This Book

JACK KELLY: "World Class coaching is not about coaching high difficulty skills, it is about coaching basic technique and applying it to high level performance."

CHAPTER 01

READ BETWEEN THE LINES

SECTION ONE
SERVING THE APPRENTICESHIP

The bibliography of trampoline gymnastics dates back to the 1940s and the birth of the sport. Early volumes describe how to somersault, twist and perform competition routines; however, there have been such advances in equipment design and athlete preparation that many of the early techniques described have become obsolete. Thankfully, the national governing bodies for gymnastics affiliated with the Federation Internationale Gymnastique (FIG) offer coach education programs with supporting literature to describe current approved methods for teaching the sport with safety. Indeed the FIG also has its own coach accreditation program.

So what can this latest book offer that doesn't already exist? The answer lies in the title ... "Over and Above!"

In writing this book, I am unconstrained by a coach education syllabus and can freely share my extensive experience of coaching and managing all levels of this increasingly popular branch of gymnastics. My expertise in developing young gymnasts is well known throughout the trampoline community, and my primary aim is to share my knowledge and experience with coaches and gymnasts aspiring to World Class performance. I hope this volume will satisfy the countless requests I have received over the years to commit my ideas to print. This book outlines

Over & Above

a process for developing world class skill with trampoline gymnasts who are setting out on their competitive journeys, but the methods described have also helped to remodel the technique of numerous advanced performers, enabling them to break through to the next level.

What follows is a compendium of theoretical and practical guidance based on my years of striving for and achieving World Class results. The information and guidance is "over and above" anything previously published, and the application of the principles and methods described should only be undertaken by those appropriately qualified by their national gymnastics governing body.

Readers should not expect detailed information on how to perform multiple somersaults with mind-blowing twist combinations. Instead, the philosophy and process I describe opens the door to the highest possible achievements in both difficulty and execution. I am offering the key to that door!

I recall one definition of education as, "all the influences on a person's life." I have therefore highlighted the most significant of these from my fifty years' education in the sport. The reader has the opportunity to benefit from my knowledge and experience without having to spend fifty years acquiring it. I am starting in biographical mode, not to tell my story like some third-rate celebrity, but to recount some of the experiences that made me into the coach I have become. I once asked an academic colleague why he had never written a book bearing in mind his international standing. He replied,

> *"As soon as you commit your current knowledge to print, it becomes outdated because you continue to learn. I don't want the things I write now, to be regarded as expressing my final views on a subject."*

I can identify with that as I embark on the dangerous path of committing my ideas to print, but believe me, I still learn every day and intend to do so for the rest of my life. But for now, here it is!

Much of what I have learned is spelled out clearly, but as the biography unfolds, there is a great deal to be gained from "reading between the lines."

Read Between the Lines

JACK KELLY: "There is a great amount to be learned from 'reading between the lines.'"

CHAPTER 02

TRAMPOLINING ... WHAT'S THAT?

SECTION ONE
SERVING THE APPRENTICESHIP

Trampoling ... What's That?

"Kelly! All you're good for is chasing round the rugby field after a piece of wind wrapped up in leather!"

Mr. Harold C. Gordon was expressing his frustration at my attempts to grasp the principles of 'O' Level mathematics at Aberdeen Grammar School, where its pupils were expected to excel academically. I was letting the side down! The harshness of his outburst has since been softened by the truth that I was indeed good at rugby as well as many other athletic pursuits at our 700-year-old school. I do however acknowledge that a little more focus on the academic would have been advisable.

That particular memory of school days endures because it was strangely predictive of the direction my career would take over the next fifty years. Although I was selected to represent Scotland Schools and enjoyed considerable success in senior rugby, it soon became clear that 1.7 meters and 67 kilos of muscle and enthusiasm were less than adequate credentials for playing at the international test level.

Three years at the Scottish School of Physical Education in Glasgow, training as a teacher, introduced me to Swedish Gymnastics, which was the basis of secondary school Physical Education during the 1950s. This system had developed out of military drills and featured team exercises performed in unison

Over & Above

— no pupil-centered approach there! At the heart of the program were exercises designed to compensate for the postural deficiencies that came from sitting at a school desk. Strength, flexibility and stamina were key elements, although a range of tumbling and vaulting skills were also featured. It was these latter activities that captured my imagination, and I was thrilled to discover a natural ability to vault, flik flak, and somersault. In addition, my physique was far more suited to these activities, and I began to face the reality that I would never lead my national team out at Murrayfield or Twickenham.

The 18-year-old author discovering "gymnastics" at Physical Education College in 1958 and looking like the somersaulting rugby player he was.

In 1961, I had to join the 'real world' after the joys of Physical Education College and started a teaching career in Aberdeen. At this point, I was totally unaware of the sport that would come to dominate my life, or indeed that it was already popular in many parts of the world, notably the USA, Germany, Switzerland, Holland, South Africa and Australia. It is even more surprising that I didn't know the Scottish Trampoline Association had been founded in 1959 or that Nissen trampolines had been manufactured in Romford Essex since 1956! Many of my younger colleagues in trampolining regard me as a pioneer of the sport and while I welcome the respect this brings, I am no George Nissen.

The late Mr. Nissen, an All-American diver, is credited with constructing the first modern trampoline in 1936. He worked with missionary zeal to develop the activity into a competitive sport that would enter the Sydney Olympic Games in 2000. When

George died at the age of 96 in April 2010, he had witnessed three Olympic trampoline competitions, and it was a moving experience to join the ovation as he was introduced to the audience in the Beijing Olympics Gymnastic Hall.

I don't intend to dwell on the history of trampoline gymnastics but aim simply to establish a context for my own involvement in the sport.

I can't remember when I first became aware of trampolining, but I certainly recall my first practical experiences. These were due to compulsion rather than choice. In 1963, I was appointed Assistant Lecturer in Physical Education at Hull University, where my duties involved training Physical Education teachers as well as assisting with the student recreation program. Prior to taking up my post, I received details of the recreation activities I was to be responsible for. There was nothing I couldn't handle with confidence and competence except ... trampolining. This was quite a challenge for a young man who had never even seen a trampoline, let alone taught others to perform on it. Underlying the apprehension was a sense of excitement and anticipation. As a schoolteacher, hadn't I played the part of the blind leading the blind before, staying one page ahead of the pupils? The strategy was clear — before the start of term, get a book from the library, go into the gym with the apparatus and have a go.

This strategy failed at stage one! Neither the city nor the university library had any books on trampolining, although to my delight and relief, I found a slim American volume with the pretentious title *The Complete Book of Gymnastics*. Three whole pages on trampolining took the unsuspecting reader on a hazardous journey from knee bounce to full twisting back somersault. This foolhardy 24-year-old was up for the trip.

The Nissen Trampoline Company had, by now, designed a range of folding trampolines with various bed sizes and materials, but the university had invested in a unit made by the Lodge Gymnastic Company. Its most distinctive feature was the fact that it was non-folding and had to be tipped up and leaned against the end wall of the gym, introducing a challenging obstacle for those playing basketball or 5-a-side football. Happily, it was just possible to get the trampoline out single-handed, allowing me to start my trampoline career in private. So armed with *The Complete Book of Gymnastics* and a naive bravado, I set about perfecting my knee bounce as a prelude to the more exciting gyrations to follow.

Over & Above

Progress was remarkably quick, with page two taking me through back and front somersaults, aided by the fact that I had performed these skills many times on the floor. Regrettably, the floor was exactly where these first efforts at trampoline somersaulting terminated. Quite clearly I was doing something wrong, but I was beginning to learn that tumbling and trampolining, although possessing similarities, were not quite the same.

Ever resourceful, I decided to relocate the trampoline into a corner of the gym so that one end and one side abutted the walls. What a brilliant idea! There were now only two places where I could fall onto the floor and if things went wrong, I reckoned that hitting the wall was the safer option.

In order to show that I was not alone in my primitive efforts to master the trampoline, let me fast-forward to 1972. In that year, I took the first-ever British team to Poland (still behind the "Iron Curtain"), to compete in a televised four-way international with Czechoslovakia and Bulgaria. The equipment was Russian-made, took a team of eight men to assemble, and had been constructed out of what appeared to be scaffolding poles. The beds were hand-stitched with 9mm webbing and the huge bore metal springs were covered by a patterned curtain material. We took this to be an important safety feature, preventing gymnasts from falling through the springs. We complimented our hosts on this innovation, as we had become used to the Nissen "77A" and "Goliath" trampolines with those genital-threatening gaps between the springs. Our hosts informed us, however, that as the springs were the most expensive part of the trampoline, the curtaining was an attempt to protect the springs, not the gymnast! This disregard for safety was reflected in the crazy, uninhibited performances of our opponents, who had no more regard for their physical well-being than those who had decided to protect springs rather than people.

After the competition, we attended the customary post-event banquet, and I had a chance to speak with Bruno, the Polish coach. He asked me how I started trampolining. I told him about *The Complete Book of Gymnastics* and my irresponsible attempts to teach myself.

"And how about you, Bruno? How did you start?"

Awaiting his reply, I observed his broken nose, cauliflower ear, and the line of stitch marks above his left eye.

"It vos da same vis me, Jack but ... no book!"

Meanwhile, back in 1963, I was confidently teaching the university students everything I knew about trampolining. Little did they know just how little I knew; a case of the partially sighted leading the blind! By my second year in the job, I had become a self-styled expert in trampolining with students of all shapes and sizes projecting themselves skyward with little regard for personal safety. The little safety awareness that did exist had been developed through my own painful learning experiences. Nonetheless, I continued to practice in private, and being isolated from any information source apart from the aforementioned book, I was discovering a brand new range of movement possibilities.

Once I was comfortable with tumbling combinations such as round off/flik flak/back somersault and round off/back somersault, transferring these to the trampoline as barani followed by immediate back somersault was a logical development. Here comes one of my first trampoline "ah-ha" moments: what would happen, I thought, if I performed the barani so high that I could no longer put my feet on the bed and suddenly tucked my legs to my chest? Would I go over twice? I debated this possibility with myself for a couple of weeks, balancing my curiosity against an innate concern for personal safety. I decided I needed to share my idea with a potential guinea pig. Having been a rugby player who would never shirk a tackle, I take no pride in the decision to persuade Hendrik, one of my overseas students, to buy into the hypothesis. Perhaps he would fancy trying it out? He did! He lived! We had just invented the barani-in back-out fliffis.

So what, I hear you say. Back in 1964, trampolinists had been doing much harder skills than that for years. But here is the point — we didn't know that! We were, in effect, replicating what was happening worldwide in this new sport with its limited access to information and its dearth of instructional literature. Divers, gymnasts, and death-wish egotists had been experimenting, just like us, and were coming up with an amazing range of "tricks" or "stunts," as we learned to call them. The sport had been driven by a challenge culture where participants strove to outdo each other without the constraints of formal competition rules. It was a "freestyle" sport. But all that changed with the first British Championships in 1959 and the inaugural World Championships in 1964.

CHAPTER 03

BITTEN BY THE BUG

SECTION ONE
SERVING THE APPRENTICESHIP

Appointed Deputy Manager of Harlow Sportcentre in 1966. The trampoline in the background hints at things to come.

In 1966, I accepted the post of Deputy Manager at Harlow Sportcentre, the first community leisure center in the UK and forerunner to thousands of facilities now commonplace. Although my prime

Over & Above

responsibility was general management and the development of sporting opportunities for young people, coaching and teaching remained my passion. The center had two trampolines that doubled my opportunities and increased my enthusiasm for the sport exponentially. However, that boost was nothing compared to the impression created when the center hosted an England Schools versus German Youth trampoline international (an annual event still being contested). The range of skills and impressive execution on display placed my efforts, as coach and gymnast, firmly in the novice category.

I had never even seen a 10-contact routine, let alone one containing 10 consecutive somersaults. Most competitors performed at least two double somersaults, some with a kind of mid-air twisting motion I couldn't follow. One British gymnast even finished his exercise with a one-and-three-quarter back somersault to stomach and then … a double back from the stomach landing! Wow! I couldn't wait to get back on the gym floor and start work with the group of 15 children I had already selected to start my trampoline club. I had optimistically named it the High Club-Harlow.

The current trampoline coach at the center was a local builder who had discovered the sport while at a seaside holiday camp. As a trained teacher, brought up within the conservative Scottish education system, I was appalled by his colorful language, more suited to a building site than the gymnastics hall. Nonetheless, Fred Wells displayed the first essential quality of anyone aiming for excellence; he loved the sport and had the desire to share his enthusiasm with everyone he taught. Unlike Fred, I had no formal trampoline coaching qualification so, despite setting up the club, I chose to play a supporting role. Together we started building the skills of our chosen group, but little did the parents of these children realize we were effectively experimenting with their cherished offspring.

In order to gain parity with my colorful colleague, I attended a two-week course at the Loughborough Summer School run by a National Coach of the British Trampoline Federation. Syd Aaron was a Senior Lecturer in Physical Education at Cardiff Teacher Training College and an acknowledged authority on the biomechanics of trampolining. His greatest asset, as far as I was concerned, was his conviction in everything he said, this being reinforced with the words, "What I'm saying simply can't be refuted!" I, for one, was not about to refute anything this muscular academic told us, and he became my hero and inspiration. Although the main objective of the course was to train qualified coaches, there were plenty opportunities to perform on trampoline – I wasted no time in picking up a range of new skills. If Syd told me I was ready to go for a move, I went for it, such was my belief in him.

Mentor and role model, the late Syd Aaron MBE, with the author at the Nissen-sponsored Trampoline Safety Conference in London, circa 1970.

On my return to Harlow as a qualified coach, I immediately assumed the lead with our young team. Fred seemed happy dropping into the supporting role, albeit with no dilution of his enthusiasm or indeed his language! The club started raising money for additional trampolines, and gradually our set-up became the envy of other local clubs. One club in particular, the Brook Club from Loughton, already had four members in the senior Great Britain team. We looked up to their coach George Stephens for guidance and inspiration to help us get closer to international standards. Unwittingly, George (or "Steve" as he was known) provided me with my biggest incentive to date. He visited our

Over & Above

club on one occasion and said, "You've got a great set-up Jack, but you'll never beat my guys because you haven't got good enough coaches!" The man was a national coach, and I respected his views … until then. Although outwardly calm and acknowledging his opinion, my inner self was saying, "Oh really? Well you just watch because you ain't seen nothin' yet!"

The High Club-Harlow 1969. Proud coaches Jack Kelly and Fred Wells flanking their first-generation trampolinists. Gymnasts mentioned in the text:

John Beer, Jan Kelly (née Allen), Alan Green, Geraldine Whiffin, Vanessa Smith. Simon Rees, Alan Hay

In the 1960s, being the best trampolinist in Britain meant you were automatically "world class" since British gymnasts had featured in the top five of both men's and women's World Championships from that first global event held in the Royal Albert Hall in 1964. America had dominated and would continue to hold the top spot in both men's and women's events for some time to come. Britain, meanwhile, picked up silver and bronze medals through gymnasts such as Dave Smith, Lynda Ball, David Curtis and Mike Williams. It was not unreasonable that The High Club and its coaches, Jack Kelly and Fred Wells, should dream of long-term international success for their young performers. Despite our contrasting backgrounds and styles of coaching, Fred and I cooperated in the development of our talented group, debriefing after every session to make sure we didn't confuse the gymnasts with conflicting information.

Fred Wells and the author making fools of themselves at an open air display circa 1968. These events raised funds for the club but also created "performance robustness" in the gymnasts, as they delivered their best work outdoors in all types of weather.

We only disagreed seriously on one occasion. Fred had given an interview to the local newspaper and was quoted as saying, "One day a World Trampoline Champion will be born and trained in Harlow!" I was furious with him. How dare he make such an outrageous statement when our senior gymnast was 12 years old and we hadn't even produced a National Age Group Champion?

When Stewart Matthews climbed the World Championship podium in 1980 and Carl Furrer did likewise in 1982, I thought to myself, "Fred, now I forgive you!"

During the initial four years with our first-generation gymnasts, I sought out any source of information that might improve the work of our pupils. Regular "topping up" visits to the Loughborough Summer School were an essential part of my development, with Syd Aaron taking on a guru-like status in my eyes. I dreamt that one day I might have a similar inspirational effect on young up-and-coming coaches and their gymnasts. That is still my motivation!

During these summer schools, I was to meet and become friendly with many prominent and influential individuals within the sport. Of particular note was my close association

Over & Above

with the late Bert Scales, when we studied and worked together to achieve Senior Advanced Coach status. Like me, Bert had a background in Physical Education, and I feel sure he would approve of the philosophy developed throughout this book. His painstaking, holistic development of the talented but temperamental Sue Shotton (later Challis) to become World Champion in 1982 was exemplary. He went on to inspire the next generation of British coaches and gymnasts through his coach education work. Indeed his widow "Biz" Scales, who was one of my National Squad in the 1970s, plays a leading role in delivering high-quality coach education and is a respected international judge.

As the High Club-Harlow gradually became a force within Great Britain, its members winning national age group titles as well as representing their country at youth level, I started to target overseas competition. I will always remember our first competitive experience with Eurotramp trampolines in Stuttgart, Germany. Having been used to the Nissen trampoline from the outset, it was hard to believe that equipment conforming to the same specifications could be so much more powerful. How could "Goliath" frames (in Nissen parlance) and half-inch webbed beds suspended on steel springs be so different? The Eurotramp "Grand Master" with a 13mm webbed bed looked the same, but my gymnasts found themselves embarrassed by the additional airtime it provided. Suddenly, the Harlow gymnasts were over-rotating every skill, and it was disconcerting to watch double somersaults, with and without twist, depositing performers on their backs. Fortunately, this all happened during a training day before the competition, giving me time to contemplate a possible solution.

This potential disaster led me to my second important "ah-ha" moment in the sport. I had heard the Americans speaking about "top" to express the appearance of impressive vertical component with less than normal rotation. Of course, it was obvious! With greater height from the more powerful equipment, the gymnast has more time. Having more time means that the rotational input during take-off can be significantly reduced. With only one training session remaining before the competition, my gymnasts started to get a feel for this unfamiliar concept and the High Club returned to Harlow with a fine collection of trophies.

By the early '70s, the High Club had become the most successful club in the UK. The gymnasts had also distinguished themselves by winning five titles at the first-ever

World Age Group Championships. As knowledge of our achievements spread, the club attracted a number of mature gymnasts who were prepared to seek local employment in order to train within this progressive and competitive environment. Prominent among these was John Beer, a former student of the legendary Syd Aaron who had been converted by Syd from successful diver into a promising trampolinist. I say "promising" because he promised much but rarely delivered a full routine. I recall John expressing his frustration.

"Look at these little kids you're coaching; they can finish routines in competition every time, and yet I can't!"

"John, how many competitions have you taken part in?"

"I don't know for sure, but probably about six."

"Well those little guys have been doing more than that each year for the last three years! You must realize you are still a beginner in this sport."

That conversation started a change of approach that led John Beer to become the most consistent competitor in the country. Whatever the execution score, John could be relied upon to deliver ten complete skills. Several years on, he was to play a different and more significant part in this story.

Over & Above

John Beer training with the High Club at Harlow Sportcentre 1970. Note the bare feet and swimming trunks. This was normal training attire for male trampoline gymnasts in those days.

As standards rose and I perceived the need to devote more hours to coaching and training, Fred Wells decided to reduce his commitment and limit himself to a small but valuable role, coaching adult beginners, several of whom developed into capable coaches. Perhaps I should have seen this reduction in commitment, largely for family reasons as an omen for future events in my own life! But I was "on a roll" and totally committed to the development of World Class performances with my athletes.

Meanwhile, another Syd Aaron product came to work in Harlow. This time the young teacher was an artistic gymnast and coach with ambitions to match my own. Although still competing, Mitch Fenner set about creating a gym club at his school but much of the training took place alongside my trampoline squad at the sports center. It wasn't long before we discovered a mutual movement philosophy, and we decided to merge our two clubs.

Mitch Fenner with some of his Bush Harlow gymnasts.

So the High Club-Harlow and Bush Harlow Gymnastics merged to become Apex-Harlow. All newcomers were exposed to a broad-based movement program before opting to take either the artistic or trampoline gymnastics route. Three of the first under-10-year-

Over & Above

olds to join were Stewart Matthews, Carl Furrer and Alan Hay. Although all displayed some early ability, they were by no means the most naturally talented of the new intake. Despite our mutual respect and cooperation, Mitch loved trying to wind me up.

"All the best trampolinists are just failed gymnasts," he would say. "Look at Dan Millman, Wayne Miller, and even Paul Luxon who gave up gymnastics because he was too stiff!"

Young Alan Hay, having undergone his introductory all-round program, initially opted for trampolining but was clearly third best behind Stewart and Carl. At this point, he "jumped ship" and joined Mitch's artistic squad, going on to win a Daily Mirror Scholarship to train in the Soviet Union before achieving Great Britain international honors as a gymnast. Now it was my turn to do the winding up!

"How is the failed trampolinist getting on Mitch?"

"Failed trampolinist" Alan Hay with Kathy Williams having won the Daily Mirror Scholarship to train in Russia. Alan went on to win senior international gymnastics selection for Great Britain.

Apex members are jumping for joy

APEX club members are jumping for joy, having just leapt into the world-class bracket of trampolining. They returned to Harlow on Friday proudly displaying five gold medals that they had won at the World Age Group championships, held in San Francisco on July 13 and 14.

Carl Furrer, aged 10, and Simon Rees, aged 17, both were triumphant in their individual age group events — and now with their gold medals and "world-champion" titles, they feel that the months of hard training before the championships were well worth all the effort.

The seven members of the trampolining section of Apex brought home a total of eight medals—and the five youngsters who took part in the tumbling events collected three medals between them.

Carl, of 185 Rundells, Harlow, and his partner Stuart Matthews, won the junior boys' title in the synchronised competition.

In the girls' synchronised events, Vanessa Smith, 13, the youngest-ever full British champion, of 88 Brays Mead, Harlow, and Geraldine Whiffen, from Sawbridgeworth, together won the gold medal in the senior girls' title,

Rhona Cotton and Jane Smith gained the gold medal in the junior synchronised event.

As a result of the San Francisco competition Apex can now boast seven world champions in trampolining, and the club also collected two silves and a bronze medal in this section.

Simon Rees collected a second medal when he took the silver in the open event, and Stuart Matthews also came second in the 11-12 year old section. Vanessa Smith, who had high hopes of winning her age group title was compensated by gaining the bronze medal in the 13-14 year event.

In the tumbling events all five competitors reached the finals, and three of them won medals. Gary Smith won a silver in the 14-15 group, Alan Hay came third in the under-12 event, and Gary Thorogood also won a bronze in the under-19 competition.

Pictured right are medal winners at San Francisco : Carl Furrer (front) ; middle row (left to right), Alan Hay, Stuart Matthews, Garry Smith and Geraldine Whiffen ;

Outstanding success for Apex-Harlow tumblers and trampolinists at the 1974 World Age Group Championships in San Francisco.

04
CHAPTER
A REALITY CHECK!

SECTION ONE
SERVING THE APPRENTICESHIP

A Reality Check!

By 1973, Apex-Harlow had begun to build an international reputation and could already boast numerous World Age Group Champions, the star performer being Simon Rees. Simon was a High Club "original," and in 1974 he would become British Men's Champion at 15 years of age. He was already Youth Champion of Europe, and his technique and stylish execution represented everything I had learned about the sport up to that point. At the European Youth Championships, he had attracted the attention of the Soviet coaches who followed all his training and competition performances with notebooks and video cameras. It served to increase my belief that we were on the path to international senior success.

Over & Above

Fourteen-year-old Simon Rees on the victory podium at the first World Age Group Championships in 1973. The following year Simon would become British Senior Men's Champion and European Youth Champion.

When the British senior team was selected for the 1973 European Championships in Edinburgh, Apex provided seven gymnasts out of the 12 strong delegation — eight if you counted my role as national coach. Simon Rees, John Beer, Alan Green, Jane Pullen, Vanessa Smith, Geraldine Whiffin and Janet Allen (now, I am proud to say, Mrs. Jan Kelly) headed north with optimism. My hopes were high that Simon Rees would win our first senior international medal. We expected strong opposition from the German and French teams whom we knew, but we had little information on the Soviets, apart from Simon beating the best of their youth. As we all posed proudly for a press photograph dressed in our Great Britain uniform, Alan Green was heard whispering, "We all won our international badges for trampolining; Jack got his for talking." Nice one Alan — at least we were all smiling when the picture was taken!

I was in for a shock. The Soviet men and women were in a totally different league than us. Their physical preparation gave their gymnasts, what I can only describe as, "hardness" throughout every contact with the bed. This led to impressive height and an appearance of momentary stillness at full depression between each element. I remember well the solid sound of their feet making contact with the bed prior to the delivery of impressive, spring-depressing power. Nonetheless, the Soviet coaches clearly felt they had something to learn from the British, and as coach for the team, I was approached in the training hall by their interpreter:

"You Great Britain coach?"

"Yes"

"Russian coach wishes to speak with you ... ask you some questions."

I meekly followed the speaker across the hall where I was introduced to the Russian coach.

"This is Great Britain coach. Meet Russian coach!"

At this point, I had many questions forming in my mind, not least of which what was his name? I waited patiently for my turn to ask about their program. My questions were totally forgotten as I was grilled about the number of gymnasts in Britain, the age at which they were selected, the hours devoted to training, and the most difficult skills we were working on in training.

After a brief pause, the interpreter said:

"Russian coach thanks you. That will be all."

I turned and started walking back to my team when I realized:

"Damn, damn, damn. I forgot to ask him anything!"

I must say, as national anthems go, the Russian has a great tune and is one of my favorites. However, by the time I had heard it five times as the Soviets were awarded gold medals for Women's individual, Men's and Women's Synchro and Men's and Women's Team, it ceased to be one of my top tunes. Only Richard Tison (FRA) spoiled the musical monopoly by winning the men's individual event.

At the post-event banquet, I made up for my earlier lapse and managed to extract as much information as possible from the Russian Head of Delegation while the gymnasts

Over & Above

danced the night away. The Soviet PR department had clearly planned a charm offensive for the evening by dressing their team in fashionable western-style party gear. A limited number of Hollywood films had clearly penetrated the Iron Curtain, creating the model for their look. Blue jeans with six-inch turn-ups and checked lumberjack shirts were indeed fashionable ... fifteen years ago!

I hadn't the heart to tell them James Dean was dead.

Returning to Harlow, having seen my number-one gymnast relegated to fourth place behind a Frenchman and two Russians was at first a discouraging experience. I had learned just how far we were off the pace. The Russians were effectively full-time gymnasts from the army or attached to a university. I shouldn't have been surprised because this had been the Soviet model for athletics, artistic gymnastics and other high profile sports since the 1950s. I calculated that Simon Rees, with academic demands and plagued by a persistent neck injury, could never replicate the time, commitment or volume of technical and conditioning work required to truly compete as a senior at this level.

Retiring from the sport at 17 could have been regarded as failure but having been British Senior Men's Champion, European Youth champion and twice World Age Group Champion, the young man had much to be proud of. What he didn't realize was how much I had learned about the technical, physical and psychological aspects of working with a gifted athlete and the way this would benefit my new guys.

Carl Furrer, age 9, and 11-year-old Stewart Matthews had been, to quote Mitch Fenner, my "secret weapons!" I had already visualized them outstripping Simon Rees to dominate world trampolining in the next ten years.

Well, think again Jack!

A Reality Check!

Seven Apex-Harlow gymnasts with the author as coach representing GBR at the third European Championships in Edinburgh.

Left to right: Jane Pullen, Geraldine Whiffin, Vanessa Smith, Simon Rees, Jan Kelly (née Allen), Alan Green, John Beer, Jack Kelly.

CHAPTER 05
RADICAL RE-THINK

SECTION ONE
SERVING THE APPRENTICESHIP

As the pain of defeat gradually subsided, my motivation returned, but I was aware that the bar had been raised significantly. Would we have to settle for being second best to the Soviets just because we couldn't match their resources or time commitment? We might have to be satisfied with being the "best of the rest." Before accepting this situation, I wanted to explore possible ways of competing with these "professionals" on our terms and within the British culture. Full-time training was not an option. I had to earn a living, and the gymnasts attended school five days a week. Our current training was two hours a day, six days a week. That gave us just 12 hours to fit in all the technical drills, competition routine repetitions and new skill development to merely achieve a competent standard. This didn't begin to address the increased level of conditioning necessary to underpin all the technical work and get us close to matching our opponents.

Within the Apex gymnastics organization, there was a competing trampoline membership of 30, looked after by four coaches and a number of occasional helpers. My own group consisted of 11 gymnasts, all Great Britain internationals, training on three trampolines. For several weeks my mind was in turmoil due to so many questions with very few answers. Was there a better way to organize the group to allow more development time with those demonstrating the potential to

Over & Above

reach the highest world standards? Could the gymnasts commit more than two hours a day to trampoline training? Could the sports center accommodate more training time for our sport? Despite the Soviets being in full-time training, surely they couldn't train all day, every day? What were they doing that could be described as essential and which elements of their programs were merely desirable? Did they possess more technical knowledge than I did? How much one-to-one technical coaching time did each gymnast receive? What was the most effective sport-specific conditioning for our sport and had the Soviets gotten that right?

Out of this mental morass came a moment of great clarity. The answer was ... time management! We didn't have the luxury of 24/7 training opportunities so we had to use the time we did have as efficiently as possible. Firstly, I wasn't using my own time effectively. Why was I trying to be all things to all people and directly coaching all club members? Hadn't I trained good assistant coaches who could accept responsibility for their own group of gymnasts, thereby restricting my role to overseeing and mentoring their work? It all seems so obvious now, but as a somewhat arrogant young coach, I didn't trust anyone to do as good a job as myself. When two of these coaches developed their own national champions for Apex, I began to realize the effectiveness of skillful mentoring and delegation. Another "ah-ha" moment perhaps? This continues to inform the work I do today at the club, national and international levels.

I started restricting much of my direct coaching to the younger gymnasts, specifically Stewart Matthews and Carl Furrer, believing these individuals had the potential to challenge the Soviets in the long term. Meanwhile, I still spent time with my senior performers John Beer, Alan Green, Bob Hughes, Clive Brigden, Jane Pullen, Geraldine Whiffin and the future Jan Kelly. However, as three of them were also qualified coaches, they were able to adopt a more self-coaching style and continued to be successful on the national stage. Although getting more of my attention, the "secret weapons" were still training alongside the seniors, and I believe there was significant benefit to both groups being able to watch each other at work.

All the major conditioning work was done using facilities outside the main sports hall, thereby protecting valuable trampoline training time. I introduced two weight training sessions (unusual for trampolinists in Great Britain at the time) that could be carried out in the sports center's body building facility. Another two sessions were dedicated to running, one for aerobic capacity and the other for sprinting and interval work aimed at the anaerobic system. These were conducted outdoors using the roads and fields around town. Although these conditioning sessions were compulsory, the "new generation" gymnasts applied themselves enthusiastically without any pressure from me. By joining in with the running and weights sessions, I was able to monitor their performance and stimulate their competitiveness while retaining my personal condition for what remained of my rugby career. Of course the initial weight training with the younger gymnasts was closely supervised, concentrating on safe and efficient lifting techniques with minimal resistance. Equally important was giving the young gymnasts an understanding of how each exercise related to the particular trampoline technique for which we were conditioning. Although the youngsters were the center of my focus, the conditioning program was open to all and embraced with varying degrees of commitment and consistency by the seniors. These program additions were supplemented by more efficient use of trampoline time and the introduction of training diaries. The subject of time management will be discussed more fully in Chapter 23.

This restructured way of working was initially aimed at closing the gap on the Soviets before addressing the challenge of overtaking them. As things stood in 1973, this meant becoming the best in Europe. Whether that equated to becoming world's best remained to be seen, as we couldn't discount the strengths of the reemerging Americans, uninhibited Australians, flamboyant French, meticulous Germans and the exciting, but inconsistent Japanese. China had yet to show any interest in applying their physical, cultural and gymnastic advantages to the trampoline and would remain an unknown quantity until the sport was accepted as an Olympic event.

There was little point in harboring world-conquering ambitions if the gymnasts were simply jumping for fun. Nonetheless, I was well aware that fun and love of the sport were essential starting points for any pursuit of excellence. I knew we had to establish a "shared vision" if we were to become the world's best, so I conducted interviews with the younger gymnasts to try and discover what they wanted to achieve in their sport. Depending on their responses, I would create appropriate targets and plans with them.

Thirty years later it was interesting to have separate conversations with Stewart Matthews and Carl Furrer and discover that, despite Carl still having all his training diaries, neither of the boys had any clear recollection of this goal-setting process taking

Over & Above

place, confirmation that it was nicely in tune with their needs at the time. Those 1973 interviews with the boys remain vividly in my memory as a landmark in my coaching career and a template for all future coaching relationships. The following accounts, while not verbatim, record the interview process and may provide a useful template for other coaches with World Class aspirations.

I asked Carl what he wanted to achieve from his sport. Perhaps I shouldn't have been surprised when all the nine-year-old could tell me was that he enjoyed trampolining and would like to be as good as possible. I resisted the temptation of leading him into the answers I wanted to hear, but the following analogy helped him understand what I wanted him to think about. It's an approach now being used by a number of the coaches I mentor.

Jack: What if you went to the station to travel by train, what would the ticket clerk ask you?

Carl: He'd ask me where I wanted to go.

Jack: Of course. Now, what if you told him you just liked going on trains and wanted to go as far as possible?

Carl: He'd still ask me where I wanted to go.

Jack: OK. Let's say you told him Edinburgh, what would the ticket clerk tell you then?

Carl: The cost of the ticket.

Jack: Correct. Now if he said it would cost £100 and you only had £10, what would you do?

Carl: I'd have to travel somewhere closer or just give up the idea of going on a train.

Jack: Right, now let's go back to my first question. How far do you want to go with your sport?

I went on to point out that, depending on how far he wanted to go with trampolining, there would be a cost in terms of time, effort and commitment. British Junior Champion would be a much shorter journey than the expedition to Senior World Champion. The commitment cost would depend on the length of the journey.

Being two years older and perhaps a little more outgoing than Carl, Stewart responded quite differently.

Jack: *What do you want to achieve from your trampolining?*

Stewart: *I want to be world champion!*

Frankly, I wasn't prepared for such a decisive response, and it took me a few seconds to gather my thoughts. Make no mistake, I was delighted, but was this just the fanciful dream of a twelve-year-old, like wanting to be a rock star or a professional footballer. We had already created a club culture where excellence was the goal, and 1972 World Champion Paul Luxon frequently dropped in for extra training. His gold medal-winning synchro partner Bob Hughes had now joined Apex so it was hardly surprising that the young Stewart Matthews already knew what he wanted!

The late, great Paul Luxon training at Harlow Sportcentre. In 1973, Paul was the first non-American in the history of the sport to become world champion. He was also the first performer to compete using straight arm twisting in single and multiple somersaults.

Over & Above

Jack: OK, Stewart, let's estimate how old you might be when you become world champion. I think the earliest would be when you are in your early 20s, so let's say 20 years old, just to give us a starting point. Your goal is therefore to be world champion in 1982. Does that sound OK to you?

(It is important to be aware that in the 1970s, World and European Championships took place on alternate years.)

Stewart: Yes, because it gives me enough time to work toward it.

Jack: In that case, what would you need to achieve at the Europeans in 1981?

Stewart: I'd have to be European champion.

Jack: Now, if you are European champion in 1981, what would you need to achieve at the Worlds in 1980?

Stewart: Probably a bronze medal.

We were both warming to the task. This was good fun!

Jack: Now let's consider the European Championships in 1979.

Stewart: Bronze or even silver?

Jack: And the Worlds in 1978?

Stewart: Top five!

I'm sure the reader can see where we were going with this and to cut a long story short, we ended up with the current year's target as winning a medal at the British Under 15 Boys Championship. Back in 1973, I freely admit I didn't know this was called goal setting, but it seemed like the right thing to do, a sensible if somewhat hypothetical exercise. Nor was I aware that we were setting outcome goals, which of course are uncontrollable due to many factors, not least of which is the progress of one's opponents.

The author with 12-year-old Stewart Matthews at the second World Age Group Championships in San Francisco.

CHAPTER 06
MAKING IT HAPPEN

SECTION ONE
SERVING THE APPRENTICESHIP

If the story so far suggests I was making things up as I went along, reacting to circumstances using a mixture of common sense, intuition and previous experience, then that is exactly right. I did however, have a creative curiosity and an open mind when it came to applying ideas picked up from a range of sources, including my conversations with leading coaches in other sports. Most productive of these was my adaptation of a concept used by a national track coach to help his athletes with visualization. This will be covered in Chapter 16.

Trampolining is a modular sport with every major skill or combination built upon pre-existing modules. Each module must therefore be solidly constructed and understood before taking its place as part of a more complex structure. Both boys had demonstrated an ability and desire to learn increasingly complex moves, but it was important to control their ambition in that area and concentrate on putting in place the techniques that would allow them to develop their difficulty with top-class execution. I had seen too many trampolinists prematurely raise their difficulty only to suffer height loss, poor execution scores, skill confusion, and sometimes complete confidence breakdown. Coaches would then spend many wasted hours trying to correct basic faults within complex routines or combinations ... a fruitless exercise. **Basic techniques can only be established or corrected within a simplified context.**

Over & Above

This is not to say my protégés were held back in any way. I simply tried to balance safe, but exciting, fun alongside a sound technique. An experienced artistic gymnastics coach once told me, "They need a diet of bread and jam, but it must be in *that* order. The coach's art is to recognize when to put a little jam on the bread and when to return to the staple diet."

My experience had already taught me the benefits of pairing up gymnasts of similar age, ability and work ethic. This had occurred spontaneously with my seniors, and it soon became apparent that, despite the two-year age difference, Stewart and Carl were beginning to gel as a training unit. I also enjoyed the benefit of having the remarkable American coach and innovator Bob Bollinger stay at my house for a week with his two 11-year-olds — son Robbie and training partner Ronnie Merriot. The Nissen Corporation had brought them over to make a presentation at the International Conference in London. These young guys were amazing, and the skills they could perform opened my eyes to what was possible when two well-matched training partners work with a dedicated and intelligent coach. Nonetheless, it was becoming clear to me that I was dealing with two contrasting personalities with differing physical and mental attributes. So while enabling them to bond, I used a different coaching style with each. Stewart was a more natural athlete with a sense of adventure and inclined to try emulating the senior men before he was technically secure. Carl, on the other hand, was what I call, a "paint-by-numbers" learner. He took longer to become secure with an element, but once it was "painted in," we could move to the next element with confidence.

The boys made good progress throughout the next few years with three World Age Group titles for Carl and World Age Group synchro titles for the pair.

Stewart Matthews and Carl Furrer win the 1974 World Age Group Synchro in San Francisco.

Stewart's early achievements were limited by his unfortunate ability to get injured just before major age group events. A broken ankle sustained when playing in the park with his pals denied him his first British junior title, but there was an interesting upside to this disappointment. Although the recovery and rehabilitation meant 12 months away from the trampoline, he still turned up at every training session to stay in contact with the sport and his teammates. Any doubts about his commitment to become the world's best were dispelled by this exceptional behavior.

In 1976, as Britain's youngest ever Men's National Champion at 14 years of age, he competed in the Senior World Championships in Tulsa, Oklahoma. To my astonishment, he was in fourth place after the set routine, a remarkable achievement for one so young. His inexperience was exposed, however, when he lost his way after six moves in the voluntary. Nonetheless, his special ability shone through as he proceeded to ad lib in impressive style, narrowly missing the final but having performed a 12-element exercise! Another injury to his ankle meant that as we travelled north to the World Age event in Cedar Rapids, Iowa (home of the Nissen Corporation), he was denied yet another title chance.

Over & Above

In Cedar Rapids, I was standing in the training hall with Wayne Miller (yes, *that* Miller!) as I supervised Carl's preparation for the age group competition. Wayne, clearly impressed by the tiny, cherubic 12-year-old who performed an adult standard routine, exclaimed,

"Man ... he's a real s-t-u-d!"

I'm not sure Carl's mum would have approved!

I don't intend to trace the progress of the next few years other than to record that when the 14-year-old Stewart Matthews beat reigning World Champion Richard Tison in a Great Britain versus France international, I knew we were on the path to the very top.

The press acclaims Stewart Matthew's victory over current World Champion Richard Tison of France in 1976.

There were many times when Carl looked as if he was closing the gap on his older training partner, but that was always the signal for Stewart to put distance between them once again.

They were a fantastic duo, constantly stimulating each other and bonding into a brilliant synchro partnership. Over the previous five years, I had ensured their basic techniques were firmly in place and reinforced this at every training session through a range of technical drills. Although further moves were still needed for the repertoire, I was confident that because we had put in all the groundwork, these young gymnasts had arrived at a point where there was nothing they couldn't learn. Both boys were comfortable with piked and tucked triffs, while Stewart had comfortably performed half in-half out triff and rudi out triff. This was a considerable achievement bearing in mind the age of the boys and the 6mm x 6mm webbed bed they were using. My responsibility was now to control the pace of more complex skill acquisition and to resist the temptation to become intoxicated by rising difficulty.

Meanwhile Apex-Harlow had become a major player in world trampolining and certainly the strongest all-round club in Great Britain.

Apex-Harlow in 1976, featuring eleven gymnasts who represented their country at senior level.

Back row (left to right): Jack Kelly, Alan Green, Jan Kelly (née Allen), Stewart Matthews, Colin Robson, John Beer, Colin Bird, Heather Brockenshaw, Peter Roberts (coach), Clive Brigden, Anne Furrer (coach).

Middle row: Amanda Richardson, Geraldine Whiffen, Kim Richardson, Carl Furrer, Chris Hilton, Mike Windsor, Sue Chandler, Rhona Cotton, Caron Duplok.

Front row: Alison Furrer, Adrienne and Jeanne Kelly (the author's daughters) Caroline Furrer, Johnny Hughes, Matthew Gill, Debbie Maidment, Tracey Jarvis.

Just as we were beginning to close in on our long-term goals, the break-up of my first marriage compelled me to change jobs and live ten miles from our training venue. This could have been catastrophic for Stewart and Carl's dreams of international success, but as I was now managing another sports center, I encouraged the boys to travel

Over & Above

there in order to maintain coaching continuity. Carl and his parents decided this was unacceptable, and he would remain at Apex-Harlow. Stewart made the journey for a short time, but I had to accept that this arrangement was unsustainable for two reasons: the successful training partnership was being broken, and Stewart had to find transport for a 20-mile round-trip to every session instead of simply walking to the gym.

My life was at a crisis point, and for the first time I had lost my life's balance. The sport had become such a big part of me that other values, such as home, relationships and career progression, had been abandoned. Coaching had become an obsession, and considering it earned me no money, I had been taking a massive risk with my future. On the other hand, I knew the highly focused commitment I had applied to the task was essential for successful World Class coaching. What I lacked was the maturity to realize that commitment and life balance do not have to be mutually exclusive.

While I struggled to come to terms with my personal life, Stewart and Carl turned to John Beer for continuing guidance within Apex-Harlow and a new coaching partnership was born. Not only had John become an experienced international performer, he had qualified as a Senior Advanced Coach who was prepared to accept the challenge of taking the boys to the next level. The arrangement had been born out of a crisis, but it turned out to be a life-changing episode for all four of us.

During the ensuing years, I had the bittersweet experience of watching "my boys" become "John's boys," going from triumph to international triumph. No doubt the reader can empathize with the mixture of pride and melancholy I experienced, knowing the significant journey the three of us had already travelled, yet being absent when the final accolades were awarded … Stewart as World Champion in 1980 and Carl as World Champion in 1982. Stewart and Carl were World Synchro Champions in 1980.

Coach John Beer in podium celebration with Stewart and Carl after they had taken gold and silver in the individual, followed by gold in the synchro at the 1980 World Championships.

John and I have always had a strong relationship within the sport and much of the work we did together as coach and gymnast surely helped in his coaching role with the two future world stars. In 2006, when he and I led the British Gymnastics World Class Trampoline Programme together, I asked him if he realized that in developing and coaching the boys to the top of the sport, we had jointly done "one helluva job!"

"Look at it this way, John," I said. "You'll never know if you could have got them to point where they were ready to start taking on the world's best, and I'll never know whether I could have taken them on the latter part of the journey. But despite some unfortunate circumstances, we both enabled those gymnasts to reach their goals."

Now *that* is what coaching is all about!

As a footnote to this chapter, you may recall my goal-setting exercise with Stewart Matthews in 1973. I had estimated he could aim to be World Champion in 1982, but the medal was hung around his neck in 1980. So much for outcome goals!

CHAPTER 07

GETTING MY ACT TOGETHER

SECTION ONE
SERVING THE APPRENTICESHIP

By 1980, my professional career as a sport center manager was back on track. I had a "proper" job, remarried and started a new trampoline club with my wife Jan at the sports center I now managed. Levitation Trampoline Club was developed from the methodology learned with Apex, drawing its initial membership from local primary schools and the broad-based recreation program at my sports center. It wasn't long before our young gymnasts were making an impact on the national stage, with the inevitable result that ambitious parents from as far as 30 miles away wanted their talented children to join us. Jan was responsible for the girls, while I coached the boys. It was gratifying when national success was achieved by both genders. I was particularly thrilled when Jan was awarded the 1987 British Trampoline Federation Coach of the Year Award for the achievements of her girls. My own high point came when the Levitation boys occupied the top four positions in the 1987 National Championships.

But where were the international stars you might ask? I was a far more experienced and knowledgeable coach, had complete management control of the facility in which we trained, and enjoyed the backing of my employers and local company sponsorship. The parents were highly supportive and the club even enjoyed the services of the Coach of the Year. This easily matched our

Over & Above

advantages when we hit the heights with Apex. So what was missing? Perhaps the children who walked into our gym weren't as talented as those in Harlow? No, we had talent in abundance and you won't have to read between the lines to learn this lesson, because here it is ... I was no longer prepared to give the level of commitment that had seen me destroy a promising career, wreck a marriage and create stress and misery for the many people I cared about! Although many successful individuals do combine World Class focus with a balanced family life, I had not been one of them! This time I was playing it safe. Coaching had to take second place.

By 1988, our children Simon, Gavin and Claire were still under 6 years of age and enjoyed being part of the Levitation trampoline "family." Like most children, they had fun on the trampoline, but we had no desire to try and turn them into champions. We decided that their needs and development had to come before chasing international success with our club. Jan gradually reduced her coaching commitment as a prelude to us winding up the club. This process took two years as I was gradually able to transfer each gymnast to a suitable alternative club. It was later gratifying to see several of these gymnasts achieve National team selection with their new clubs, confirming that we had established sound technique as the basis for future success.

Getting My Act Together

Levitation GBR international Michele Miles with the Kelly children. This was the closest they came to becoming trampoline gymnasts!

CHAPTER 08

SEEING THE BIGGER PICTURE

SECTION ONE
SERVING THE APPRENTICESHIP

Seeing the Bigger Picture

By 1990, my life had become a rich mix of family, career and part time coach education. By helping coaches through the British Gymnastics Coaching Award structure, I found I could add significantly to the formal syllabus as a result of my experience — over and above, one might say. At the same time, as satisfying as my missionary tendencies, the education work kept me in touch with but at arm's length from individual ambitious gymnasts who might draw me back into the World Class performance maelstrom. Also, my own children had become involved with competitive swimming, and it wasn't long before the head coach of their club discovered I was also qualified in that sport and invited me to help poolside. Twelve years later, I was to become a head swim coach, training my own squad of swimmers, including a future Olympian and my own daughter, to national standard. Ah well, once a coach, always a coach.

Over & Above

Claire Kelly competing in the 800m Freestyle at the 2001 Scottish National Championships.

Trampoline coach education and competitive swim coaching were totally compatible for a time, giving me new insights into both sports. As a relative newcomer to swim coaching, I had an "outsider's" perspective on the nature of the training and coaching I witnessed. I was surprised by the low percentage of time spent on technical efficiency and the heavy emphasis on all aspects of fitness. I found that many young children had the "gift" of being able to swim fast with crude technique, just as some were naturally fast runners. These children were then selected for club training and a remorseless escalation of distance, speed and stamina work with little regard for technical efficiency. Although this process often resulted in swimmers having early success, a point was reached where natural talent and fitness were not enough. Technical flaws had become too ingrained to rectify, and most coaches seemed obsessed with conditioning the "energy systems." Hadn't they considered that every meter swum with flawed technique off set advantages gained from physical preparation?

I witnessed too many fast, young swimmers fail to maximize their potential through this shortsighted approach. I was nonetheless impressed by the swim coaches' understanding of physiology, which was in direct contrast to my experience in trampolining. Their training programs were based on sound scientific principles, but I couldn't help thinking they might as well have been training racehorses.

It is ironic that as a swimming coach I now had an "outsider's" perspective on the current state of British trampolining. I was still delivering trampoline coach courses at all levels and frequently worked with coaches aspiring to high performance. Trainees were required to attend with a gymnast of appropriate standard, and I was shocked by what I saw! The gymnasts were having their learning accelerated according to the coach's need to obtain the next level of qualification! To progress through the levels, student coaches had to be able to teach a specified group of moves, increasing in difficulty with each award. There is nothing wrong with that as a principle, but the missing ingredient can be summed up as follows:

High-level coaching is not about high difficulty moves; it is about **coaching basic skill** with an understanding of its **significance to high-level performance.**

There was a presumption by many, that by applying the recommended series of progressions, the pupil would "learn" the desired move. Inevitably, when these new moves were prematurely inserted into competition routines to raise the difficulty, lack of control in more fundamental elements frequently proved to be the limiting factor. This could be as basic as a gymnast's inability to jump with balance and consistency prior to attempting the targeted skill. Natural aptitude, confidence and fast learning were disguising the fact that these gymnasts, like many young swimmers, were being escorted down a blind alley.

When delivering coach education courses at different venues throughout the country, I had the opportunity to work one-on-one with a number of current British internationals. Again, I was shocked by the poor level of basic skill possessed by gymnasts attempting routines of World Class difficulty (at that time, 15.0-16.0 for men and 13.0-14.0 for women). Compared to the frequency and volume of swim training, many of the current Great Britain trampoline team members were training as few as eight hours a week. In addition to their technical shortcomings, they were unaware of the significant role played by the energy systems in their sport. Many coaches had no understanding of how to create the physical adaptations needed to improve competitive performance or enough training time in which to do it! I was amazed that these gymnasts were as good as they were, considering this technical and physiological naivety. On the other hand, it was becoming clear why Great Britain (with a few notable exceptions) was beginning to fall behind the rest of the world at the senior level.

Over & Above

Most disappointing of all was that in 2003 most of the gymnasts and coaches I met were failing to match, let alone develop, the work we had introduced 30 years earlier. Nonetheless, Britain had still managed to produce global trampoline stars throughout the 1980s and into the 1990s. Sue Shotton, Andrea Holmes, Kirsten Lawton, Claire Wright, Nigel Rendell, Theo Kypri, Paul Smith and Daniel Neale kept Britain in the top flight, but these "top end" successes were achieved independently by individual coaches rather than as a product of a national "system." Apparent success at this level simply masked the deep malaise threatening the overall health of the sport in the UK. We were fast gaining a reputation as a nation with promising juniors (as seen from World Age and European Youth results) but failing to convert age group successes into senior world honors. From my newfound "outsider's" perspective, it was clear that too many internationally aspiring coaches were being seduced by the ease in which high difficulty moves could be "learned." The situation wasn't improved when bonus points were awarded in selection events for higher levels of difficulty. I took this as a clear sign that the British trampoline gymnastics hierarchy was conscious of the problem and looking for immediate solutions. The strategy was shortsighted and simply undermined the already shaky basic technique of most gymnasts aspiring to international selection. The juniors were succeeding largely due to high difficulty levels that masked the lack of underpinning stability and control needed long term. Trampoline beds had improved massively since the 1980s to the point where, even without sound basic skill, highly complex moves could be performed. That may sound contradictory, but it was only when these moves came to be placed in routines that the folly of "fast tracking" became evident.

I was becoming frustrated that my technical and development message, delivered through the formal coach education structure, was failing to reach the "producing" coaches. I needed to get into a position where I could directly influence those coaches working with talented juniors but who seemed unaware of how to develop them into top seniors. Consequently, I contacted the British Gymnastics Performance Director and John Beer (now the Trampoline Technical Director) to offer my help on a part-time basis, perhaps by assisting at national training camps. I was totally unprepared for what happened next!

Unknown to me, there had been a recent resignation among the High Performance Coaching staff, and following a meeting with the Performance Director, I found myself with a full-time job as a High Performance Coach on the UK Sport-funded, World Class Programme. Six years prior, I had taken early retirement from my Leisure Development post and at 64 was one year away from the old age pension and winter fuel allowance! Perhaps I was foolish to accept the challenge, but I was now in a position to start exerting influence. Wasn't that what I had wanted?

JACK KELLY: "Height=Time=Opportunity"

09 CHAPTER
NEW CHALLENGE

SECTION ONE
SERVING THE APPRENTICESHIP

I was now working in a small coaching team led by John Beer as Technical Director. This was an interesting juxtaposition bearing in mind our previous coach/gymnast relationship, but I was sure we shared similar technical philosophies that had been borne out by the way he skillfully steered Stewart Matthews and Carl Furrer to their World Titles. My belief that we could work together was enhanced by the knowledge that we had been an effective half-back partnership on the rugby field with Hertford Pacemakers, the Hertford Rugby Club's unbeaten veteran team.

It wasn't long before I began to understand the complex set of issues facing British trampolining. Since my previous involvement, the British Trampoline Federation had been successfully absorbed into British Gymnastics but many of the experienced coaches were uncomfortable with the new structure and some of the decisions being taken by the professional officers. Perhaps most damaging of all, coaches who had consistently produced World Class gymnasts seemed to be at odds with each other as well as with the crop of younger, ambitious coaches eager for recognition. Nonetheless, I focused on contributing what I could to my assigned group of six athletes on the World Class Programme and tried to exert a technical influence on those coaches who were open to change.

Over & Above

Meanwhile, unknown to me, the funding agency, UK Sport, was conducting a review of the Trampoline World Class Programme ahead of the Beijing Olympics and had sought the views of those unhappy leading coaches. This, I believe, had a significant effect on the governing body's subsequent actions.

The system of peripatetic High Performance Coaches, working under a Technical Director was dismantled, rendering those posts redundant. Instead, there were to be two posts of equal status, described as National Technical Managers, and the existing team members were free to apply. Following formal interviews, John and I were offered the jobs. On the face of it, it made sense to put together a proven partnership to take British trampolining forward through the next Olympic Cycle.

Each post carried a subtitle — either "Performance," with responsibility for overseeing the small group of potential Olympians, or "Development," with a goal to nurture the younger performers to the point where they could aspire to senior international representation. Bearing in mind our individual track records, it was clear to me that John would be in charge of performance, and I would play the development role. To my astonishment, I was offered the performance job … or nothing! That left John with development, leading me to conclude there must have been some political or financial motivation behind such an illogical decision! Before accepting this appointment, I knew that John and I would have to talk because, as Britain's coach at the last two Olympics, I couldn't believe he would relish that development role.

For me, the options were clear: either reject the inappropriate appointment and return to the obscurity of retirement, or accept the offer but take "nominal" responsibility for performance. Meanwhile, I pondered, would it be possible to work unofficially with John to start changing the philosophy and methods of coaches developing the next generation gymnasts?

New Challenge

JACK KELLY: "Difficulty must be easy!"

CHAPTER 10
STARTING THE PROCESS

SECTION ONE
SERVING THE APPRENTICESHIP

Stage one was to draw up a SWOT analysis in order to identify national strengths and weaknesses as a basis for creating a credible action plan. I perceived two major strengths within the sport. Firstly, there were experienced coaches who had already achieved international success for Great Britain. Secondly, numerous enthusiastic younger coaches were keen to make their mark on the world stage. I saw these as major resources that required the right kind of leadership to get them working together instead of falling out with the governing body and with each other. In order to realize that untapped potential, we had to address what I saw as our major weakness — the total absence of a technical policy that everyone could buy into.

Over & Above

The subsequent action plan was straightforward in concept but would require careful handling.

1. Produce a document in consultation with my colleague John Beer, spelling out the technical principles essential for developing World Class trampolinists and sustaining their international success.

2. Meet with the leading club coaches to highlight the importance of working together for the benefit of Team GB.

3. Present the technical document to the coaches and identify areas of agreement or controversy.

4. Collate the points of agreement and gain acceptance that these would form the basis of the National Technical Policy.

5. Launch the finished policy document with the World Class Squad and distribute it regionally through the newly established "Cluster" Programme, the brainchild of Technical Chair Martin Laws.

To my astonishment and delight, the coaches agreed upon the content of the document (National Technical Priorities for Aspiring World Class Coaches and Gymnasts). This was a restructured version of the printed handout I had been giving my club coaches since the 1980s outlining the technical principles we aimed to establish with our gymnasts. They acknowledged that GBR had a generation of what I chose to call "difficulty-damaged" young performers who were unlikely to mature into top seniors. This was a mistake not to be repeated. Some coaches claimed that the development principles I put forward described exactly what they had already been doing. It was clear from the quality of their gymnasts that this was not the case; the claim was nothing more than ego protection. The most encouraging reaction came from several experienced coaches who acknowledged that, although they agreed with the principles, they had lost sight of these in the misguided chase after high difficulty. We were on our way!

Just as the ocean liner can take a couple miles to turn around after the command is issued, so I knew the adoption of a unified technical policy would take several years to deliver international results. But at least we had started to turn the steering wheel.

Seven years later the British women became World Team Champions. Could 'turning the wheel' and helping the leading coaches to re-focus on key technical aspects have some bearing on subsequent international successes? I simply pose the question!

As I transfer from biographical to technical mode, the reader should already have obtained some insights into my coaching philosophy.

Did you manage to read between the lines and recognize the lessons I learned during the formative years?

- Adapt successful methods to suit your own situation rather than try to copy.
- Match your goals to your resources or change your resources to match your goals.
- Don't expect gymnasts to automatically share your ambitions.
- Outcome goals are pointless without a performance plan.
- Optimize the work/rest ratio.
- Be prepared to make changes based on experience.
- Pair up gymnasts who have similar ambitions.
- Adapt your coaching style to match the personality of your athletes.
- Question your own attitude and be prepared to make positive changes.
- Maximize effectiveness through team coaching.
- Passion and commitment are necessary in the pursuit of excellence and *can* be compatible with a balanced life.

CHAPTER 11

THE TECHNIQUE/EQUIPMENT RELATIONSHIP

SECTION TWO
TECHNICAL CONCEPTS

The Technique/Equipment Relationship

The principles and techniques promoted within this book have evolved along with the gradual refinement of the trampoline itself. Many technical faults can still be traced to a lack of understanding about the nature of the apparatus, resulting in a gymnast's failure to harness its potential. Since the characteristics of the sport are dictated by the potential of the equipment, a brief study of how the apparatus has developed can be technically rewarding for both coach and gymnast.

In the early days of the sport, most serious participants were either competitive divers or gymnasts with a repertoire of tumbling skills. Divers adapted to the new apparatus more comfortably than tumblers because of their familiarity with jumping and somersaulting from a highly flexible surface that enhanced airtime. Tumblers and gymnasts, on the other hand, were used to jumping off a far less obliging surface, the sprung floor and tumble track being many years from realization.

The first trampoline beds were made of a double thick nylon sheet suspended on rubber cords. They were capable of deep depression but prone to "bottoming out" as the shock cords reached full length. A personal memory of this "solid" bed is the constant draft of cold air created by the jumping gymnast. Warm clothing and even

Over & Above

gloves had to be worn while waiting around the trampoline in an unheated gymnasium! The introduction of one-and-three-quarter-inch webbing and high tensile steel springs removed much of the air resistance and draft, while giving a more predictable rebound. This solved one problem but created another. The soft flexible nature of the solid nylon bed with its bungee-cord suspension had created a sensation of "loading up" the trampoline, similar to drawing back an archery bow. A clear delay could be felt as the bed sunk to full depression before recoiling upward, propelling the gymnast into the air. The webbed beds gave a more immediate hard, short, rebound phase that felt similar to jumping from the floor. Herein lay the problem!

This sensation of jumping from the floor, albeit with enhanced flight time, encouraged many of the sport's pioneers to simply adapt their knowledge of tumbling, thereby failing to employ the equipment's "bow and arrow" potential. The reader may recall how my personal attempts at trampoline somersaults ended up on the floor, leading to a realization that the horizontal nature of tumbling must somehow be modified for the trampoline. The solution recommended by experts at the time was to initiate somersaults using an excessive forward or backward displacement of the hips during bed contact. This created rotation but kept the gymnast's center of mass above the feet throughout the take-off process, thereby avoiding catastrophic travel. Consecutive somersaults were now possible "on the spot" without the need to topple off-balance and create travel. The resultant visual and aural effect of consecutive somersaulting was a swinging rhythm that could also be felt by the performer. It is hardly surprising then that this became known as performing in "swingtime."

In naming his new apparatus, George Nissen apparently coined the word "trampoline" from the Spanish *trampolin* or "springboard." There is also anecdotal evidence that a French trapeze artist was called DuTrampolin because of his spectacular rebounds from the catch-net at the end of his act. Surely the name for the new sport would be "trampolining," but there were those who thought this failed to describe the excitement and potential of the equipment. Although the apparatus was called a trampoline, the sport became known as "rebound tumbling," a name that persisted in many places until the early 1970s.

By this time, the equipment used for competitive trampoline gymnastics consisted of half-inch (13mm) webbed beds powered by steel springs suspended on a frame high enough to prevent the gymnast from touching the floor at full depression. Despite the improvement in equipment, the concept of rebound tumbling persisted and the understandable desire to remain in the center of the trampoline took precedence over the real potential of the equipment to send the gymnast high into the air.

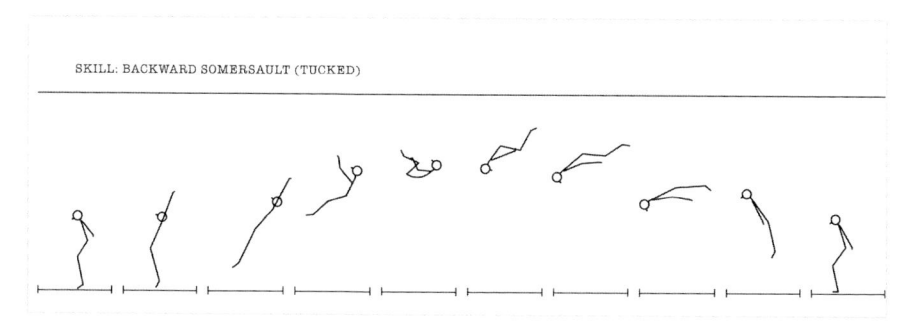

SKILL: BACKWARD SOMERSAULT (TUCKED)

A typical illustration from a 1970s coaching manual showing forward hip displacement during bed contact to create backward rotation. The subsequent sequence, while intending to show each separate stage in the somersault, actually implied there was a need to travel. This was misleading and failed to show the vertical nature of trampolining.

The 13mm beds gradually gave way to 9mm and 6mm webbing until the present day when 4mm and "string" beds have been used at major championships. The main objective of this evolution has been to send the gymnast higher while maintaining stability. It is not unusual to see the world's top trampoline gymnasts performing close to eight meters above the arena floor and enjoying around two seconds of flight time per element. One of the earliest books on the sport, published in 1954, was *This Is Trampolining: Two Seconds of Freedom* by Frank La Due and Jim Norman. Bearing in mind the limitations of the apparatus at that time, the subtitle was either a flight of fantasy or an inspired prediction of things to come.

Over & Above

"Since we are on the subject of rather difficult stunts, we may as well mention a group of stunts which we call 'triffles' or twisting triple somersaults. Actually, the triple somersault is considered to be next to impossible on present trampolines. Theoretically, the only thing preventing us from performing such stunts is the lack of height or time in the air." (p.137)

The authors finally comment:

"We won't attempt to list all these stunts here, but the student should realize that in time he may witness such tricks." (p.138)

The "landmark" 1950s publication from the Nissen Trampoline Company of Cedar Rapids, Iowa. It would be 50 years before trampolinists regularly attained "two seconds" of airtime, but what an inspired prediction!

Even the most basic trampoline has the capacity to impart vertical force to the performer who, in order to somersault, must create a degree of turning force while in contact with the bed. The greater the vertical component, the less rotational force the gymnast needs in order to achieve the desired somersault. Conversely, a low vertical component requires a greater input of rotational force to achieve a similar degree of somersault rotation. Larry Griswold wrote in his 1948 publication, *Trampoline Tumbling*, that in order to perform a front somersault:

"Thrust the hips back on take-off."

The Technique/Equipment Relationship

His recommended technique for creating a back somersault was:

"Swing the arms up and thrust hips forward on take-off."

This was, at the time, the best advice available. Those "rebound tumblers" of the 1940s through the early 1970s tended to maximize the rotational component at the expense of the vertical, motivated by the natural fear that in failing to impart sufficient rotation they might not "get round!"

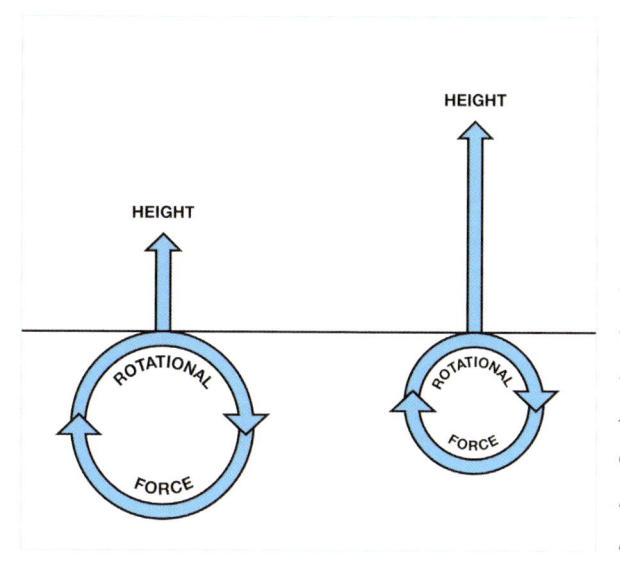

The vertical/rotational force relationship.

Restricted jump height requires a large amount of rotational force during bed contact to produce a given degree of somersault. By increasing jump height, the same degree of somersault can be achieved with less rotational input during bed contact.

This understandable concern still bedevils many of today's trampoline performances. In my experience, gymnasts will always tend to "overcook" the rotational component in preference to the vertical. As I say to young performers,

"High and slow is the way to go! Low and fast, your routine won't last!"

The powerful and stable nature of modern competition trampolines allows the gymnast to employ techniques that maximize vertical force while minimizing rotational input. To employ the techniques involved, the coach must enable the gymnast to understand how this distribution of force is created during bed contact. Becoming familiar with

Over & Above

the height/rotation balance as early as possible during development is one of the keys to eventual World Class performance. The process of acquiring maximal height with minimal rotation takes a significant degree of initial courage and has the added benefit of identifying those who relish airtime, an essential component in the World Class Potential Package. High marks for visual impression depend on the gymnast's ability to maximize time in the air, which comes from appreciating this vertical/rotational balance.

Spectacular aerial **outcomes** are simply the result of efficient **inputs** created by the gymnast **during the bed contact phases**. Everything that follows is written with that as the underlying principle.

The Technique/Equipment Relationship

JACK KELLY: "Impressive aerial form is the product of efficient work during bed contact."

CHAPTER 12

TRAMPOLINING IS TOO EASY!

SECTION TWO
TECHNICAL CONCEPTS

Trampolining is Too Easy!

A controversial statement perhaps, but this is at the root of most technical problems experienced sooner or later in the trampoline gymnast's career. Although the trampoline is now a well-established discipline within the Olympic program, its initial appeal tends to be based on having fun rather than the pursuit of excellence. The proliferation of backyard trampolines supports this assertion. When comparing trampoline with artistic gymnastics, it is easy to see their generic similarity, especially when performed by experts. However, the starting point for the two disciplines reveals a stark contrast. To be able to perform simple competition work on beam, pommel horse, bars or even floor, artistic gymnasts must first acquire competence at a wide range of body management skills. They must understand the specific nature and potential of each apparatus in order to perform with control and continuity. Furthermore, the attainment of strength and flexibility must keep pace with new skill acquisition. Simple elements, such as back walkover on floor or upstart on bars, cannot be performed without both physical and technical preparation. On the trampoline however, it is possible to execute forward and backward somersaults with only the courage born out of ignorance and ambition. This is the seductive quality of the apparatus, which beguiles coaches and would-be performers alike, breeding excitement and fueling further misguided ambition.

Over & Above

The necessity to acquire sound fundamentals before meaningful progress can be made creates a culture within artistic gymnastics where establishing and revisiting basics always precede more complex work. This puts great onus on gymnastic coaches and their pupils to accept that initial progress may appear slow. Those who attempt to speed up the process by omitting technical or conditioning fundamentals, quickly discover they have entered a movement dead end.

Trampolining, on the other hand, can be very attractive to those in pursuit of instant gratification because any pupil with a degree of natural physical ability can make quick progress after paying only "lip service" to the fundamentals. Should you need convincing, check out the plethora of would-be acrobats displaying their "skills" on round trampolines on YouTube. Coaches too, can be flattered by their apparent effectiveness in "teaching" talented pupils a burgeoning repertoire of skills. In the artistic disciplines, the absence of any technical or conditioning fundamental becomes obvious at an early stage in the gymnast's development — not so on the trampoline.

A talented newcomer to trampoline can, with enough time, ambition and supportive coaching, achieve a remarkable level of performance with limited awareness and control of fundamentals. I use "supportive" to describe such coaching because all that is required is encouragement and basic feedback. This type of coach simply shares in the gymnast's intoxication with fast progress and purely experiential learning. My colleague Johnny Tenn describes this as "Neanderthal coaching."

Because trampolining is a modular sport enabling complex skills to be developed through joining together simpler elements, it is reasonable to expect that each module should be perfected before inserting it into a compound situation. The performer's range of technical competencies may be likened to a car engine, which is made up of many components. When the car breaks down, it is rarely because the whole engine suddenly explodes and disintegrates. The cause will inevitably be a small component malfunction or even a loose connection! In all my years of watching and working with some of the world's best, I have never seen a failure caused by the comprehensive disintegration of a single move. The culprit is usually a fundamental error or technical misjudgment. Often it is a "loose connection."

The most common cause of competition failure is the gymnast's inability to react proportionately to an initial error, leading to over-correction thereby compounding the mistake. This won't always lead to the immediate termination of a routine, but there will be a consequential loss of execution marks from every element following the error. What is being exposed here, in both the initial error and subsequent over-correction, is a breakdown in the gymnast's ability to control the response of the trampoline bed to his or her actions. That is surely the most fundamental of fundamentals! Whether the error appears during a multiple twisting double somersault or a simple tucked jump, the cause can generally be traced to the failure of a fundamental skill component.

So trampolining is too easy! The unwary coach or gymnast becomes sucked into a quagmire of half-learned techniques and skills, prematurely inserted into competition routines. This is destined to bring progress to a frustrating end before true potential can been reached.

CHAPTER 13

WHEN IS 'THE TAKE-OFF' NOT 'THE TAKE-OFF'?

SECTION TWO
TECHNICAL CONCEPTS

When is 'the Take-Off' Not 'the Take-Off'?

As the aircraft gathers speed down the runway, we become acutely aware of dramatic acceleration. Our bodies are forced more deeply into our seats, take off is imminent; or has the process already begun? Certainly we have yet to feel that distinct sensation indicating the actual moment when the wheels part company with the tarmac and we become truly airborne. Should we define the take-off as that particular instant or is it simply the culmination of the take-off process? Likewise, when the aircraft lands, there is an instant when the wheels first touch the runway but perhaps the plane has not landed until it comes to rest outside the terminal. When has the plane landed? When has it taken off?

In this chapter, I will answer these questions in the context of trampoline gymnastics and highlight the importance of understanding the concept in order to communicate accurately with our gymnasts.

Over & Above

A typical illustration from a coach education manual still in circulation during the 1990s showing the bed as a straight line with the implication that it is similar to the floor surface.

When an illustration like this appears in the official manuals for trainee coaches, it is hardly surprising that the most fundamental part of trampoline gymnastics is the least understood. The drawing purports to illustrate the basic take-off and landing of a straight jump. At best, it may be said to represent the actions of the gymnast, but what about the actions of the trampoline bed and the adaptations the gymnast must make in relation to that? This simplistic little drawing symbolizes much that is wrong with the way trampoline gymnastics has been taught, coached and spoken about over the years. Happily, British Gymnastics has begun to rectify this in their most recent publications, but legions of currently practicing coaches, trained under the old concept, have yet to catch up with reality.

Coaches and gymnasts constantly refer to "*the* take-off" or "*the* landing." The gymnast might comment:

"I felt I landed a bit short." The coach might say:

"Your take-off needs to be stronger."

What exactly do they mean? Try to answer this question:

When exactly has the trampolinist landed?

a) When the feet make first contact with the bed?

or

b) When the bed has been fully depressed?

Neither answer is totally right or indeed totally wrong because the question can't be answered in such simple terms. To some extent, it is a trick question. In reality, there is a **landing phase** that starts at first contact with the trampoline bed and continues until the bed is fully depressed. So the landing is not an **instant** but a **process**! The same principle applies to take-off, with the process starting at full bed depression and continuing until the gymnast loses contact with the bed — the **take-off phase**.

THE "LANDING PHASE" is from FIRST CONTACT to FULL DEPRESSION

THE "TAKE-OFF PHASE" is from FULL DEPRESSION to LAST CONTACT.

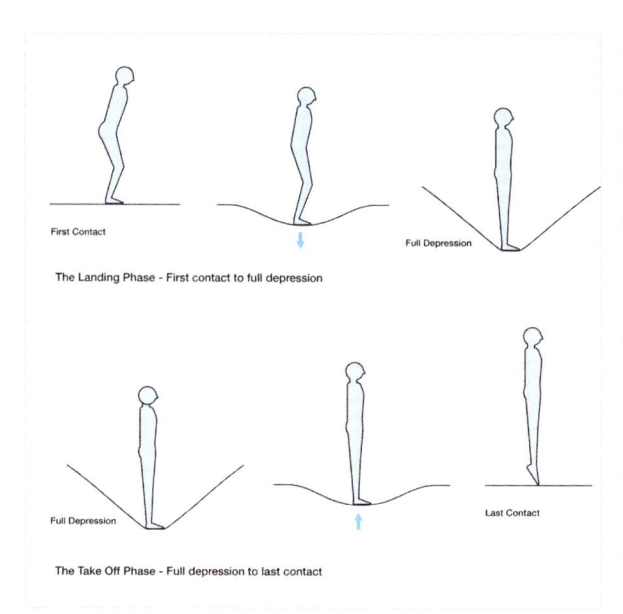

The Landing Phase - First contact to full depression

All coaching should relate to these two distinct phases so the gymnast begins to feel and understand the delay during bed contact.

The Take Off Phase - Full depression to last contact

In my experience, most coaches work with the **"at"** take-off and **"on"** landing concept. Whether or not they *understand* the principle of the take-off and landing **phases**, their coaching is flawed by using this form of communication with the gymnast.

When very young children are learning to jump on a trampoline, they are unlikely to experience the sensation of these two distinct phases due to the brevity of bed contact. However, as strength and body weight increase resulting in greater height capability, the coach should make the developing gymnast aware of the delay between first

Over & Above

contact and full depression and correspondingly, full depression to last contact. The coach has a responsibility to help the pupil "tune in" to this critical factor, although there will always be a few gifted young gymnasts who may not be able to describe it but intuitively perceive it. Once the gymnast appreciates this "feel," the changes in posture and body angle in relation to the fall and rise of the bed start to become the coaching focus. Following first contact or "touchdown" as I prefer to call it, the aim is to progressively adjust the body angle until arrival at full depression is achieved with the torso as upright as possible. The landing phase has now been completed and the take-off phase can begin when the bed starts to recoil. In the early stages of development, coaches should encourage their pupils to imagine they are arrows about to be shot from a bow. I have found this to be a simplistic but potent analogy.

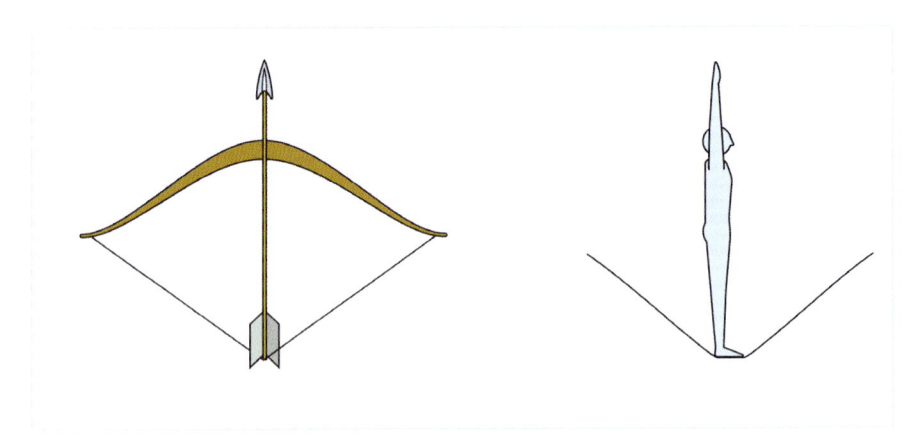

The gymnast becomes a human arrow in response to the depression and recoil of the bed.

A new form of language should be adopted to express the landing and take-off processes. "When you landed" should become, for example, "as you first contacted the bed," or "when you touched down." The end of the landing phase should be, "as you reached full depression," or "when you touched bottom." Instead of saying, "when you take-off," try saying, "just as you left the bed" or, "as the bed started to rise," depending on which point in the process is being referred to. But the key to giving the gymnast relevant feedback depends on the coach recognizing **what** is happening and **when** it is happening. This presupposes that the coach understands what should be happening. It is all very well adopting a new form of words, but sharp observation is also required so the coach can make a mental comparison with the ideal model before

When is 'the Take-Off' Not 'the Take-Off'?

entering a dialogue with the performer. Accurate feedback, which is expressed through the appropriate words, enhances the pupil's understanding of that crucial quality — timing. This involves the performer making appropriate postural and dynamic responses at the right moment in the fall and rise of the bed in order to harness the potential of the apparatus.

JACK KELLY: "The trampoline is the bow and the gymnast is the arrow."

CHAPTER 14

EVERY TAKE-OFF IS SIMPLY A MODIFIED STRAIGHT JUMP

SECTION TWO
TECHNICAL CONCEPTS

Every Take-Off is Simply a Modified Straight Jump

During my period as a High Performance Coach with British Gymnastics, a great pleasure was working with National Squad gymnasts alongside their personal coaches in their own gyms. During these sessions, I aimed to contribute to the development of both coach and gymnast, but I learned a great deal in return. One of the most enlightening environments was the Edgebarrow Trampoline club in Bracknell. Head Coach Sue Lawton and I had many fascinating discussions about the technical and psychological aspects of developing World Class skill, and we were clearly in agreement on most things. A bonus on these visits was the opportunity to debate biomechanical principles with one of Sue's younger coaches Jake Bailey, now lecturing in biomechanics at the University of Wales in Cardiff. I recall Jake distilling the complexities of trampoline technique with the statement:

> *"Every take-off is simply a modified straight jump."*

Take a moment to consider that statement, but for now exclude the fact that some skills are created from the seat, stomach or back. The straight jump from feet is the basic skill in trampolining, just as push-and-glide leads to sound swimming strokes or the grip on the club determines the golfer's ability to hit

Over & Above

accurate shots. Coaches of gymnastics and diving have long understood that efficient swinging on the apparatus or hurdle stepping on the springboard hold the key to skillful performances in their particular sports. In my experience, most trampoline coaches will say they appreciate the importance of straight jumping as the key fundamental, but it is rare for the technique to be given the full attention it requires.

The straight jump is not simply a means of becoming airborne to the requisite height; it is the essence of **every single** take-off. Let me expand the original statement: all trampoline take-offs are simply straight jumps with various modifications, made a) while in the air, if a simple jump with shape is required or, b) in contact with the bed if any degree of somersault rotation is intended.

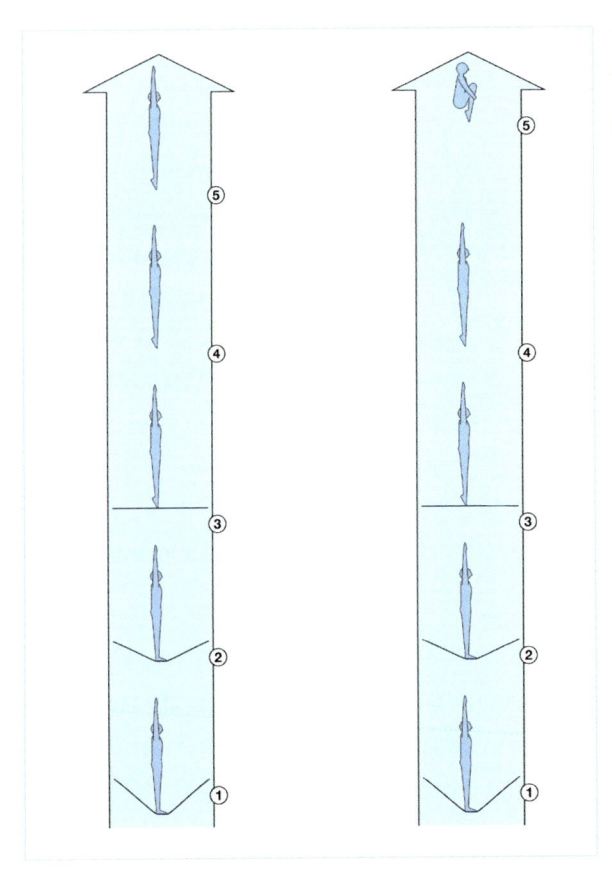

The straight jump is "modified" during flight producing a tucked jump.

Every Take-Off is Simply a Modified Straight Jump

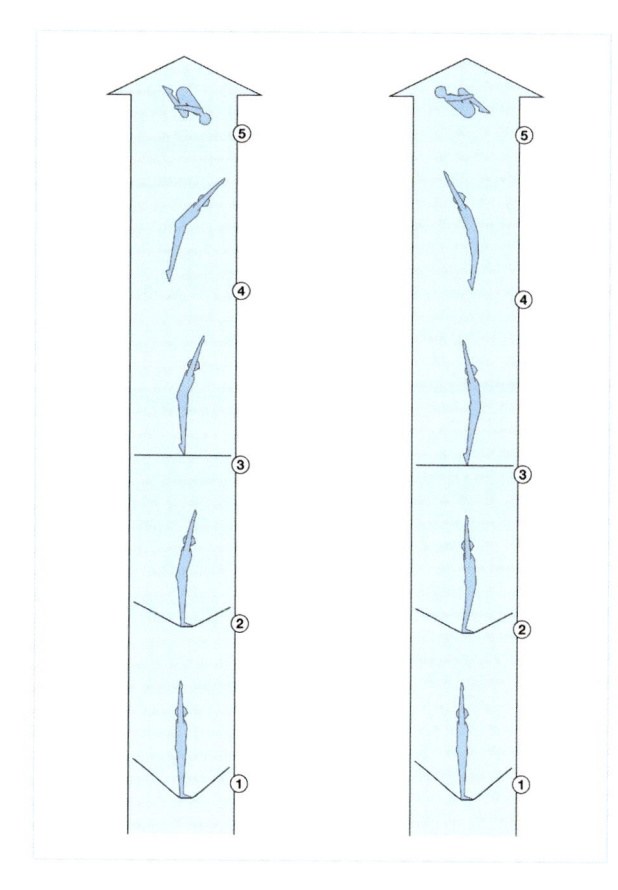

The straight jump is "modified" as late as possible during the recoil of the bed to create forward or backward rotation with a high vertical component.

If this principle is accepted, it follows that the skill of performing straight jumps with height, control, direction, placement and balance is fundamental to the gymnast's progress toward World Class. Am I advocating that the potential World Class gymnast be restricted to basic straight jumping until the technique is perfected? Of course not! Very few beginners would remain committed to the sport if such a restriction were imposed, but here is the start of a dilemma that will recur throughout the coach's career-long relationship with the athlete – just how much disciplined work should be devoted to mastering the fundamentals as opposed to the more exciting aspects of skill acquisition?

Our sport must be filled with fun, excitement and perceived progress, but the acquisition of technical fundamentals must be nurtured alongside safe progressive experimentation. The "bread and jam" dilemma again!

Regrettably, I see too many coaches spending their gymnast's development years acquiring an increasingly complex repertoire of skills and combinations for competition purposes. If **every take-off is indeed a straight jump with a modification**, then once that basic skill has been consolidated, all the gymnast needs to do is judge the

Over & Above

magnitude and timing of the appropriate modification. It's that simple! There are many "key" skills that open the doors to further progress, but **straight jumping with balance and control is the "master key."** It opens **all** the doors to **all** the rooms that contain **every possible skill and combination**. Unless the gymnast has earned the possession of this "master key," control of the advanced skills will remain behind a locked door.

However there is a way to access those skills without possession of the "master key." The coach and gymnast can kick the metaphorical door down and raid the room. The problem is that the "stolen property" will never truly belong, and in the end "crime doesn't pay!"

Every Take-Off is Simply a Modified Straight Jump

JAKE BAILEY: "Every take-off is simply a modified straight jump."

CHAPTER 15

THE STRAIGHT JUMP

SECTION THREE
TECHNICAL APPLICATION

The Straight Jump

Notwithstanding the important safety requirement that a beginner must learn body landings from minimal height, the aspiring World Class coach must fully understand the technical issues relating to skillful performance of straight jumping, which should display the following qualities:

1. Height
2. Balance/Control
3. Accuracy
4. Consistency

Height is number one on this list because it is often the defining factor in competition as the Time of Flight score is added to the total. Furthermore, the gymnast who achieves the greatest height has the most available time in which to deliver perfect execution.

HEIGHT = TIME
= OPPORTUNITY
(to display immaculate execution and perform high difficulty)

Consider the implications of time in most areas of life, including its significance to skillful sporting performance. Everyone understands that doing things hurriedly tends to cause mistakes. The soccer defender attempts to control the brilliant ball-playing

Over & Above

attacker by "closing him down." The aim is to apply sufficient pressure to cut down the time available for skillful performance and to force the attacker into mistakes. Happily, trampoline gymnasts do not have to contend with defenders trying to limit their performance through tackling or physical pressure. However, a coach may inadvertently act as an opposing "defender'" by failing to enable the gymnast to achieve sufficient height and therefore time to deliver excellent performance. Like the skillful soccer player, the gymnast becomes pressured into mistakes through lack of time to perform.

The 2011 World Championships produced a remarkable example of height as the defining factor. Lu Chunlong (CHN) beat his countryman Dong Dong to the Men's title by a mere 0.70. Dong Dong had superior difficulty, but Lu beat him on execution, making the total points score exactly equal. However, Lu registered an additional 0.70 in time of flight to come out ahead. Was it a coincidence that Lu also had the higher execution mark or did the time of flight he obtained also give him the opportunity to display cleaner form?

	Execution	Difficulty	Time of Flight	Score
Lu Chunlong	27.000	17.100	18.045	62.145
Dong Dong	26.300	17.800	17.360	61.460

2011 World Championships Men's Final Routine – height with control makes the difference.

Having made the case for height, let me stress that this is not a raw quality and paradoxically, the acquisition of **usable** height is totally dependent upon **balance/control, accuracy** and **consistency**, all of which appear on my list as subsidiary factors. It would be madness to fit a Formula One engine into a family car without improving the construction, steering, transmission and brakes to cope with such raw power. The gymnast must therefore acquire balance, control, accuracy and consistency as a means of **harnessing their height capability**.

That said, in the long term ... height **is** king!

TOPPLE, LOCOMOTION AND TRAVEL

This fundamental human movement principle has a major impact on control, stability and consistency. I therefore make no apology for spelling it out in simplistic terms before proceeding to examine the roles of the various body parts in straight jumping.

Try this. Stand on the floor and topple forward off balance. You will either fall on your face or take a forward step in order to regain your balance. I feel sure you will choose the more intelligent option! With that single balancing step, you have just replicated what you experienced when you were approximately one year old. That is how we all learned to walk. Watch any child making progress from crawling to walking – they crawl to a piece of furniture or grasp the hands of a parent before rising from all fours to a supported standing position. Gradually, unsupported standing can be learned. At this point, all exhortation for junior to "walk to mummy/daddy" will be met by an inelegant descent to a seated position on the floor. If instead, "mummy/daddy" holds the infant's hands and gently pulls forward, the first stumbling steps can be taken. The child will not walk unattended until the confidence to manage tipping forward off balance has been gained, thereby enabling a series of balance-maintaining steps to be taken. This is the process by which we humans create locomotion, and it is displayed in spectacular fashion by the tumblers as they topple continuously down the track, inserting hand and foot contacts to maintain control of their particular form of locomotion.

I have taken the trouble to describe this process because it highlights exactly what is needed in order to remain in the center of the trampoline during a series of straight jumps. The body weight must be kept directly above the feet throughout contact with the bed. Any degree of "topple" in any direction during bed contact will, unsurprisingly, result in locomotion in the direction of that topple. Yes, it's that simple, yet most trampolinists and their coaches fail to address a jumping control problem through this basic but highly effective diagnosis.

Over & Above

BALANCE AND CONTROL

It may be recalled that height provides time and therefore opportunity to demonstrate beautiful execution and high difficulty. There is a downside however, because any mistake made during bed contact will result in a problem during the airborne phase in proportion to the height (and therefore time) available. A small on-bed error will produce a large aerial outcome if the jump is high. However, during low jumping, quite a large on-bed error can be more easily tolerated. Because straight jumping is simply a microcosm of more complex take-offs (and I hope the reader has already accepted this premise), the gymnast must first be capable of total control during this fundamental skill. It follows that without complete mastery of straight jumping, the execution of a complex ten-contact routine is likely to become a gymnastic version of Russian Roulette!

It must be understood that imbalance cannot be **caused** once airborne. The **effect** of losing balance during bed contact will however be **perceived** by the performer once airborne. This can lead to the misconception that some airborne action has actually caused the problem. However, if one's center of mass remains above the base of support (in this case the feet) throughout bed contact then balance will be sensed, resulting in the gymnast feeling stable when airborne. If the center of mass starts to move forward, backward or sideways because the gymnast leans in that direction during bed contact then balance will be compromised in that direction leading to travel. But does the gymnast understand what is meant by "leaning?" There is a difference between "leaning" and "bending." The latter will not necessarily cause loss of balance, but a whole-body "lean" will certainly set up a traveling flight.

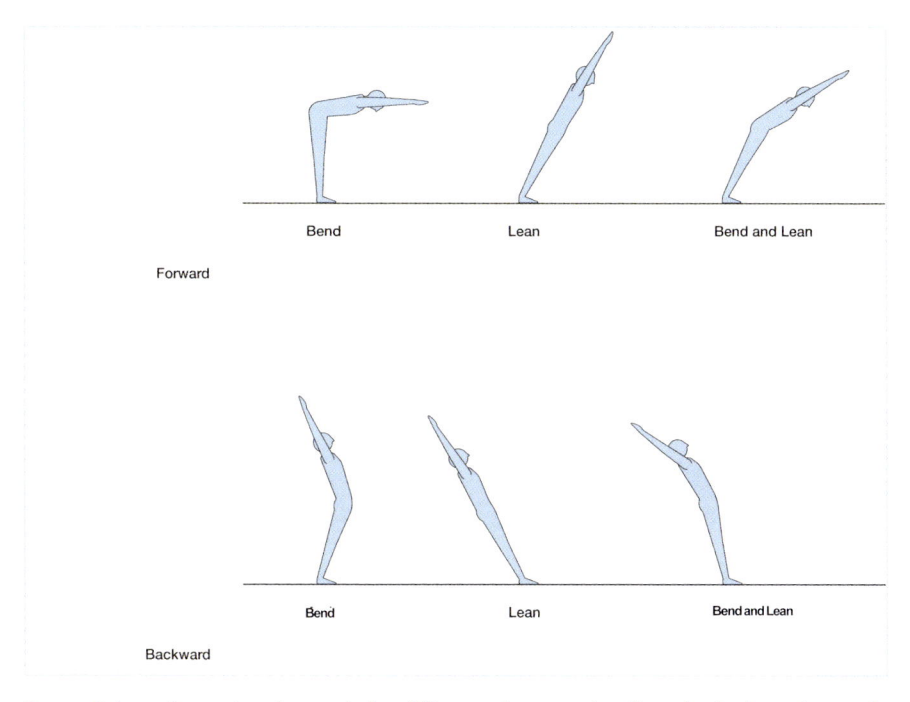

	Bend	Lean	Bend and Lean
Forward			
Backward	Bend	Lean	Bend and Lean

Trampolinists often misunderstand the difference between bending the body and actually toppling off balance, i.e., "leaning." The gymnast may feel a "lean" when it is actually a "bend." It is of course possible to do both at the same time, but coaches need to help the gymnast differentiate between what is felt and what is actually happening. This understanding is crucial to the gymnast's ability to cause or arrest travel.

Very often a gymnast exhibits signs of instability during the aerial phase of a straight jump; this is characterized either by a cycling action with the legs or a circling action with the arms. Too often both coach and gymnast try to rectify this in the airborne phase, but the problem actually originates during bed contact. The rotary action of the limbs is the gymnast's unconscious reaction to small degrees of rotation inadvertently created during bed contact. The gymnast is intuitively complying with the law of conservation of angular momentum and trying to absorb the body's rotation by cycling the limbs. Watch the expert long jumper cycle their arms and legs during the flight phase of the jump. They are deliberately performing this action to absorb unwanted forward rotation that will prevent a distance-maximizing "leg shoot."

Over & Above

Let us consider the common problem of a gymnast who has difficulty performing a series of jumps without travelling forwards, backwards or sideways, unable to consistently touch down at the same spot on the bed. The gymnast must first understand that travel in any direction can **only occur because there was some degree of directional lean during the bed contact phase**. When the gymnast and the coach fully understand and apply this concept, it is possible to eliminate those frustrating episodes of erratic and unproductive jumping. I wish I had a euro for every occasion I experienced the following dialogue.

Jack: Now that you understand **why** you traveled forward, you have the means to correct it. So, if accidentally leaning forward during contact with the bed caused you to travel forward, how might you return to your original jumping zone?

Gymnast: Lean backward?

Jack: Yes, but **when** are you going to lean backwards?

Gymnast: When I realize I'm travelling.

Jack: Of course you must immediately **recognize** the mistake, but can you travel backwards while still airborne? Have you the gift of flight?

Gymnast: No, I have to wait till I next contact the bed, then I can make the correction.

Jack: That's absolutely right. Man cannot fly! So, sense the travel **immediately** and be ready to make the appropriate correction during the **very next bed contact**. You also need to be subtle and sensitive to make the corrective lean in proportion to the initial one that made you travel. Over-correct and you'll travel back too far and once again be out of your jump zone.

In my experience, the prime cause of poorly controlled straight jumping is ignorance of the principles just described or a failure to apply the understanding of simple biomechanics taught in every first-grade coaching course. I frequently hear coaches blaming irrelevant factors like poor core stability, looking in the wrong place, or dropping the shoulders. Let's keep it simple because once this control mechanism is learned in straight jumping, the principle can be developed into the positional control of increasingly complex elements and combinations. Why? (You've heard this before!) Because every trampoline take-off is simply a modified straight jump.

The Straight Jump

My long-time coaching colleague Johnny Tenn uses the analogy of a pyramid to encourage gymnasts to feel securely balanced during bed contact and then inverts the pyramid to emphasize lack of stability. I have developed this idea in the following illustration to highlight the priority of technical components that combine to make up the pyramid.

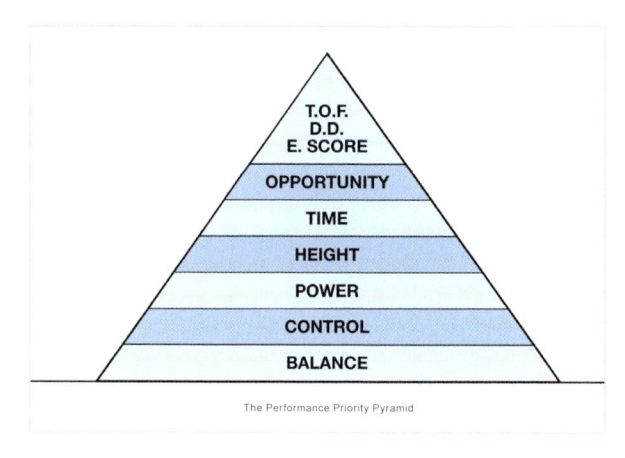

High-level performance must be built upon a solid technical foundation where each layer provides the secure base upon which every subsequent layer can be constructed. The pyramid is a formidable structure!

The Performance Priority Pyramid

If coach and gymnast prioritize Degree of Difficulty (DD), execution and time of flight as opposed to balance and control then the pyramid will tend to fall over.

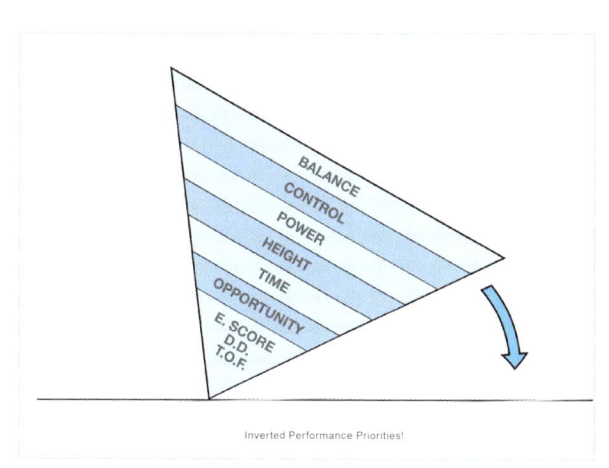

Prioritizing the "scoring" elements when developing high performance is likely to result in long-term instability and frustration. It is folly to try and improve basic technique after the gymnast has become used to throwing high DD and trying to conform to execution criteria.

Inverted Performance Priorities!

So there it is, right there! The key to World Class execution, even in the most complex of routines, is to master the control of balance during straight jumping.

Having considered the general aspects of straight jumping, let me turn to the role of the individual body parts in the process.

Over & Above

THE FEET

The grip on a golf club or tennis racket is the means of making contact with the implement; its efficiency determines the quality of subsequent strokes and shots. In trampolining, it is the feet that make contact with the equipment and as such their positions and actions are fundamental to all other parts of jumping technique. They must be flat as first contact is made in order to maximize the transfer of bed-depressing power from the legs. The flatness must remain during the bed's descent (landing phase), providing a stable base throughout. As the bed rises, the feet must remain flat in order to provide sufficient surface area for balance and the transfer of power. The feet act as the notch at the end of the arrow that receives the full force of the released bowstring. Unlike the inanimate arrow however, the gymnast can powerfully plantar flex the feet as the bed approaches last contact, adding further impetus to the upward flight, an action characterized by the familiar toe point.

There are different schools of thought regarding the amount of space between the feet during bed contact. It is argued by some, that the feet should be together throughout this period, as it increases the possibility of showing a "legs-together" position in the early part of the flight. There may also be a mechanical advantage because the closer together the feet are, the more likely it is that the downward and upward forces will be applied vertically through the gymnast's center of mass. The major drawback is the compromising of lateral stability due to the reduced base of support.

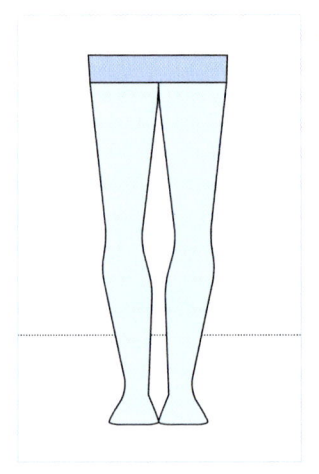

Jumping with feet together can look great and makes the best use of vertical force, but lateral stability may be compromised.

Conversely, greater lateral stability can be achieved when the feet are wider apart during the contact phase but the gymnast may have more difficulty showing "legs-together" form at the moment of becoming airborne. It could also be argued that the force applied into the bed will be less well directed with the feet wider apart. The resultant recoil may also be compromised with a possible reduction in height capability.

The Straight Jump

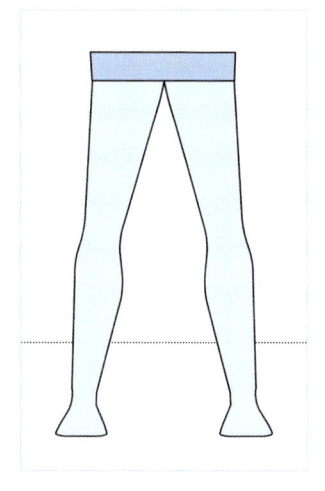

Jumping with feet apart enhances lateral stability but may diffuse vertical force and create a problem with showing a "legs-together" flight phase.

Initially, I recommend a compromise. If the gymnast imagines they have three legs instead of two, the right and left feet should be just wide enough apart to allow space for the imaginary third foot. A degree of improved lateral control is combined with the potential to apply and receive vertically directed power, as well as facilitate the closure of the legs on becoming airborne.

If this foot placement is taught initially, it provides the best of both worlds and can be modified toward a "feet together" stance when the gymnast has reached an appropriate stage in development.

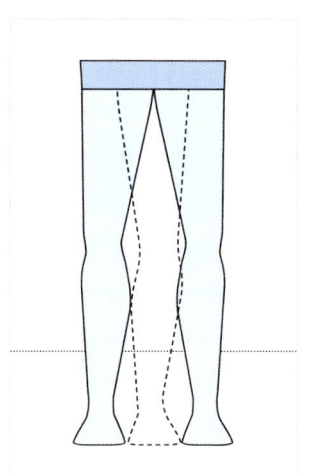

Compromised foot spacing gives a degree of lateral stability with effective vertical force application and the potential to display "legs-together" execution.

Over & Above

THE LEGS

Many accomplished trampoline performers report that once a degree of height is achieved, they feel a sensation of jumping **from** the bed, and yet the leg action required to gain height is quite the opposite. A jump from the floor requires a powerful leg drive against a firm, solid surface, while a jump from the trampoline depends on the gymnast driving the bed **downward** to stretch the springs and create the potential for powerful recoil. Why then, do many gymnasts feel they are jumping **from** the bed in the same way they jump from the floor? There is a need for detailed research into this, but here is my hypothesis.

The gymnast gains height as a result of the gradually increasing downward force of the legs depressing the bed and stretching the springs. It has been shown that an adult performer can experience a peak loading of thirteen times their bodyweight during this process. It would be impossible for a human athlete to fully straighten their legs against such a load, so it could be concluded that, as the bed reaches full depression, the legs still retain a few degrees of flexion. As the bed begins to recoil upward, it becomes similar to a solid floor, enabling the gymnast to "jump" the legs fully straight against it. We know that the feet are forcefully plantar flexed as the final action before losing contact with the bed and this combination of factors contributes to the feeling of jumping **from** the trampoline. Coaches however, must focus the gymnast's attention on the powerful **downward** action of the legs to create the greatest possible depression. This requires a flexion at the knee of approximately sixty degrees just prior to first contact. It is common to see young trampolinists vainly attempting to gain height but keeping their legs almost straight during bed contact. This, I believe is the result of a misplaced desire to show straight leg form to the judges and the coach's fear that their pupil will "stamp" the bed inefficiently. This is a hangover from the days of half-inch (13mm) webbed beds. The modern 4mm webbing responds well to a leg action that would have once been condemned as "stamping." The skilled performer will not simply flex and extend the legs but will do so with precise timing in relation to their descent to first contact and the resultant depression of the bed.

THE TORSO

The posture of the upper body has an important bearing on the effectiveness of the leg drive, and upon examining many of the world's top performers, a variety of styles can be observed. Some gymnasts maintain a largely upright posture as they make first contact, while others bend forward at the hips prior to touch-down. The upright posture and flat back will assist the transfer of power through the legs, similar to the technique of a weightlifter snatching the barbell from the floor. On closer inspection however, it can be seen that although the back is flat there is a flexion at the hip as first contact is made. Again, depending on efficient timing, a powerful upward extension from the hip can contribute considerably to the downward force into the bed using the principle of action and reaction. When the performer "stands up" as the bed goes down, the upward movement of the trunk creates a downward force into the bed. The result is a deeper depression than would have been achieved by the leg drive alone. Probably the most extreme example of this is exhibited by Shanshan Huang (CHN) with her inelegant preliminary jumps that border on the grotesque. However, that description only applies to the descent phase toward the bed as she curls her body and bends her knees prior to first contact. Once the contact has been made, she can be seen to drive down with the legs and powerfully raise her body to maximize the depressive force into the bed. The product of this unconventional style is impressive height and two beautifully poised straight jumps prior to her "arm set."

What many coaches forget is that there are no marks for aesthetically pleasing preliminary jumps – the focus should be on adopting the most mechanically effective technique to create height with balance and control. I am certainly not recommending the adoption of the "Shanshan method" because simply copying the aerial appearance of such a great performer will not transfer automatically into the attainment of greater height. The key to her acquisition of height is not **how she looks** but **what she does** from first contact to full depression. Having said that, as the **early build-up** to height is taking place, don't be afraid to "jump ugly!"

Over & Above

THE ARMS

There tends to be a disproportionate amount of attention given to the role of the arms in straight jumping, yet their action contributes least to height attainment. Their main function is to assist in balance during bed contact and to enhance the sense of tempo experienced as the bed descends and recoils. The arm movements when airborne will be discussed soon but first let us consider their contribution to height attainment.

Once the feet have contacted the bed and the downward leg drive has started, only then do the arms start make a contribution. Slow motion studies of many World Class performers show a delay in arm lift until just after full depression. It is interesting to note that these gymnasts reach full depression with arms down by their sides. This is similar to the posture I recommend in the "arm-less" jumping drills, adding credence to this as a drilled exercise. When they are lifted they display a dynamic but relatively short, upward "punchy" action similar to that which might be used when jumping from the floor. Indeed when the bed has started to rise following full depression, it will act just like the firm floor. The upward path of the arms will stop initially just below the chest area. Once the gymnast has left the bed, the arms can be lifted to reach high above the head in readiness for the "arm set." From the top of the jump, where the gymnast resembles an arrow, the arms must travel downward, keeping as close to the body as possible, in readiness for the next contact.

The arm actions employed by many of the world's best performers are highly individual and Ueyama (JPN) even makes his initial arm lift upward and behind the line of his body. This is reminiscent of the "reverse lift" somersault technique used by the much-admired Japanese male artistic gymnasts in the early '70s. The Japanese preferred this style of floor take-off because it encouraged the maintenance of a high chest, thereby delivering a front somersault of impressive height. I suspect Ueyama's employment of this arm action is no coincidence. Whatever limb path is employed, two common factors can be discerned. The action to drive the bed down is short and dynamic while the aerial phase aims to culminate in an arrow-like shape by the time the top of the jump is reached.

The Straight Jump

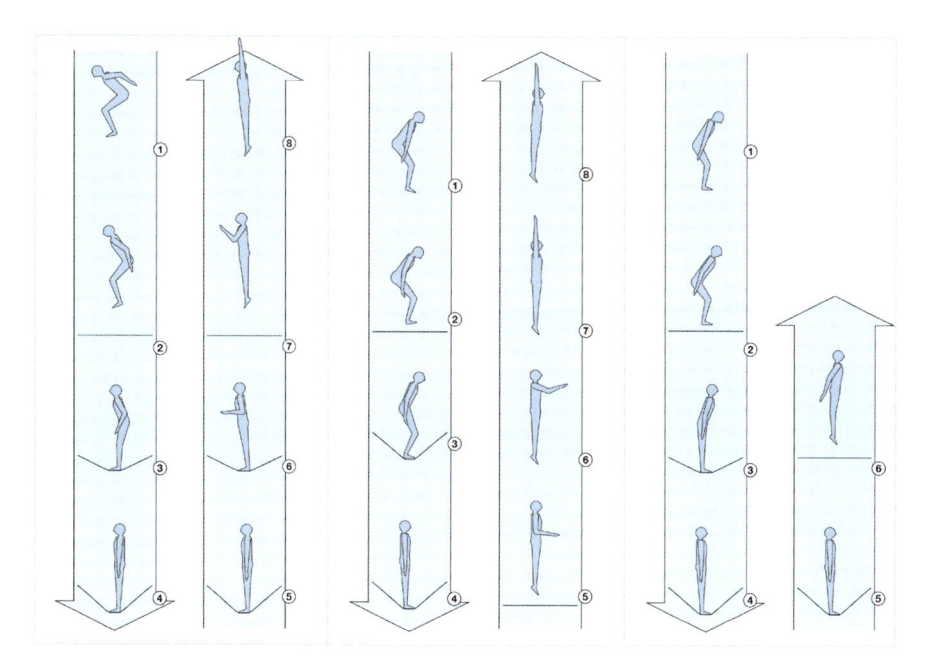

Jumping method of three World Class trampolinists.

Left to right: Huang Shanshan (CHN), Dong Dong (CHN), and Ueyama (JPN). Despite the individual differences, there are important common factors. 1 – Legs bend in preparation for first contact. 2 – Feet flatten prior to first contact. 3 – A degree of forward bend (not "lean") is seen at the hips as the bed is being driven down with the legs. 4 – This bend straightens out as the bed goes down. 5 – At full depression, the posture is erect with arms by the side. 6 – Initial arm lift during recoil is restricted. 7 – In the case of Shanshan and Dong Dong, the "arrow" shape takes place well after last contact has occurred.

The Ueyama method is distinctive for the "reverse lift" of the arms as recoil takes place. He, too, reaches the "arrow" shape (not shown) well after departure from the bed.

Over & Above

If, on becoming airborne in the "arrow" shape with the arms stretched overhead, the gymnast allows them to stray forward or backward, this will cause a piking or arching of the body in proportion to the force, range and direction of that extraneous arm movement. The body is simply conforming to the law of conservation of angular momentum. The action of the arms alone will have a slight effect on piking and arching, but it tends to be accompanied by a forward or backward movement of the shoulders and sometimes the head, which will cause a significant reaction from the legs.

Feelings and the appearance of instability in straight jumping are frequently caused by extraneous arm, head, and shoulder movements during flight. The forward and backward action of the arms and shoulders will cause piking and arching in proportion to the magnitude of the initial action.

While these airborne corrections may look unsightly, they are not as damaging as many coaches fear. The main practical problem is the tendency to mentally unsettle the gymnast and create a distraction, when all the concentration should be on composure and poise for the start of the routine. The net result may be a hurried entry into the first skill and, as already highlighted, actions that become hurried lend themselves to error. This is certainly not what is wanted before delivering a competition exercise. It may appear that these extraneous aerial arm movements cause the gymnast to lose balance but that may also be the gymnast's erroneous perception. However, because balance cannot **actually** be lost as a result of actions that take place **after** leaving the bed, the coach should be primarily concerned with addressing the stability of the gymnast during bed contact.

It could be argued that the arm action in straight jumping should be the same as when performing a 10-jump routine. This would suggest that the arms should be kept straight and swung through as the bed depresses in contrast to the shorter, bent arm punch action I have recommended. I confess that I was an early advocate of this straight arm swing before concluding that the swinging of straight arms during the bed contact phase of straight jumping adversely affects the body's center of mass. Furthermore, as the performer becomes airborne, a straight arm swing that is a little erratic will be inclined to induce the undesirable piking and arching already discussed.

Before describing a series of drills designed to improve the major aspects of the straight jump, I feel compelled to stress that drills by themselves, no matter how regularly they are practiced, do not guarantee the improvement of a particular technique. A training drill is simply a tool by which the craftsperson (in this case, the coach) fashions the product. The best tool for the job must be selected and applied with both skill and a clear vision of the desired finished article. The strength of any drill depends on the coach's ability to select the most appropriate practice and use it in enabling the gymnast to "get the message." The next step is to help the gymnast understand how to apply the drilled technique to a specific trampoline move or combination. This is known as transfer of training. The coach should always make an honest and realistic appraisal of whether the drill work being undertaken is indeed transferring properly.

Over & Above

JUMPING DRILL ONE

Aim: Help the gymnast feel the effects of balance and imbalance during the bed contact phase and come to terms with the means of jumping accurately in the target zone.

Preparation: Mark three jumping zones on the frame pad using chalk or tape. A slightly more laborious but effective method is to weave a length of colored yarn or tape between the strands of bed webbing. The zones are as shown below.

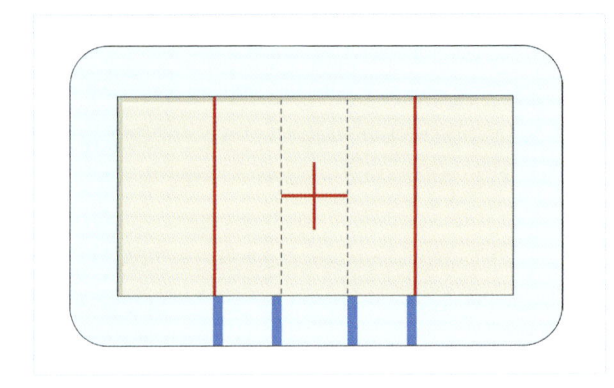

Target zones for positional jumping drills.

If working with younger gymnasts, only the central zone should be used, but more experienced performers may have acquired the habit of working just in front or behind the cross. The coach must decide whether the effort required to break such a strongly formed habit is likely to be cost effective in terms of time management.

Process: The gymnast must first declare within which zone they will be jumping. The drill should be performed with the gymnast standing erect, arms *strictly* by the side of the body, and eyes looking forward and slightly down focusing on the end frame pad. The arms must be kept by the sides to focus all the attention on posture and the actions of the feet and legs, revealing even the smallest degree of topple or inadvertent rotation. If the arms are allowed to break away from the gymnast's side, it is possible for the gymnast to disguise the small elements of imbalance that the drill is designed to address. For effective transfer of training, the coach must therefore insist on *strict compliance*. (Remember the lack of arm action at full depression displayed by Shanshan, Dong and Ueyama in the illustration on page 111.)

The gymnast performs their normal straight jumping technique in every respect, apart from using the arms. Twenty jumps are performed while attempting to remain within the designated zone. Jump height can be modified to facilitate accuracy, but the long-term target is to remain in the designated zone while jumping close to full height. This can be very demanding without the stabilizing benefit of the arms.

Evaluation: If the gymnast touches one of the imaginary extended lines which define their declared jumping zone then a point is lost. In this drill, the coach should assess only forward and backward faults. Deduct the number of faults from 20; thus if it results in, say 10, then the gymnast has achieved 50% accuracy. This should be recorded in the training diary. Frequent practice of the drill should see the score rise to 100%, which is exactly what the gymnast requires in a competition situation. The coach's role, apart from scoring, is to ensure that the gymnast begins to recognize the association between a small degree of topple and travel away from the target zone. Once a high level of accuracy is achieved consistently, then the 20 jumps can be timed by stopwatch and recorded alongside the accuracy score. It is likely that the longer the time taken, the less accurate the jump will be. However the aim is to reduce the deductions whie also increasing the jump time.

JUMPING DRILL TWO

Aim: Before working on this drill, the gymnast must have fully grasped the relevance of topple in traveling away from the target zone. The objective of the drill is to demonstrate this understanding by deliberately moving from one zone to another using complete control and awareness. Once this level of control has been mastered, if the gymnast loses bed position during the preparatory jumps in a competition situation, they can instantly recognize the nature and degree of the error and make an appropriate correction. This level of composed competence has a significant benefit in saving energy and stress during the nervous pre-performance jumping. The author frequently sees promising gymnasts undermine their mental and physical equilibrium in competition by failing to control their preliminary jumps, yet coaches are often reluctant to do the work that can have a massive beneficial effect on competition performance. I recall a conversation as I worked with a world-ranked male gymnast.

Over & Above

Jack: You are wasting so much energy and getting seriously stressed by your inability to jump with height, control and placement before starting your routine. Tell me what you are aiming to do with your pre-routine jumps. What are you thinking about?

Gymnast: I'm thinking, jump as high as I need to for the first move.

Jack: Ok, but how do you know when you're ready to take off?

Gymnast: Well, I just jump around until I manage to hit my spot, then I go!

Needless to say we immediately started addressing this random approach that I have found to be surprisingly typical.

Preparation: The gymnast starts within the chosen zone and jumps, as before, with *arms tightly by the sides*.

Process: Jump to a controllable height in the starting zone then, on a signal from the coach, perform five more jumps in that zone before taking two controlled jumps to arrive in the next zone. Clearly this will be relative to the starting zone, but let us assume the gymnast begins in the middle. The first objective is to arrive at the forward zone by using controlled forward topple. Five jumps are then performed in the forward zone before employing controlled topple (backwards this time) to returning to the starting zone. Five jumps are then performed before controlling the topple to arrive at the rear zone. The coach can vary the starting zone as well as place conditions on the drill to suit the needs of the individual. I recommend the employment of two small incremental transition jumps to help the gymnast appreciate **gradual correction**. Frequently, the performer will make the transition in one jump, but this can so easily be overdone and should be discouraged for the sake of effective transfer to the competition situation.

Evaluation: Check whether the gymnast is moving zone to zone with conscious control or simply being accidentally projected in that direction. This is a good example of a drill being used as a tool with which the coach fashions a quality product. If this drill is performed without the gymnast acquiring the awareness and competence to react appropriately then little is likely to be achieved. The gymnast should record the results of each attempt in the training diary. Regular repetition will provide a picture of the gymnast's increasing awareness and control.

Development: The next stage is to perform the two drills using a full arm action, but there are many variations that can be used to good effect. In Drill One, for example, the first 10 jumps can be performed with arms by the sides and the second 10 with full arm action. This can be varied by jumping 5 times with no arms and then 15 with full arm action. The total number of jumps can be extended to 30, with alternating groups of 5 jumps without arms then with full arm action. That is a particularly interesting challenge because as soon as the gymnast has to cease the full arm action and revert to holding the arms down, the slightest lean will become uncomfortably evident. I could have written a whole range of training variations, but my aim is to stimulate the coach's imagination and creativity in designing their own drills based on the template I have provided.

Regarding frequency and duration, I would use jumping drills at the beginning of every session following the warm-up, although the recording of scores should be limited to a monthly monitor. I am a firm believer in testing and measuring technical progress, but if testing becomes too frequent, it can have a discouraging effect. The amount of time per session devoted to this work has to be at the coach's discretion depending on the session length, and the number of gymnasts per trampoline.

Trainee coaches frequently ask me for definitive advice on what to do with their gymnasts, how long to do it for and at what frequency. Frankly, that is for each coach to decide based on their particular goals and training conditions. All I can do is indicate what to prioritize and how to recognize when quality performance is being achieved. There is no magic formula but since high, accurate, balanced straight jumping is the top priority, jumping drills must feature in every training session. Coaches therefore need to be inventive and introduce variety and interest into this work.

CHAPTER 16

THE PERFORMANCE CHIMNEY

SECTION THREE
TECHNICAL APPLICATION

The Performance Chimney

Readers may have recognized my fondness for relating trampoline gymnastics to other sports and how we can learn from the way they are performed and coached. Over the years, swimming, golf, artistic gymnastics and even fencing have stimulated my lateral thinking and provided many effective analogies. I would therefore urge ambitious coaches to broaden their quest for knowledge by developing an open mind to ideas from the wider sporting world. Sometimes the connection with our sport is immediately striking, but more often time and creative thinking are required to translate them into a usable format. The discovery of the "Performance Chimney," as I have come to call it, occurred in a most unlikely place but totally transformed my coaching focus and the quality of my trampolinists' work. It has remained my number one focus since 1970.

While watching a nationally renowned sprint coach working with his athletes on the track at Harlow Sportcentre, I became fascinated by the vision he was presenting to his group. It involved the sprinter visualizing the track lane, not as a two-dimensional surface but as a three-dimensional gun barrel. The aim, he said, was to explode from the blocks like a bullet and feel the force projecting them along the gun barrel into the circle of light they could see at the end. I don't know how effectively this concept worked for the

Over & Above

sprinters, but it had a profound effect on my thinking about trampoline performance. Yet another "ah-ha" moment!

Surely, I thought, the trampolinist aims to achieve the same as the sprinter, but the gun barrel points vertically instead of horizontally. However, the gymnast doesn't aim to be projected out of the gun barrel like the sprinter bursting into the daylight as the tape is broken. The aim is simply to reach its end at the top of every jump. So Instead of a gun barrel, the idea of a tall factory chimney made more sense to me in terms of trampolining because of its vertical and more spacious structure. I started working with my gymnasts to visualize jumping up and down inside a transparent factory chimney aiming to reach the top, not only on every preliminary jump, but with every skill in the routine. To hit the top on a straight jump was straightforward, but performing somersault skills that reached that same point was only achievable once the concept was modified as I will describe presently.

We know that without clear goals, practice becomes ill-directed, and a line from a George Harrison song, released after his death, expresses this beautifully:

"If you don't know where you're going, any road will take you there!"

The most immediate impact of the performance chimney on my gymnasts came from presenting them with a positive perceptual target for every single take-off. To parody the former Beatle, "Once you know where you're going, you know which road to take!"

THE CONCEPT

In order to apply the concept effectively, the coach must ensure that the gymnast has the ability to jump consistently within a designated area with a radius that does not exceed 30 cm. This is effectively the area of the center cross, if a circle were described around its extremities. Imagine therefore, a chimney-like structure extending upward from that circular base.

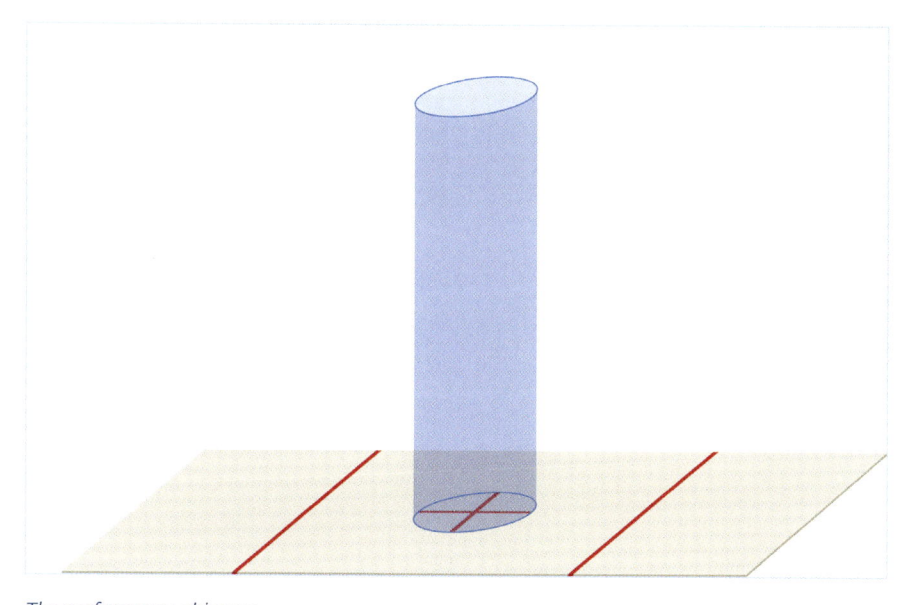

The performance chimney.

It is simple enough for the older gymnast to understand the concept of jumping and performing inside the chimney, but with younger children, standing them inside a hoop while holding another just above the head to simulate the chimney works particularly well.

Over & Above

Younger gymnasts can be helped to visualize the three-dimensional nature of the performance chimney by the coach raising a hoop from the bed to overhead.

Visualizing the base of the chimney is only the starting point because the height of the chimney must also be defined. The chimney is in fact as high as the performer chooses to jump, which means the top of each gymnast's chimney will be specific to the individual. Whatever height the gymnast is jumping, there will be an instant when they have stopped going up but not yet started to come down. I hope biomechanists will forgive the artistic license in that description! The gymnast should be directed to "feel" that moment in space and perceive it as the point reached by the top of their head. It is a moment of stillness at the top of each jump. It is that "magic moment." It is the top of the chimney!

The objective is to hit the top of this personalized chimney on all skills while remaining in the center of the trampoline. This can be readily achieved on straight jumps and jumps with non-rotating, airborne-created shapes because only vertical force is involved. However as soon as the gymnast has to introduce a degree of rotation around an axis while in contact with the bed, some height will be lost due to the need to redirect force around the axis in question. This will result in a failure to hit the top of the chimney previously established in the straight jumping. So does this effectively invalidate the performance chimney concept for all somersaulting and contact-twisting skills?

That would indeed be the case if the gymnast were setting the chimney top (henceforth to be called "the top") by jumping to their maximum height. It is not technically possible to reach the pre-set top with a somersaulting skill. *But here is the key to the success of the concept.* If the gymnast jumps at, say 80-85% of their maximum, it becomes technically possible to hit the top on jumps, twists **and** somersaults. The coach and gymnast must therefore *determine a realistic top* that can be attained using all the skills from the gymnast's repertoire. I have used the phrase "technically possible" because there are a number of challenges for gymnast and coach to overcome in mastering the technique.

1. The gymnast must be able to jump with unerring accuracy within the confines of the chimney. (Hence my detailed analysis of balance, topple and travel in Chapter 15.)

2. The gymnast must develop a keen and consistent awareness of that "magic moment" when the top is reached.

3. The gymnast must relish that moment of stillness between going up and coming down. This can be a decisive factor in identifying young gymnasts with the potential to reach World Class ... part of the "talent package."

4. The gymnast must be able to recognize the difference between maximum jump height and the still-powerful but more controlled 80-85%.

5. Most importantly, the coach must embrace the concept, learn to recognize when the top has been reached and "sell" the vision to the pupil so that both can clearly recognize the difference between attainment and failure.

I have already expressed concern that many coaches and their gymnasts are unaware of the landing phase and take-off phase processes, referring to them as if they were instants. When I work with gymnasts, even those competing at international level, I am

Over & Above

frequently astounded to discover that many are also unaware of the "magic moment" when the top of a jump has been reached. Why does this happen? Once again we have an example of the "trampolining-is-too-easy" mindset. Coach and gymnast have never thought about it. I liken this to the novice swimmer being unaware of where the pool bottom is. It is a critical reference point, in the same way that the high jumper must be focused on the high point above the bar. Young gymnasts on a World Class pathway should be familiar with the importance of "top" long before they are taught to somersault. This is such a fundamental piece of awareness, I am inclined to use the cliché, "it's not rocket science!"

However, upon reflection, it is very like rocket science!

"TOP" DRILL ONE

The gymnast performs a series of straight jumps **strictly inside the chimney**. The coach stands on the floor and relates the top of each jump to some visual marker on the wall (e.g., pipe, window ledge, line of bricks, edge of the balcony). The top of the head is the point to focus on. When the high point in **each jump** is reached, the coach calls, "Top!" The gymnast stops jumping and the coach asks, "Do you agree that when I called, you were at the top of the jump?"

"TOP" DRILL TWO

Having ascertained that the performer understands and agrees with the coach's perception of the top, the drill is repeated with the pupil now calling "top" when they feel that point has been reached. The coach needs to provide feedback as to whether the gymnast is calling at the right moment. The underlying philosophy is to empower the gymnast into feeling the top for themselves.

"TOP" DRILL THREE

The gymnast now executes a tucked jump following a series of straight jumps where either the coach or performer calls "top." The aim is to show the tucked shape exactly at the highest point. It must be noted that the action of tucking needs to start significantly before the top is reached, otherwise, the completed shape will be seen on the descent. Nonetheless, the start of the tucking action must be postponed until the gymnast is off the bed or vertical force will be compromised, resulting in a failure to hit the top with the shape being displayed at the desired point in space. This drill can have a high degree of transfer to somersaults, which **appear to be created** in the air. But it requires the "craftsman" to use this "tool" skillfully. The drill can be developed to include the other jump shapes, singly or in combination. The coach needs to remind the gymnast, as I remind you now, that "every take-off is simply a modified straight jump!"

"TOP" DRILL FOUR

Here is where the real challenge begins — hitting the top while performing a take-off with a rotational element. The gymnast must again jump **within the chimney**, but now they will be operating at 80-85% of maximum height to allow for the fact that the rotational force will prevent absolute maximum height from being reached.

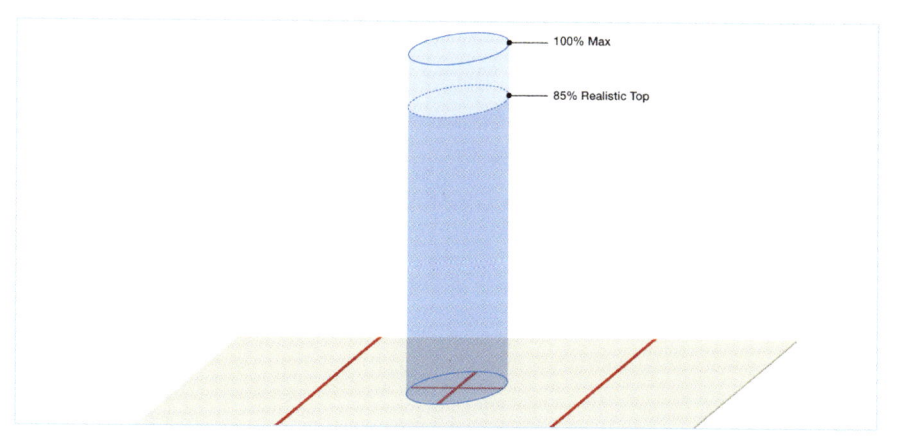

The performance chimney indicates a realistic target height for the execution of ten skills in a competition routine.

Over & Above

Once again, the coach reminds the gymnast of that "magic moment" when the top is reached. Because this take-off will produce a rotating skill, the coach should now use the gymnast's waistband (the approximate location of the center of mass) as a visual guide against the wall marker. The gymnast, on the other hand, still uses the top of their head as the reference point in order to maintain that **feeling** of hitting the top. This is a classic example of a coaching scenario where the coach is trying to create an accurate biomechanical performance yet is asking the gymnast to feel a sensation that is biomechanically incorrect. Following a series of jumps, a seat drop is performed. Did the gymnast hit the top? The coach needs to assess what was **seen**, but the gymnast must judge success by what was **felt**.

The reader should note my deliberate use of the term "seat **drop**," as opposed to "seat **landing**" in order to maintain consistency with my statement (Chapter 13) that there is no such thing as a landing; there is a landing phase! If the gymnast hits the top following this particular take-off, there is no doubt that they will indeed drop. Go straight up, and you'll come straight down! I even use the phrase "top, stop, then drop!" This is **exactly what is wanted*!**

"TOP" DRILL FIVE

Because our intention is a gradual progression toward the performance of a tucked back somersault, the next logical step is to repeat drill four, but introduce marginally more rotation by creating a back drop. In my experience, it is rare for a performer to get this on the first time and, if they do, it may cause slight alarm due to the rotation feeling slower than usual. It may help to overcome initial reluctance if the push-in mat is used. Once again, did the coach see the waistline of the gymnast reach the same point at the top of the back rotating skill as was seen in the 80-85% max preliminary jumps? Did the gymnast feel they had taken the top of their head up to the same place?

---

*The use of the word "landing" as opposed to "drop" is meaningful when encouraging beginners to jump up before making bed contact on the seat, the back or the front rather than "dropping" straight down to the body contact.

"TOP" DRILL SIX

Once consistent success is achieved with drills four and five then work can begin to reach the top on a tucked back somersault. I hasten to add that the gymnast must already be competent and confident in performing back somersaults before this final drill is introduced. The aim of the drill is to reconfigure the existing somersault into one that hits the top. "Top" drills one to five can be introduced very early in the gymnast's development and before complete 360-degree somersaults are taught.

There are a number of reasons why a pupil may have difficulty with Drill Six.

1. If the gymnast has already been taught to show a somersault with a straight kick out, this will almost certainly result in a fast somersault with the top cut off. A difficult habit to change.

2. It is disconcerting to take off with less rotation and greater vertical force if the somersault has not been originally taught in that way.

3. The gymnast may be used to somersaulting with a degree of travel. If we relate it to the chimney concept, this would equate to breaking through the back wall of the chimney! Even a small amount of travel will result in failure to hit the top.

Drill Six is a highly revealing exercise that often exposes the fact that the gymnast has been allowed to perform seat drops and back drops with varying degrees of travel. This can be exacerbated by the idea that these two backward rotating skills are, in fact, landings. The crucial point is **not the landing but the direction of the take-off**! These are effectively straight jumps with a slight modification during take-off. The gymnast should feel their head has reached the top before descending onto the appropriate body part.

Clearly, the same process can be employed using the front somersault as the target skill. Once again, the somersault microcosm (in this case, front drop) should have been learned with a clear feeling (by the gymnast) and with appearance (to the coach) of hitting the top of the chimney. The drill sequence just described is suitable for pupils in the early stages of development or as a remedial process for mature, higher-level gymnasts. Judicious use of the push-in mat is recommended for all drills where the gymnast is likely to be exploring a new mix of vertical and rotational inputs.

Over & Above

BEWARE THE SELF-DESTRUCTIVE CHAIN!

Following the concept and process just outlined requires a clear vision of what will eventually be possible rather than a desire for a short-term result (see Chapter 11 "Trampolining is Too Easy!") In the early days of developing my gymnasts, I resisted the temptation to improve execution marks by complying with the International Rules for Trampoline Gymnastics. I know that sounds paradoxical, but let me explain. In most sports, the rules of the game and the equipment for young developing athletes are modified to suit age, stature and skill level. This is not so in trampolining. Certainly there can be difficulty limits imposed and a grading structure based on age or ability, but children are still judged by the same criteria as competitors at World and Olympic level. That is folly in development terms.

The two major features of performance that appear to concern most coaches are avoidance of travel and showing somersault exits at 12 o'clock. Both qualities can be achieved by the gymnast through spinning fast and keeping the center of mass approximately above their feet during every take-off. For a ten-year-old to somersault "on the spot" **and** exit at 12 o'clock requires damaging technical "shortcuts." Attempting to prioritize the FIG judging criteria before the young gymnast has the strength and height to cope tends to create the following counter-productive chain of consequences.

EMPHASIS ON "FORM" ———— *LOSS OF HEIGHT* ———— *LOSS OF TIME* ————
INCREASED PRESSURE ———— *LOSS OF EXECUTION MARKS*

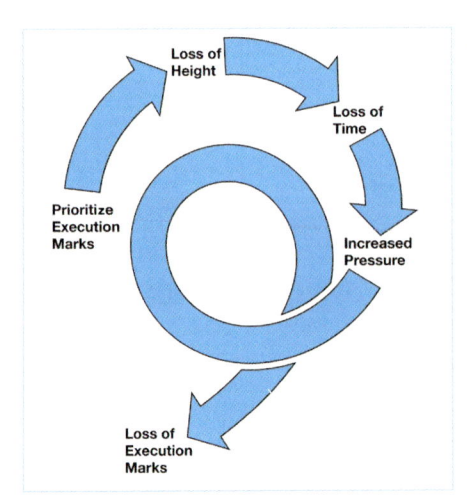

A counterproductive downward spiral can result if coaching is too focused on the "cosmetic" requirements of the Code of Points.

By following the Performance Chimney process, where the emphasis is on achieving the top on every jump, we can break this damaging sequence. Somersaults will be high and remain in the center of the trampoline, permitting the gymnast to perform with **time to**

think and control the work through all ten consecutive skills. There will be a need for the developing gymnast to concede **some** deductions for failing to exit at 12 o'clock, but the height maintenance throughout all ten skills in the routine can offset this concession to a large extent. Look at the long-term creative "production chain" we create with this approach:

EMPHASIS ON "TOP" ——— MAINTENANCE OF HEIGHT ——— LACK OF TRAVEL ——— TIME ——— POTENTIAL FOR LONG-TERM WORLD CLASS DEVELOPMENT

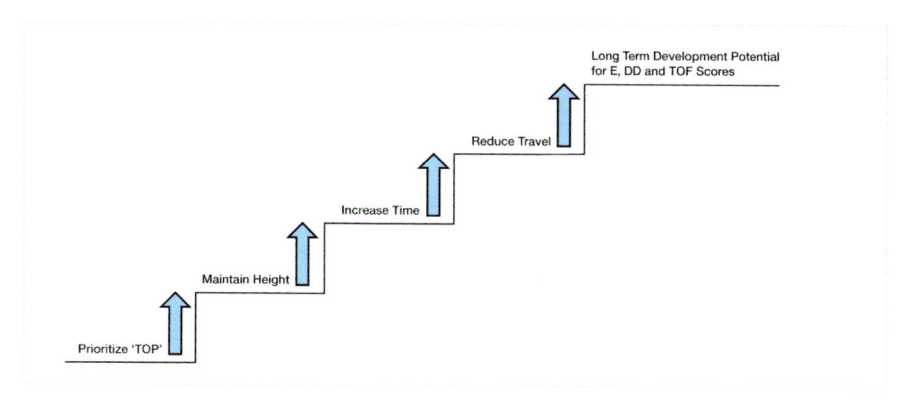

The positive development "escalator."

I work with juniors to maximize the top and perform somersaults that show clarity of shape followed by a straight-legged but somewhat piked exit. If patience is exercised during the development period, the maturing gymnast gradually learns that, as their jump height increases, so their somersault exits begin to conform more closely to FIG criteria. Furthermore, the time element they have been brought up to enjoy lends itself to increasing difficulty. I call that a win-win situation!

The introduction of time of flight scoring may discourage the damaging "spin and kick out" obsession, but coaches should see beyond improving time of flight simply as a means of increasing that particular score. Working up to the top of the performance chimney has much greater long-term benefits to offer.

Over & Above

IMPLICATIONS FOR SHAPING

One of the ironies resulting from teaching young gymnasts how to impart excessive rotational force to enable a 12 o'clock exit is that the exaggerated body action during the take-off phase destroys the possibility of creating a compact shape in the early part of the flight. So we tend to see a fast, ill-shaped skill with what coach and gymnast may regard as the required straight exit. There is no point in a straight exit if the required shape of the somersault has been compromised. I recall a discussion on this subject with Nigel Rendell, coach to Britain's 2008 Olympian. He knew I was inclined to express key coaching points by means of snappy sayings or rhymes to make them memorable. He was determined to show he could do the same.

Nigel: What you're trying to say is, "if you take off steep, your shape will be deep!"

Jack: Nice one, Nigel, I really like that. But the opposite is also true. Take off with travel, and your shape will unravel.

Many a true word is spoken in jest, and I confess my response wasn't quite as immediate as that sounds!

The gymnast who takes off with the goal of hitting the top of the chimney will feel short of rotational force, which in turn will require a tighter shape in the air to accelerate the somersault. It must be remembered that the execution judges will penalize loosely held shapes as well as incomplete exits, so a vertical take-off still has a potential short-term form advantage despite the absence of a straight exit.

The Performance Chimney

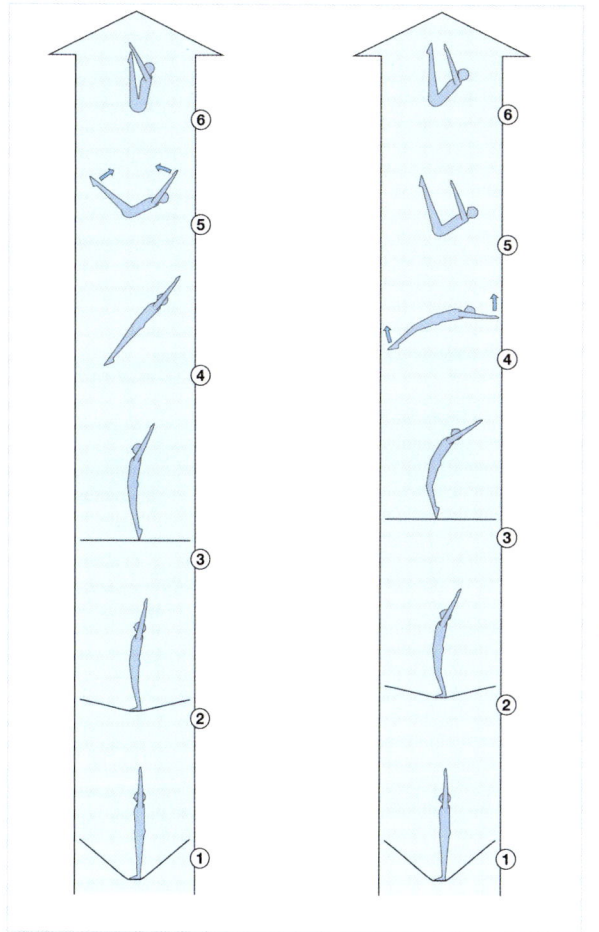

Left: "Steep" take-off using principle of a modified straight jump, aiming to hit the top of the chimney resulting in close pike.

Right: "Soft" take-off prioritizing rotational force rather than vertical direction resulting in loose, ill-defined piked shape. These shapes will also have a bearing on the gymnast's ability to show a straight exit.

"Take-off steep, and your shape will be deep!"

CHAPTER 17

TUNE IN TO TEMPO

Tune in to Tempo

SECTION THREE
TECHNICAL APPLICATION

The performance chimney and awareness of the top are powerful concepts, but too often gymnasts and coaches will only work with such an idea for a short time, thinking, "we've done that," before moving on to the next gimmick or "quick fix" idea. It is important to sustain the objective with constant reminders in order to create a long-term benefit. Sometimes both coach and pupil stop doing what is successful, either because they believe that the gymnast has now "got it" or because both parties become bored with the constant repetition. Let us look at another equally effective piece of imagery that targets a different part of the gymnast's technique yet brings a fresh approach to the objective of hitting the top.

You may recall that in the early days of the sport we called the process of joining a series of skills together "performing in **swing time**." We would even say things like, "Now that you can do a back somersault in all three shapes, let's see you **swing** them together." This use of the word "swing" has an immediate rhythmical reference to music that I find appealing. Over the years, I have developed a preference for the musical term "tempo" to describe evenness of bounce and maintenance of height. My preference for "tempo" as opposed to "swing" or even "rhythm" is not so much in the meaning, but the onomatopoeic effect of the two syllables. TEM ... PO has an affinity with the "down-up"

133

Over & Above

feeling we want the gymnast to appreciate during the depression and recoil of the bed. This may strike you as an irrelevant detail, but the communication of an idea to the gymnast can be greatly enhanced by appropriately clever word selection. That is just one example.

Imagine a typical scenario in which the trampolinist is starting to perform a routine. The preliminary jumps are high, well placed, and the posture is good. The first skill takes off and, although displaying stylish form, loses a small amount of height. As the routine progresses, further height loss is seen, resulting in a pattern of travel, recovery and a scramble to the finish. The following conversation ensues:

Jack: What did you think of that routine?

Gymnast: I could feel myself rushing, but I managed to finish.

Jack: OK, let's deal with the loss of height because that is what made you rush and make mistakes. Where did that start?

Gymnast: I think it began to go wrong around move four.

Jack: What about move one?

Gymnast: It felt like that looked good.

Jack: Yes, but **that** was where you began to lose height.

Gymnast: How could that be when it was only the first move?

Jack: You were hitting the top of the chimney on each preliminary jump but broke through the front wall of the chimney on the first move!

It is a common misconception among trampoline gymnasts that height loss starts **after** the first skill rather than in the transition between preliminary jumps and the start of the routine. If the gymnast has learned to jump at 80-85% of their maximum and is aware of the chimney top before taking off for the first move, they can and should expect the first skill in the routine to start at the same height as those preliminary jumps.

The conversation continues:

Jack: Do you listen to music?

Gymnast: Yes.

Jack: Does your music have a definite beat?

Gymnast: Yeah!

Jack: Imagine you're listening to the intro of one of your favorite tracks. The beat is being laid down, and you can feel the groove. Suddenly, the singer comes in ahead of the beat. Unthinkable, huh?

Gymnast: (Thinks) ... He's right, but the old boy has really lost it and is just trying to appear cool!

Jack: As you performed the preliminary jumps before your routine, I was enjoying the height, balance and rhythm of those jumps ... feeling the groove, you might say. But can you imagine how my senses were offended when you suddenly started the first move ahead of that tempo? Arrgh!

Gymnast: OK, I get it now!

Jack: Right, let's do the preliminary jumps again, but this time listen to the sound of the bed and feel the beat you are laying down. It starts quickly with the low early jumps but soon builds to a regular tempo in readiness for the start of the routine. Can you feel that?

Gymnast: (Jumping) Yes, I can feel it.

Jack: As you make first contact with the bed, say "down," and as the bed starts to recoil, say "up." So we have a tempo that goes "down-up, down-up, down–up, etc."

Gymnast: (Jumping) Down-up, down-up, down-up.

Jack: Next time when you reach the highest point of your jump, say "top." So now we have "down-up ... top, down-up ... top." That is the tempo we will maintain, not only through the first move in the routine but for all of the following nine moves to the end.

This approach has been remarkably successful over the years, and gymnasts who read that little cameo may recognize a conversation they had with me. The objective is, of course, to feel the take-off for the first move as being right on the tempo created by

Over & Above

the preliminary jumps. I have known this method to produce spectacular results, but a word of warning is required. Sometimes the gymnast who has a habit of "chopping" the top off the first move will perform so spectacularly on their first attempt when focusing on tempo, that they become alarmed by the additional flight time created. With this type of reaction, some patience is required to develop the process into a permanent part of their technical competence. The push-in mat may be advised depending on the temperament and attitude of the performer, so don't expect a quick fix with everyone.

DEVELOPING TEMPO AWARENESS

To increase the awareness of tempo and the way it is exhibited by the world's best performers, I have used the following introduction to a tempo session with national squads. I share it here with you.

Obtain some video recordings of the world's leading performers, both male and female. Make sure the video has reasonable sound quality so that the noise of the gymnast contacting the bed and the corresponding recoil of springs can clearly be heard. Each gymnast in the session should have a pen and paper to write down notes during the exercise. The gymnasts sit facing **away** from the screen and use their hearing to recognize whether a performer is jumping. As each competitor on the video starts to jump, the lead coach calls out, "Competitor One," etc. The squad gymnasts have to place a tick on their paper every time they hear the gymnast jump. A distinct two-beat "CHA- JUM" should be audible during every bed contact. When they think the sound indicates the first skill of the routine has taken off, the squad members must place a cross instead of a tick. This is repeated with as many competitors as deemed necessary to make an impact. The videos are played once more with the squad group actually watching and comparing their answers with what is seen on the screen. On the several occasions I have conducted this exercise, it is only by luck if the gymnast (and indeed the assistant coaches) gets more than a couple correct. It will be found that the world's best performers maintain a strict tempo through the prelim jumps and into the routine. It will also be observed that the best routines adhere very closely to the established tempo from moves one through ten.

Once the significance of tempo to World Class performance has been established, the gymnasts can go through a series of tempo drills on the trampoline. Let me remind you that drills are only tools by which the skilled coach shapes the "product." They do not, in themselves, guarantee progress and require total engagement from the gymnast to be effective. The drills need to be worked on progressively, moving to the next drill only when the previous one has been satisfactorily undertaken. Indeed, it is unlikely that the following worksheet can be satisfactorily completed in a single session, and it may take several weeks to master the range of combinations listed. Coaches can use this Tempo Drill Worksheet as a template from which to devise their own personalized work.

Tempo Drill Worksheet

1. 20 x straight jumps. Concentrate on feeling/hearing the tempo DOWN ——— UP ———————————— TOP.

2. Repeat with every second jump as a tucked jump, e.g., straight jump, tuck jump, straight jump, etc. DOWN ——— UP ———————————— TOP.

3. Repeat with every second jump as a straddle jump. (Listen and feel the even tempo).

4. Repeat with every second jump as a piked jump.

5. Six preparatory jumps then tuck/pike/straddle x 3.

6. Six preparatory jumps then tuck/pike/straddle/half twist jump x 3. (Maintain feel and sound of tempo even when twisting. Delicate twist action required.)

7. Six preparatory jumps then tuck/pike/straddle/full twist jump x 3. (Full twist jump will tend to break the tempo so emphasize vertical direction and delicate twist.)

8. Six preparatory jumps to establish tempo then back somersault (T) /straight jump/ back somersault (T)/ straight jump x 3. (Note the direction of each straight jump. It should go straight up to the top.) DOWN ——— UP ———————————— TOP throughout!

9. Repeat drill 7 with insertion of piked back somersault.

10. Repeat drill 7 with insertion of straight back somersault.

Over & Above

11. Single somersault combinations of no more than five skills with an intermediate straight jump. (Own choice but include barani.) Can you still feel the tempo?

12. Repeat drill 11 but include at least one backward single somersault with twist.

13. (Throughout the above process, gradually replace the straight jumps with shaped jumps and/or somersaults depending on progress.)

14. Single and double somersault combinations of five moves. (Own choice.) DOWN ——— UP ——————————— TOP!

15. Double somersault combinations for five moves. (Own choice.)

16. First five moves of current set routine.

17. Develop theme of TEMPO within own competition routines.

Don't expect to complete the worksheet in one session, but select drills from the list appropriate to the level of competence of the gymnast. Progress only when the appreciation of regular tempo is demonstrated consistently.

The renowned classical music composer Claude Debussy is reputed to have observed that it is not the notes that make a piece of music; it is the space **between the notes**! Think about that!

Now let me state my belief that *it's not the moves that make a quality trampoline routine — IT IS THE **SPACE BETWEEN** THE MOVES. That is what I mean by TEMPO!*

Tune in to Tempo

JACK KELLY: *"Bed down…Body up!"*

CHAPTER 18

ARM SETTING

SECTION THREE
TECHNICAL APPLICATION

Arm Setting

Arm setting is the process by which the gymnast changes the action of the arms on the final straight jump prior to the take-off for a skill, sequence, or full routine. Despite many idiosyncratic variations, the arm action during straight jumping approximates to a backward circling motion. While this pattern of arm movement can be appropriate to the take-off for all basic skills and even single somersaults, it is poorly suited to the gymnast working at height and about to take off for a multiple rotating skill. It makes sense however for the young aspiring gymnast to learn the process of arm setting at an early stage in their development. In normal straight jumping, the arms will be rising as the gymnast leaves the bed, and this can certainly lend itself to efficient backward rotating skills since the arms are already rotating backwards as they reach up. If this action is used during the take-off for a forward somersault, however, the arms will rotate contrary to the direction of the somersault.

Over & Above

This arm action was in general use for forward take-offs until the 1970s, but it was very inefficient when attempting multiple rotations without dramatic loss of height. The technique (and the limited power from 13mm beds) accounted for the limited number of male gymnasts using triffs and the complete absence of triples in women's competition.

As 6mm webbing became more prevalent during the 1970s, I was concerned with developing a more effective arm action for the initiation of triple forward rotations at the start of competitive routines with a focus on improving direction and height maintenance. My guinea pig for these experiments was 15-year-old Simon Rees, World Age Group, European Youth and British Senior Men's Champion. The technique we evolved is now standard practice throughout the world for both forward and backward take-offs. That is not to say that coaches in other parts of the world were not having similar thoughts. It is interesting to note that when Simon won the European Youth Championship in 1974, he was the only one using what we now recognize as the "arm set" technique. Even the technically aware Soviets were relying on the traditional contrary arm action for their forward take-offs. However, they were quick to recognize the benefits of what we had developed. By the next major championship, every Soviet gymnast was using the arm set technique. I now accept that imitation is the sincerest form of a compliment.

The arm set also replicates the timing of the arm action, which develops naturally when consecutive somersaults are linked together. This enables the coach to ask the gymnast to finish a given skill at full depression "exactly as if it were an arm set." The essence of the technique is to set the arms overhead at some time during the final descent to the bed or even during the actual process of depression prior to the first skill take-off. It is a relatively simple matter to stop the standard arm action used in straight jumping and holding the arms overhead throughout the drop toward the bed. To incorporate this rhythmically within the final descent takes practice and exquisite timing to produce the best results. There are many variations in the timing of the arm set, which I will examine later in the chapter. Unfortunately, many young trampolinists can be seen interrupting their arm swing and holding their arms overhead for the entire final descent to the bed for the first take-off. This can lead to a loss of stability on first contact and increases the potential for injury to the lower back when bed depression takes place. This should be discouraged!

TEACHING METHOD

The method I employed with Simon Rees was developed by setting up a tucked jump before the first take-off. Many young trampolinists will learn the arm set simply by copying, but I still prefer to use the following process. It has the advantage of adapting a well-known skill rather than introducing a totally new pattern of arm movement.

1. The gymnast performs a tucked jump followed by a straight jump. They may exit the tucked jump with the arms directly overhead or with the arms down before reaching them overhead. At this stage, either is acceptable as long as the arms are up by the time full depression is reached after the tuck jump has touched down. Care must be taken to ensure the gymnast contacts the bed with the torso in a strong upright posture. Making first contact with the back slightly arched will cause discomfort, instability, and possible injury. Height should be limited on these early attempts.

2. Once this can be done with accuracy and stability, the task is to repeat the arm action and minimize the leg tucking action. This is done by the gymnast calling "tuck" as the arms touch the knees and "jump" as the legs drop down and the arms start to rise overhead. This apparently silly exercise is very helpful in establishing the rhythm and timing of the arm drop and subsequent lift overhead. The verbalized tuck and kick out are followed by a straight jump as before.

3. The exercise is repeated with the tuck jump, arm drop and lift but with the leg action being minimized to a slight knee bend only. The gymnast continues to call "tuck" as the knees bend and the arms drop, followed by "jump" as the arms are raised overhead.

Over & Above

4. By now, the leg bend will be minimal and the arms will be dropping by the gymnast's side rather than reaching for the knees. The calling of "tuck" and "jump" may still be necessary to ensure good timing, and the drill should be completed with a straight jump.

5. Finally, the gymnast will maintain straight legs throughout but should be encouraged to visualize the previously established tuck then jump timing. We now have an arm set that can be used to produce straight jumps to the top of the chimney as well as back and front somersaults with top.

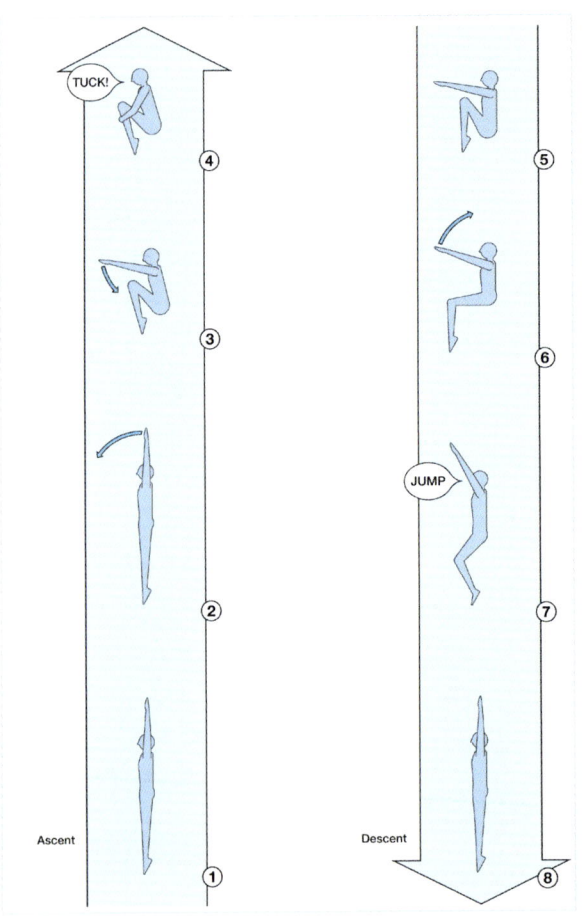

The teaching of an arm set action through the conversion of a known skill – the tucked jump. This teaching process will result in an "early" arm set, and there may be a need to slightly adjust the timing as the technique comes into general use.

Although I have introduced the arm set as a single technique, it can and is used with various distinct timings depending on the preference and needs of the gymnast. I have identified two distinct categories of timing within the arm setting.

Arm Setting

1. Early Arm Set—This causes me some concern, particularly because it is prevalent among younger gymnasts and inexperienced coaches who have largely imitated what they believe is being done by the top performers. In this version of the technique, the arms have been raised overhead by the top of the jump, resulting in the gymnast descending all the way to the bed with arms raised. This renders the arms totally impotent as far as contributing to the actual take-off and leaves them unable to assist with the gymnast's stability as the bed depresses. Indeed, it places the gymnast in a highly vulnerable situation in terms of balance and control. My comments about the potential for back injury described in stage one of the teaching method also apply here.

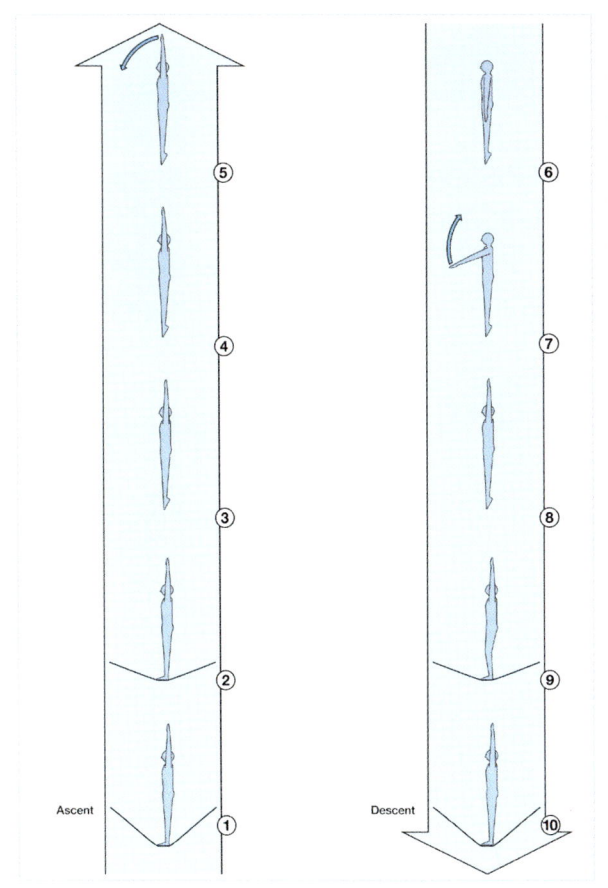

The "early" arm set involves the arms being "set" overhead just after the beginning of the descent to the bed for take-off. However, if the arms are directly overhead at any point before bed contact, it still constitutes an "early" arm set.

2. Late Arm Set—In this timing, the arms will drop after the gymnast has reached the top of the jump and will be held alongside the body during the descent toward first contact. Although I have designated this as "late," wide variations in the timing can be employed. A range of timing between early and late can be seen among the world's top performers with variations such as the arms being swung behind the hips on the descent in order to absorb excessive time on the way down to first contact. Ueyama (JPN) typifies this variation. Dong Dong

Over & Above

(CHN) on the other hand often allows the arms to start rising before first contact is made. So much depends on the height of jumping as well as the stature and stage of development of the gymnast. My main concern is to eliminate the inefficient and potentially damaging early arm set. I strongly recommend the development of a "late" arm set with appropriate fine-tuning to suit the needs and abilities of each individual performer.

I have defined only two categories of arm set timing for the sake of simplicity but there is of course a range of timings possible within each.

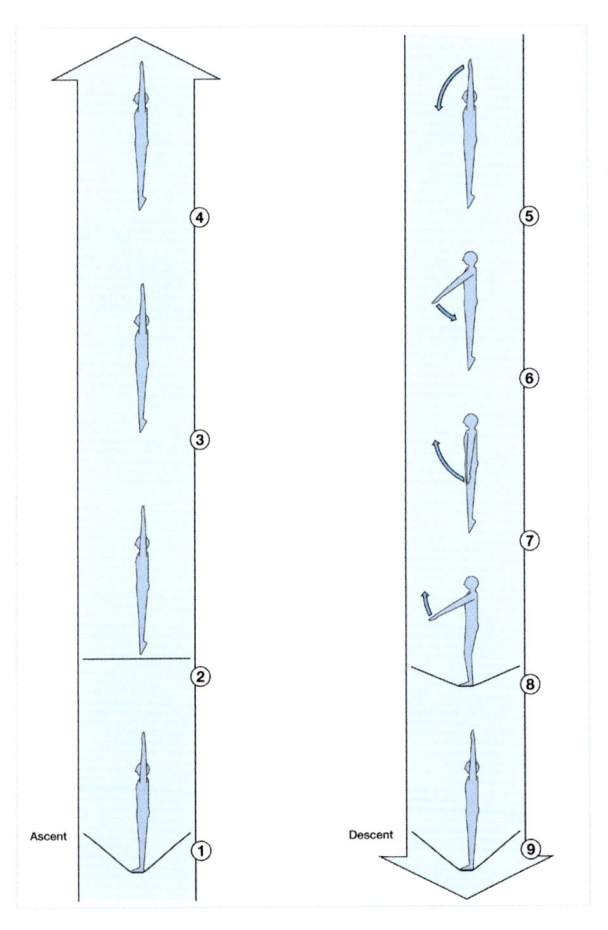

The "late" arm set involves the arms being dropped to the gymnast's side during the descent toward the bed for take-off. The arms are held in position until just before the bed is contacted and dynamically swung overhead. This "late" arm swing enhances balance during bed depression and also creates an additional downward force. The gymnast arrives at full depression in the classic arrow posture.

Arm Setting

JACK KELLY: *"A piked shape is best created through the natural body 'fold' which results from a well-directed take off."*

CHAPTER 19

THINKING ABOUT LINKING

SECTION THREE
TECHNICAL APPLICATION

Thinking About Linking

My own early attempts to perform on the trampoline always focused on learning new individual skills to add to my repertoire. This remained the case until I came under the mentorship of the great Syd Aaron. He showed me that the essence of George Nissen's invention was the potential to put skills into linked sequences, unlike the limitation imposed in diving. As soon as a beginner can perform two different skills, they should be encouraged to link them together. The late Bert Scales developed this idea with his club members and also with the British National Squad. He created a check-off matrix to record each gymnast's ability to link every move with every other move in their repertoire. His objective was to develop versatility and improve competition robustness. Coaches can create their own check-off matrix relative to the current repertoire of their gymnasts, both as an incentive and achievement record.

Over & Above

	Back s/s Tucked	Back s/s Piked	Back s/s Straight	Back s/s Full Twist	Back s/s Double Twist	Barani Tucked	Barani Piked	Barani Straight	Double Back Tucked	Double Back Piked	Half Out Tucked	Half Out Piked
Back s/s Tucked												
Back s/s Piked												
Back s/s Straight												
Back s/s Full Twist												
Back s/s Double Twist												
Barani Tucked												
Barani Piked												
Barani Straight												
Double Back Tucked												
Double Back Piked												
Half Out Tucked												
Half Out Piked												

This is an example of a skill check-off matrix to encourage performance versatility. These can be designed to suit the development stage of the gymnast or training group.

Throughout this book, I have promoted the principle of acquiring sound, basic techniques from the earliest possible stage. The prerequisites required to enable efficient and confident linking include balance, control and height in straight jumping, an appreciation of the chimney concept, and an affinity for tempo. Listed like that, it sounds as if progress toward the linking of somersaults would be somewhat protracted, but I haven't found that to be so. The basics of straight jumping, hitting the top, and appreciating tempo can be incorporated easily within sessions for beginners, which are filled with fun and progression. The linking of skills with sound height -maintaining technique develops naturally as a result.

If you have read this far, I hope you will have accepted the primary principle that every take-off is simply a modified straight jump. It therefore follows that the first linked sequence we perform on trampoline is a series of straight jumps that display consistent height, balance, and accurate placement, supported by visual and kinesthetic awareness of each jump. That combination of qualities — consistent height, balance and accurate placement supported by visual and kinesthetic awareness — was just as relevant to China's Dong Dong as he performed a 17-plus DD to become Olympic Champion. Indeed, I venture to suggest that his amazing voluntary routines, which hit the chimney top with almost every skill, were developed through a total mastery of linking consecutive straight jumps. We may marvel at the excellence of the top Chinese trampolinists, but I believe they are simply putting into practice much of what is written in this book. In order to emulate their performance, we must adopt a single-minded commitment to the principles. The good news is that my advice is not written in Mandarin!

Perhaps surprisingly, there are only two types of somersaulting links in trampoline gymnastics:

1. Back-to-back

2. Back-to-front

Have I forgotten about front-to-front? Not at all! Once a certain level of competence is reached, all forward somersaults, whether they are single, double, triple, or even quadruple, exit with a multiple of a half-twist resulting in a touchdown where the gymnast is facing opposite to the starting direction. This forward-initiated skill ends up as a backward touchdown for the purpose of linking to the next move. I appreciate that the young gymnast with a limited repertoire may find it useful to combine a piked front somersault with a tucked front somersault, which is indeed a front-to-front combination. However, that expedient is soon left behind, eliminating the need for a long-term front-to-front link. Lest you think I have also forgotten such combinations as piked half-out/tucked half-out where both skills take off in a forward direction, this is not a front-to-front link in technique terms. The first half-out touches down in the manner of a backward rotating skill. Thus, that particular link becomes a back-to-front combination.

By simplifying the links into only two categories, we can obtain a significant benefit by using a generic technique when developing combinations involving multiple rotations and twists. It enables us to go from a simple combination to a more challenging one, tapping into what the gymnast already understands. It also means that when striving to connect a series of high difficulty moves, the gymnast can simulate the connections involved by practicing a modified version that involves the same directional links.

Over & Above

I recall working with a leading member of the British Team who was having difficulty maintaining height and direction on the following combination — piked half-out, half-in rudi out piked. We took the combination back to basics and worked barani piked followed by back somersault piked. The gymnast began to understand the connection process, and we gradually increased the challenge through various simulations until we could revisit the original problematic combination. Afterward, he said to me:

"Jack, why didn't I learn the technique this way all those years ago before going for the big stuff?"

I rest my case!

THE BACK-TO-BACK CONNECTION

One of the most comforting things about dropping into first contact as the body rotates backwards is the opportunity to see where touchdown will take place, giving an opportunity to make appropriate adjustments before actual contact occurs. One marvels at the artistic gymnasts who often exit a tumble or vault by landing facing forward. This, in trampoline parlance, would be landing blind. Contemplate the visual and sensory challenges faced by Valery Gorbunov competing in the first Russian National Championship in 1964. Here is his silver medal winning exercise!

1. Back somersault with double twist
2. Forward one and a quarter somersault
3. Back Cody
4. Back somersault with full twist
5. Barani
6. Forward somersault (tucked)
7. Forward somersault with full twist
8. Straddle jump

9. Double forward somersault

10. Double backward somersault

There are a couple of interesting combinations where Mr. Gorbunov must have been relying totally on his kinesthetic awareness because he could not have seen the bed.

I like to stress two key factors in the linking of skills, firstly:

"Direction before connection."

The gymnast must direct the first skill in any combination up to the top of the chimney. In doing so, the reward will be a vertical drop toward the bed giving the best opportunity to create the right conditions for the execution of the skill to follow.

Secondly:

"Vision before decision."

The gymnast needs to be aware of seeing the bed during the exit phase of the backward somersault in order to inform the decision-making process for executing the most efficient touchdown and subsequent take-off.

Having made those two points, let me use the tucked back somersault as an example of the set-up move in a back-to-back combination. Of course the principles described apply to any backward finishing skill as defined earlier. Can you remember the very first time you supported a gymnast for a back somersault, or indeed the first time you performed your own back somersault unaided? The natural instinct is to prioritize the pupil's safety or indeed guarantee one's own personal survival with a complete feet to feet rotation. A safe, upright landing is usually greeted with a mixture of relief and pride. But wait a minute — did I say landing? In Chapter 13, I declared there to be no such thing as a landing. There is however a landing phase, which begins with first contact (touchdown) and ends at full depression. During the beginner's first few attempts, neither coach nor pupil need be aware of this, focused as they are on completing the rotation safely. A typical first contact for a beginner will see the pupil

Over & Above

in an upright posture, but because it is simplistically perceived to be **the landing**, it establishes a habit that has to be undone before the successful linking of back-to-back combinations can be achieved. In linking terms, this somersault has actually over rotated!

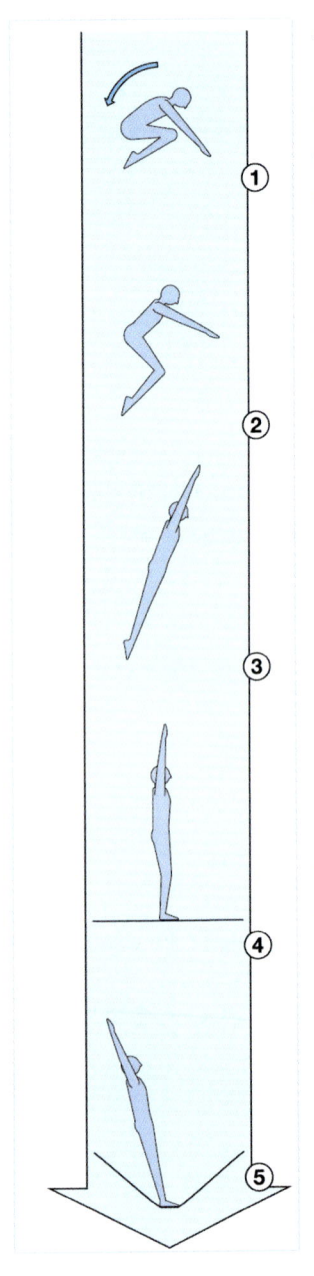

Although the somersault rotates around the center of mass while in the air, it must be realized that when the feet touch the bed, the rotation continues, but with the feet acting as the pivot point. This means that the apparently successful upright "landing" does not constitute the end of the somersault. Such a touchdown will result in the gymnast losing balance in a backward direction, rendering it unwise to attempt a second backward somersault. The coach stepping in to catch a beginner should be ready to place a strong arm behind the gymnast to prevent this resultant backward travel and continued rotation. However, the difficulties don't end there because the landing surface does not remain stable like the floor. It effectively gives way under the weight of the landing gymnast. So now we have a somersault that is over-rotated and also drops into the "hole" created by the gymnast, increasing the hazard. The illustration shows the consequences when the bed depresses beneath the feet of the still-rotating gymnast.

A backward rotating skill arriving at first contact in an upright posture followed by the inevitable consequences when full depression is reached.

If a second back somersault is attempted in these circumstances, the best outcome will be dramatic travel and height loss. Novice performers who are learning to link the back-to-back combination may instinctively try to "save" the connection as the bed is contacted by thrusting the hips forward and buckling the knees. The coach needs to anticipate this and be able to recognize when this "saving" action is taking place in order to help the young performer achieve the ideal connection. These "saving" actions do slightly arrest the backward movement of the center of mass, but there is a high risk of injury to the back as the power of the trampoline's recoil is unleashed against a weakened body posture. I have highlighted this process because it can also be seen in high-level competition where the experienced gymnast may employ the technique (indeed it is a technique at this level) when a backward touchdown is over-rotated. The skilled performer will use the "save" with varying degrees of subtlety, depending on the magnitude of the over-rotation. If it has to be employed too often in a routine, there will be a cumulative loss of height, which not only damages the time of flight score but puts pressure on all the following skills. It worries me that many of our talented young performers are allowed to over-rotate their back somersaults unchecked and begin to use this natural but undesirable compensatory technique.

Let us return to the case of the young gymnast performing a back somersault and over-rotating to guarantee safety. This is, of course, totally acceptable during early attempts, but as soon as practicable, the coach must encourage the gymnast to see the bed as they drop into first contact and aim to create a touchdown that feels relatively "short." The gymnast's sight of the bed is critical in the development of this shorter touchdown and will be enhanced if the somersault has hit the top before dropping toward the bed. By the time the pupil is ready to attempt the back-to-back link, hitting the top should have become second nature.

It is important for the gymnast to make an assessment of the likely touchdown position while still in the airborne phase. This is done primarily by seeing the bed during the descent ("vision before decision"). Coaches should be encouraged to call, "look," rather than simply assuming the pupil is using their vision to the fullest. Be aware of the gymnast who, when apparently heading for a perfect touchdown, may interpret the impending first contact as too short. They will instinctively try to correct this by a variety of means, including excessive piking toward the bed or even a bending of the knees prior to touchdown. Both of these actions cause an acceleration of the somersault rotation, resulting in the gymnast feeling comfortable at first contact but actually too

Over & Above

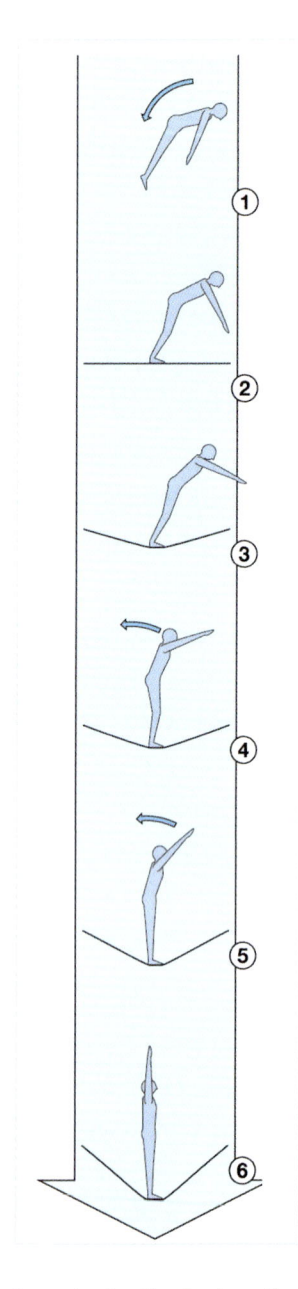

upright. If we have coached the pupil to appreciate that first contact is simply the initial stage in the landing phase, which involves the bed going down, then they will be more inclined to accept the shorter, but initially alien, touchdown as appropriate.

A first contact that feels slightly "short" to the gymnast will result in the perfect position at full depression if the physical actions performed as the bed goes down conform to "bed down, body up!"

At touchdown, the weight should be slightly in front of the feet in order to compensate for the backward pivoting effect. The arms will be somewhere below shoulder height, but it is important to realize that this is not a position, per se. It is part of a dynamic process, and the arms will be moving through a forward and upward arc as the bed sinks. As the gymnast drops deeper into the "hole" and the arms continue their upward path, the torso will be extending toward an erect posture until full depression is achieved. The gymnast is now standing up in the classic "bow and arrow" configuration. It is interesting to note that an efficient upward action of the arms and elevation of the torso triggers an action and reaction effect, adding further bed depression. This has the potential to enhance vertical force into the following skill, although the deliberate harnessing of this technique is a sophisticated development.

The coach should stress: "Bed down, body up!"

I emphasize the body action rather than the arms because the greater mass of the torso has a more significant mechanical effect on the bed. Additionally, the torso being brought upright as the bed goes down tends to encourage the arms to swing automatically overhead into the "arrow" position. I hear coaches emphasizing the reach with the arms as the primary action, but this is secondary to that of the torso. I have found that if the gymnast focuses on swinging the arms up, the body doesn't automatically follow. We can then find the gymnast in the unhelpful posture shown in the illustration. The arms have swung up above the head but the torso and head have not been raised first. Ironically, the gymnast will feel that they have complied with the coach's demand to swing the arms above the head. What they don't realize is that the head is not upright.

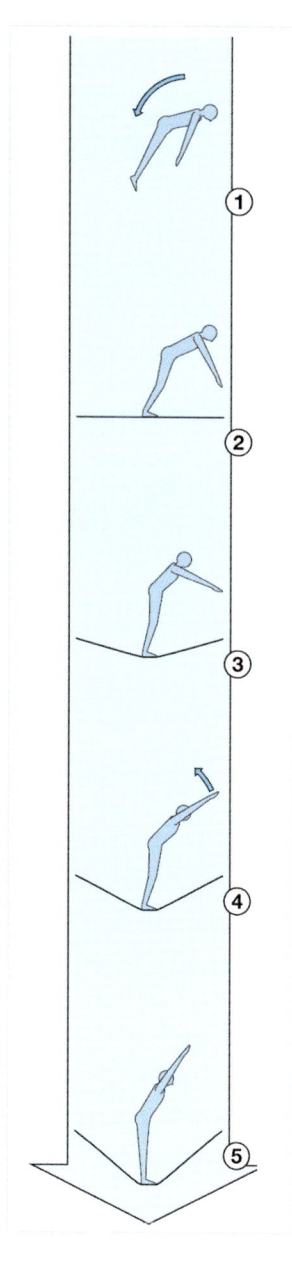

As the gymnast depresses the bed from a "short" first contact and tries to lift the arms, it is likely that the torso will remain static creating a poor posture at full depression. The gymnast may nonetheless feel as if their arms are overhead.

This position at full depression will be catastrophic for the prospect of a strong vertical second backward rotating skill. The aim is to reach full depression in the perfect starting position for a straight jump that goes directly up to the top of the chimney. Because (oh no, not again!) every take-off is simply a modified straight jump!

The younger, lighter performers will usually be able to touch down slightly more upright than the heavier, more mature gymnasts due to the smaller depression on the bed. Coaches need to be aware that as the gymnast becomes stronger, jumps higher and depresses the bed more, they will have to modify the timing of body and arm actions to accommodate these changing conditions. Don't be surprised when a gymnast who has been performing with exquisite timing gradually experiences problems as their particular stage of physical development changes.

Over & Above

The following worksheet distills the technical points already discussed and provides a practical step-by-step process through which the gymnast can develop their skills and understanding of the back-to-back connection.

Back-to-Back Connection Drill Worksheet

1. Tucked back (TB) somersault to hit the top followed by a straight jump. (The touchdown should be relatively short, with the gymnast seeing the bed and appreciating the necessity to drop into the "hole" before arriving upright at full depression.)

2. Repeat drill 1. Insist that the straight jump also hits the top and therefore remains within the performance chimney.

3. Repeat drill 2 but initiate **minimal** backward rotation to create a take-off that hits the top but drops on the **seat**, e.g., the gymnast simply "modifies" the straight jump.

4. Repeat drill 3 but initiate **minimal** backward rotation to create a take-off that hits the top but drops on the **back**. (The use of a push-on mat is advised to give the gymnast confidence and protection in the event of over-rotation.)

5. TB followed by one straight jump then a second TB followed by one straight jump. (Maintain short touchdowns and accuracy of straight jumps.)

6. TB followed by a straight jump that is converted to a tucked jump once the gymnast has become airborne. (The tucked jump is now simulating the second TB, and the gymnast should be visualizing this as the next step.)

7. TB, tucked jump, TB, straight jump. (Each somersault to hit the top and each tucked jump to leave the bed as a straight jump.)

8. TB, TB, straight jump, followed by three straight jumps before repeating TB, TB, straight jump. (Only continue this drill if the quality of the early somersaults and linkage is acceptable, with each somersault hitting the top, and the drill is contained within the chimney.)

Thinking About Linking

This drill sequence can be developed, with the first skill on each occasion being changed to piked back somersault, straight back somersault and the three shapes of barani. Indeed it lends itself to developing the full range of back-to-back connections, including doubles. I offer this worksheet as a framework for the coach to use and adapt as appropriate to the standard and age of the gymnast.

THE BACK-TO-FRONT CONNECTION

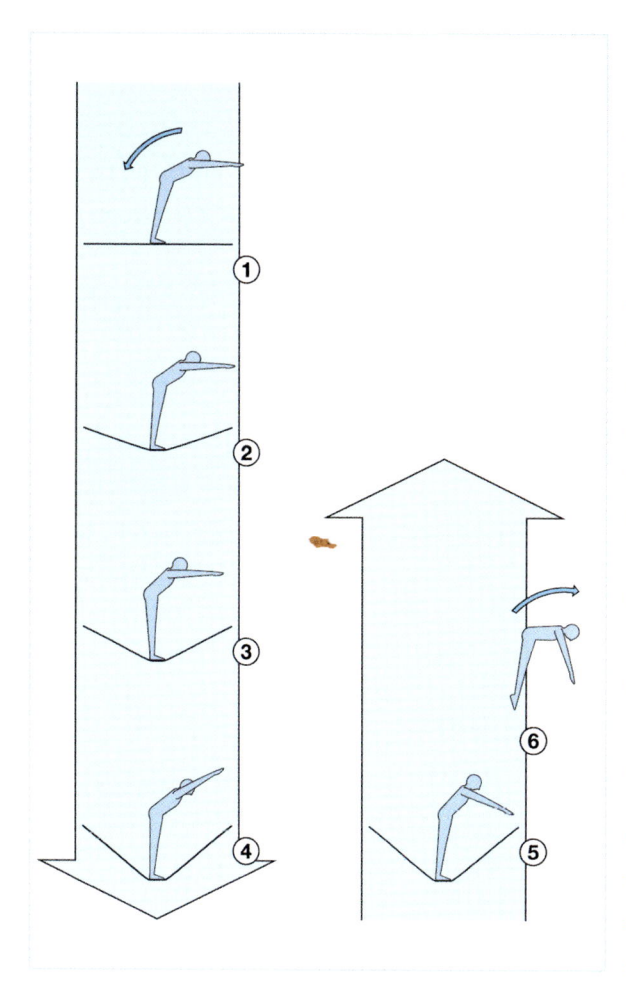

Returning to my favorite theme that "trampolining is too easy," this has a particular relevance to the back-to-front connection. Indeed coaches often choose this as the first somersault connection they teach because it is indeed "easy" compared to a back-to-back link. The rationale is straightforward — the touchdown from the backward-facing somersault allows complete sight of the bed and facilitates anticipation of the forward take-off to follow.

It is too easy to touch down from backward rotation and simply "fall" into a forward somersault take-off.

159

Over & Above

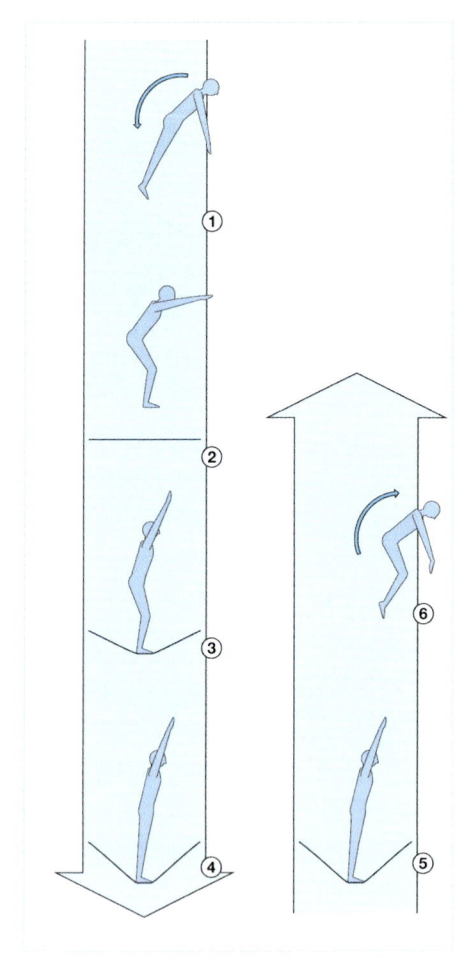

It is too easy for the gymnast to touch down following the back somersault and simply topple into a forward rotating skill without completing the landing phase of the back somersault. If this back-to-front connection is introduced as the first somersault link, it is liable to create a technical habit that is difficult to eradicate, damaging the potential to learn both back-to-front and back-to-back combinations **without height loss**. This highly visual linkage, which can cause height loss and travel, can be seen even among the world's best performers. The adjacent illustration shows that during a high difficulty voluntary, there is a tendency to "play it safe" and allow a small degree of forward lean during a back-to-front linkage.

This World Class gymnast is seen linking a challenging back-to-front connection by "playing it safe" and accepting a slight forward lean into the forward rotating skill. This will result in a degree of travel and loss of height.

Having made that point, I nonetheless understand the challenge facing the gymnast in connecting a backward landing phase into a forward take-off phase without dropping the shoulders before the bed has started to recoil. In an ideal scenario, the performer would touch down slightly short (as described in the back-to-back connection), then employ the residual rotation and descent of the bed to arrive at full depression in the classic "bow and arrow" posture. This becomes the ideal starting point for harnessing the vertical force from the bed. It replicates the take-off posture at full depression, which should have become automatic through the habitual use of an effective arm set. As the bed recoils, the off-center force that creates the forward rotation should be resisted as long as possible in order to maximize the vertical component, thereby delivering a forward-rotating skill without height loss. This is a challenging connection to make because as full depression is reached and the gymnast brings their torso upright, a degree of anxiety will be experienced that it may be too late to initiate forward rotation. It is rare for a gymnast to achieve the perfect back-to-front connection in voluntary routines due to this anxiety. Nonetheless, coaches and gymnasts must be aware of the ideal scenario and work toward it if World Class performance is the goal. The best examples can be seen in set routines when the level of difficulty is reduced.

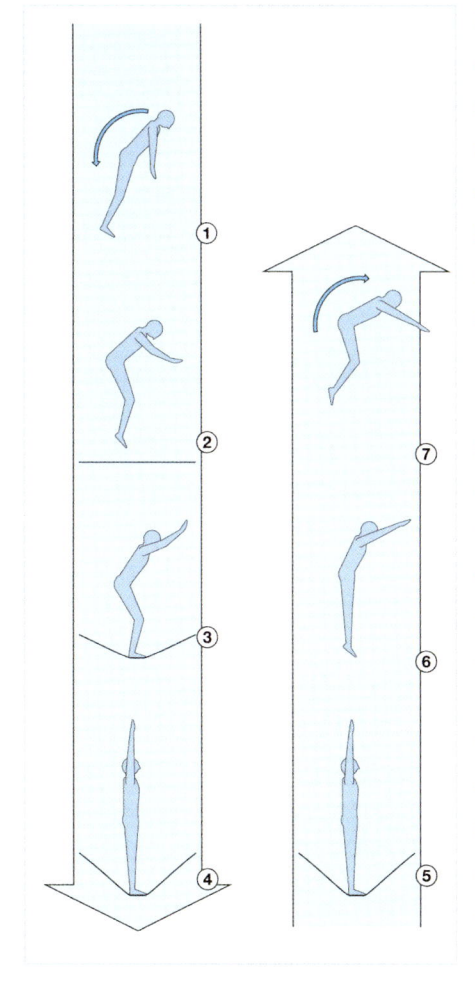

The World Class performer previously shown executes a back-to-front connection in a set routine of limited difficulty. The gymnast is seen to finish the back rotation at full depression in the classic "arrow" posture before delivering a high and central forward skill in contrast to the less risky connection used in the voluntary.

The following worksheet uses the same principles of progression followed in the Back-to-Back example but focuses specifically on the barani as the forward-rotating skill. It will be noted that in the Back-to-Back worksheet, I used the seat and back drops as initial "modified" straight jumps to give the gymnast the feel for hitting the top with minimal rotation as a prelude to a complete backward somersault. In the following worksheet, I have used the straight front drop as the model for learning to modify the straight jump with minimal forward

Over & Above

rotation. This progression may be unacceptable to some gymnasts and extreme care must be taken by the coach to protect any over- or under-rotated attempts. Frequent use of a push-in mat should be employed and indeed the front drop progression could be bypassed with progress going straight to the three-quarter front.

Back-to-Front Connection Drill Worksheet 1 (Barani)

1. Tucked back somersault to hit the top followed by a straight jump to hit the top.

2. Repeat drill 1 but follow the straight jump with a straight front drop that hits the top. (A push-in mat should be used to protect the front drop landing and encourage the vertical component.)

3. Repeat drill 2 but perform a three-quarter front somersault (straight) after the straight jump. This additional skill should also hit the top. (A push-in mat to be used at coach's/gymnast's discretion.)

4. Repeat drill 3 but replace the straight jump with an immediate straight front drop stressing the front drop take-off as a slightly modified straight jump. (A push-in mat is essential to protect the front drop and provide gymnast confidence to aim for the top.)

5. Repeat drill 4 but replace the straight front drop with a three-quarter front somersault (straight). Again, stress the take-off as a modified straight jump.

6. When drill 5 can be performed consistently, replace the three-quarter front with a high slow-tucked front somersault to hit the top.

7. Once consistent direction and connection are achieved with drill 6, change the somersault to a tucked barani.

8. Develop drill 7 to include piked and straight baranis but only if the top is being hit consistently.

9. Replace the "setting up" tucked back somersault with piked and straight somersaults.

Back-to-Front Connection Drill Worksheet 2 (Introducing doubles)

Drills 1 to 6 remain as above but when drill 6 can be performed consistently with the front somersault hitting the top, progress to one-and-a-quarter front. (The push-in mat is essential to protect the one-and-a-quarter front landing.)

7. Repeat the previous drill but perform a one-and-three-quarter front that hits the top of the chimney. (Push-in mat at coach's/gymnast's discretion.)

8. Repeat the previous drill but perform a tucked half-out showing the same quality of top.

9. Gradually develop through all other fliffs in the repertoire and progressively replace the backward "setting up" skill with the full range of single then double somersaults.

Once again, these drills are simply a framework for coaches to customize for the benefit of their own gymnasts, leading to the development of a sound and well-directed back-to-front connection. The coach must make appropriate judgments as to the gymnast's readiness to progress to each increasingly challenging combination. The principle of progression can be developed through drills of increasing difficulty until double and triple somersaults are involved. Conversely, a problematic back-to-front connection such as full-in, full-out, followed by full-in half-out, can be practiced using any of the single somersault drills as a simulation. The technique involved in that particular major combination could be practiced using a back somersault with full twist followed by a barani. Through this simplified combination, it will be seen whether the gymnast understands and can apply the connection principle before returning cautiously to the original link.

In my experience, it is folly to try and improve a particular link using high difficulty skills before the technique has been "automated" and understood in a simplified form.

CHAPTER 20

TRAINING TO INCREASE TIME OF FLIGHT

SECTION THREE
TECHNICAL APPLICATION

Training to Increase Time of Flight

Before undertaking specific training to increase time of flight, it is important to have mastered all the techniques and principles I have described up to this point. Flight time/height is totally dependent upon having strong control of balance and direction. The acquisition of tempo and top awareness will automatically lend itself to the production of height. In addition, the ability to link somersaults efficiently will aid the process further.

When designing a set of progressive drills to target a particular quality in the gymnast's performance, the coach should devise some way of measuring effectiveness and the following test drill does exactly that.

METHOD

The starting point for this particular process assumes the coach and gymnast have accepted the principle that every take-off is simply a modified straight jump. The simplest ten-bounce routine is therefore ten straight jumps. However, if we start the 10 jumps from a stationary bed, this does not simulate a competition routine. The gymnast must therefore perform sufficient preliminary jumps to reach what they regard as "working height" before commencing the ten-straight-jump "routine." When working height is reached, the gymnast calls "Ready!" at the

Over & Above

top of the jump indicating that the next touchdown is the start of the routine. The stopwatch is started and the gymnast continues to perform ten high accurate jumps as if it were a competitive routine. On the final contact, the timing stops and the score for the routine is recorded. The objective is to increase the time taken for the ten jumps with each attempt recorded in the training log. It will be realized that if timing by stopwatch, the result represents total time, including bed contact time, and not time of flight. An approximate time of flight measurement can be obtained however by deducting 3 seconds from the recorded time. If the coach is lucky enough to have access to a time of flight machine or a computer program such as "Silicone Coach" or "Dartfish," actual flight time can be recorded. It should be obvious that, regardless of which method is used, in order to obtain meaningful data the recording must always be done by the same process, preferably using the same trampoline.

Having ascertained the time for a ten jump routine with zero content, the gymnast performs Test Drill A. This consists of ten shaped jumps, none of which require any modification during bed contact compared to the ten straight jumps. If the gymnast has truly acquired the technique we seek to promote, then it should be possible for the drill time to match the time for performing the ten straight jumps originally tested. I have, however, rarely found this to be the case on initial testing, revealing the fact that the gymnast is either holding back because of a desire for more control or indeed they are modifying the take-off before leaving the bed at last contact. Either way, the first principle of trampolining has not been demonstrated. There is of course a way to cheat the test, which is by performing the initial ten jumps at less than full height and then increasing the effort on Test Drill A. This process therefore needs strong management with both coach and gymnast fully engaged in achieving the true objective of the exercise, which is where the ten-jump-zero-content exercise gradually improves and challenges the gymnast to do likewise during Test Drill A.

Despite the simplicity of the skills within this test drill, I have not restricted its use to young developing performers. It has been applied to senior international gymnasts who can benefit in terms of control and time of flight awareness. Indeed the exercise often exposes weaknesses in basic technique that can be an embarrassment to gymnasts who feel they are too advanced to be concerned with such fundamentals.

TEST DRILL A

1. Tucked jump
2. Straddle jump
3. Piked jump
4. Tucked jump
5. Straddle jump
6. Piked jump
7. Tucked jump
8. Straddle jump
9. Piked jump
10. Straight jump

For recording purposes, the Drill A time can be expressed as a percentage of the straight jump time; this relative measure can be developed and eventually applied to set and voluntary routines. The benchmark must always be the ten straight jump time and a training program should be directed at increasing that, as well as increasing the time taken for the drill. Monitoring the separate times and trying to improve each, as well as reducing the percentage difference, can supply the coach with much useful information to help the gymnast progress.

We now move to Test Drill B, which can be seen to involve simple twisting jumps interspersed with shapes. The gymnast will now be tested on their conviction that "every take-off is simply a straight jump" and "the twist is the easy bit." Put those two technical pillars in place, and the time for Drill "B" can be very close to the ten straight jump time. It would be unreasonable to expect a 100% result, particularly because of the two full twists that will require some torque during bed contact. This drill provides an excellent opportunity to encourage subtlety of twist action, which becomes even more important in the execution of early twisting in multi-somersault situations.

Over & Above

TEST DRILL B

1. Tucked jump
2. Straddle jump
3. Piked jump
4. Half twist jump
5. Tucked jump
6. Straddle jump
7. Piked jump
8. Full twist jump
9. Tucked jump
10. Full twist jump

Once Test Drill B can be performed at 95% of the ten straight jump time, the gymnast can be challenged with Test Drill C. This drill is the link between the two technical pillars and the performance of competition routines with somersaults and twists. It also sees the introduction of two consecutive somersaults, which will present a new challenge in maintaining height. The previous chapter on linking somersaults has an important bearing on this. The drill shown is simply what I have used, and it is my hope that coaches will create their own variations to suit their priorities and those of their gymnasts.

TEST DRILL C

1. Back somersault (coach to determine shape)
2. Tucked jump
3. Back somersault (coach to determine shape)
4. Tucked jump
5. Back somersault (coach to determine shape)
6. Tucked jump
7. Barani (Tucked)
8. Tucked jump
9. Back somersault (Tucked)
10. Barani (Tucked)

It is clear that each of the jumps could have different shapes or they could, for example, all be piked jumps providing a revealing test in itself. At this stage, I would be disinclined to use the straddle jump, as it eventually becomes obsolete, but I hope readers can see the patterns and develop their own variations. The main objective, however, must be kept in view, namely to maintain the ability to perform the drills at over 90% of the ten jump time.

I have employed this process with senior and youth national squads using 10 jump drills of gradually escalating difficulty until the gymnasts clearly understand the process. The gymnasts were then tested on their set and voluntary routines in order to ascertain the percentage difference between the routine and the ten straight jump maximum. Interestingly, this method was introduced long before the advent of time of flight measurement and shows the emphasis **I have always placed on height and the trampolinist's best friend ... time!**

The procedure can be used both as a test and a useful drill in its own right for developing time of flight and can be performed using sets and repetitions to build the performance endurance necessary for height consistency. This work needs to be supported by regular repetition of up to thirty maximum height jumps, which can be timed and monitored for positional accuracy within the base of the performance chimney. Appropriate weight training will also increase leg power to increase absolute jump height, but leg strength and endurance are no substitute for skillfully applied technique. Impressive bed-depressing power that is poorly directed becomes an embarrassment to the gymnast, resulting in control difficulties (see Chapter 24 – Principles of Fitness Training for Trampoline). Coaches also need to be aware of the possibility that growing gymnasts may become temporarily unable to match previous jump heights. Regular testing of jump height can become a disincentive in such circumstances. While testing and monitoring are important, discretion is needed to assess the regularity that will be of greatest benefit to individual gymnasts. Testing on a weekly basis, for example, gives the gymnast a training interval during which strength and technical improvements may become measurable. The effect of growth spurts or changes in strength to bodyweight ratios may require a longer period for adjustment to take place and measurement to become valid.

CHAPTER 21

THE TWIST IS THE EASY BIT!

SECTION THREE
TECHNICAL APPLICATION

To simplify the process of developing the myriad of skills available to the trampoline gymnast, my longtime friend and colleague in the sport, the late Bert Scales used to say, "Learn a skill then add a twist." That simple little phrase distills the process beautifully. It prioritizes the core skill and treats the twist as an additional factor. If we take the statement literally and apply it to any twisting move ... it works! The simplest of all twisting moves, the half twist jump, requires the gymnast to perform a straight jump and insert a half twist within it. The full twist jump likewise is a straight jump that contains a full twist. The rudi out triffis is a triff that just happens to contain one and a half twists in the third somersault. Bert was absolutely right, learn the skill ... then add a twist!

If it's that simple, why do twisting skills present so many challenges to gymnasts? There are several reasons for this:

1. Very often the gymnast has not followed the first part of the statement "learn the skill." Yes, they can do the skill but has it been learned to the level of mastery required? For example, how competent is the straight jump into which the full twist will be added?

2. The names by which we describe twisting moves contain a subliminal message to the gymnast that the most important

Over & Above

element in the move is the twist. Even a half twist jump mentions the twist before the jump! Rudi out triff tells the unwary gymnast they must focus on the rudi, because it is named first! It takes a strong-minded and skillfully coached gymnast to reverse the significance of those elements in their mind. We risk putting the 'cart before the horse'. Perhaps we should be thinking and saying, "a jump with full twist" or "a triff rudi out" if we want to put the horse back in front of the cart. The British Gymnastics coach education literature has made a couple of helpful modifications, such as "ball out barani" as opposed to the colloquial "barani ball out," but we are a long way from changing the perception of coaches and gymnasts.

3. Humans are challenged when they have to perform two contrasting actions at the same time. You may have tried the trick of patting the top of your head with one hand while rubbing your belly with the other. That somewhat simplistic, non life-threatening coordination challenge contrasts with the potentially hazardous enterprise of launching oneself into the air with the intention to somersault and twist. If you pat your head at a different speed from the belly rub, you get even closer to the task of trying to perform a somersault with power and commitment while introducing a subtle, well-timed amount of twist. The technical challenge is formidable enough without having to try and ignore the consequences of getting it wrong!

Bert's original theory can be expanded as follows:

In any trampoline skill involving twist, the twist is the easy bit. The difficult bit is creating the right amount of height and somersault rotation to provide enough time spent in the correct body shape to allow the twist to work.

That definition is pretty watertight as it can be applied equally to the extremes of half twist jump or the rudi out triff. To perform a half twist jump the gymnast must indeed be high enough (not very high as it happens) and create the **right** amount of somersault, which on this occasion, is **none**. The time to execute the twist is provided by the height, while the straight body shape allows the twist to work. To perform the rudi out triff, much more height is needed to provide enough time to execute the move. The amount of somersault rotation is considerable and the time created by the height combines to allow a straight body shape in the third somersault to enable the twist to work. This may be easy for the coach to comprehend standing on terra firma, but our job is to help the gymnast retain mental composure up to and during that moment of departure from the trampoline.

Before looking at ways to develop twist and assist the gymnast to maintain the right mindset, I will dwell a little longer on the difficulties experienced by our athletes. Many beginners have difficulty with the full twist jump, which is often used to start a compulsory routine at the lower levels. The most common scenario sees the gymnast perform an apparently competent take-off with all the expected style considerations, only to touch down and fall off balance, making the performance of the next skill impossible. This frustrating problem can prove difficult to solve until its source is appreciated. In creating twist during bed contact, the gymnast has inadvertently created a tiny amount of somersault-type rotation. If the jump is very low then the resultant balance loss on touchdown may be manageable, but normally there will be enough height (and therefore time) for the unwanted rotation to manifest into a significant degree of somersault. This is a classic example of an apparent **technical problem** actually being a **perception issue** on the part of the gymnast. The full twist is simply a microcosm of all the complex, multiple early twisting skills, making it an essential fundamental skill for the developing World Class performer to master.

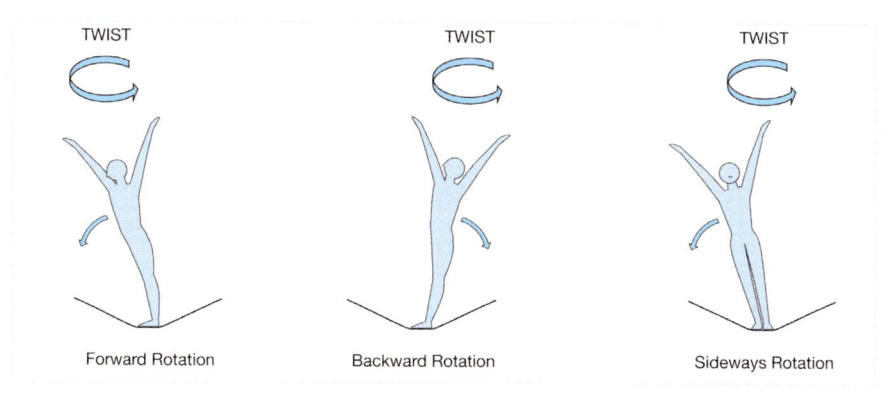

TWIST	TWIST	TWIST
Forward Rotation	Backward Rotation	Sideways Rotation

A common difficulty gymnasts experience when initiating twisting skills during bed contact is vividly demonstrated in the full twist jump. In this skill, rotation should only take place around the longitudinal (twist) axis, but it is easy for the performer to accidentally create some rotation around the somersault axis at the same time. This will result in the full twist being completed but the gymnast falling over when first contact is regained. By learning to isolate the twisting action through balance and erect posture in this basic skill, the gymnast can establish subtlety of twist in the more complex twisting singles and doubles where contact twist is involved.

Over & Above

My experience tells me that the gymnast's thinking is tainted by the following:

a) The word "full" implies "complete" or "total," thus inspiring the gymnast to create too much twisting force.

b) The gymnast will already have performed a half twist jump, and it seems logical that the full twist will require double that amount of twisting action.

c) Placing "full" before the words "twist" and "jump" gives it apparent priority in terms of the physical actions required.

These issues need to be rationalized during the development years in order to permit the right balance of twist and somersault rotation to become natural during the execution of World Class difficulty.

The barani and the full twisting back somersault can also be subject to the gymnast's mistaken perception because both of these moves are likely to be the first occasions when the pupil has tried to combine twist with complete somersault rotation. Coaches must be aware that the gymnast is likely to let the new component in the skill dominate their thinking, even to the point of anxiety. This has implications for how we protect the early attempts at twisting somersaults because there is a real risk of massive twist and poor somersault input, resulting in a dangerously under-rotated skill. A typical example can occur during the learning of a ball out barani. The pupil may have a competent tucked ball out from a three quarter front (straight) and appears ready to add a half twist, thereby producing the ball out barani. Understandably, the gymnast's predominant thought will be about adding the twist, but in the anxiety to achieve this, they are likely to twist early instead of waiting for the sighting point. The best-case scenario is that a "baby" fliffis is performed; at worst, they experience an overturned, early twisting cradle to land head first. Even if arrival on the feet is achieved safely, the trampolinist can be "freaked out" by the unexpected, unfamiliar feeling and blind landing. This could have far-reaching implications for the development of this particular move and the range of more complex but related twisting double somersaults to follow.

The barani (in all three shapes) can also go badly wrong because of the gymnast's mistaken perception of what is required. The learner may anticipate the timing of the twist or indeed fail to create enough initial somersault rotation. The outcome can involve diagonal casting across the bed, a dangerously short landing or, most alarming of all, twisting so early as to go over backwards. Having said that, the early rebound tumblers would perform this trick deliberately, and it was known as a "Jonah Back."

A related hazard lies in wait for gymnasts and inexperienced coaches when learning the half-out fliffis. The gymnast will already be familiar with the one-and-three-quarter front and probably the double front somersault. Adding a half twist in the second somersault is not at all **technically** difficult, but maintaining the **mental composure** to wait for the checkpoint or sighting point before twisting is by far the greater challenge. Coaches must be aware of the real possibility that the developing gymnast may under-commit to the double somersault and also initiate the twist too early before dropping head first onto the bed. Extreme caution, and suitable support and catching must therefore be in place throughout the development of the half-out fliffis.

The moves I have described are simply examples of a generic problem facing the aspiring coach and gymnast as they tackle every skill where twist and somersault are combined. The coach must develop awareness and sensitivity toward the performer's thinking as they come to terms with this somersault/twist dichotomy. One incident of confusion during the learning stage could slow down and even arrest progress toward the intended World Class objective. The whole process of introducing twist and combining it with somersault rotation should be linked to the principles already established — the performance chimney, awareness of top, and sensitivity to tempo. With these principles underpinning all future learning, the young gymnast will have the potential to proceed unhindered toward excellence.

Coaches reading this will no doubt already be aware of the three methods for creating twist:

1. Contact or torque

2. Counter-rotation or "hula"

3. Tilt

Over & Above

Yes, three **methods**, but only two **types** of twist – contact and aerial. Clearly method 1 above involves initiating twist during bed contact, while methods 2 and 3 are strictly for aerial initiation. I have no intention of repeating the excellent descriptions in coach education resource material, but my extensive experience enables me to offer a great deal of practical advice that coaches may wish to follow.

Let us be clear that if a performer wishes to twist while performing any amount of somersault rotation, whichever method is used, the body will assume a sideways tilt during the process. So, while tilt twisting is highlighted as a particular method, the act of tilting around the dorso-ventral axis is common to all three methods. Torque and counter-rotation are simply different ways of creating the necessary tilt to start the body twisting. Each technique can be used in isolation when performing particular skills, or may be applied in conjunction with any one of the others. Indeed, all three techniques could be operating within the same twisting somersault.

1. CONTACT TWIST

As the name indicates, this is created by turning one or more parts of the body in the direction of the desired twist while in contact with the bed. Apart from skills without somersault rotation, its most practical application is for single rotations or, if delicately executed, the first somersault in an early twisting fliffis, triffis or quadriffis. It may be used for half twists through to multiples of a full twist – indeed a back somersault with six twists can be performed although this is unlikely to have any current competitive application. The disadvantage of contact twist is the requirement to contort the body posture during bed contact, potentially inhibiting the height and speed of the desired somersault(s). Using contact twist effectively demands great skill and sensitivity from the gymnast because of the requirement to balance three distinct components that can conflict with each other. The gymnast must create height, requiring a powerful vertical force, and somersault rotation requiring torque around the transverse axis while initiating a delicate amount of twist rotation around the longitudinal axis. All three components have to be performed almost simultaneously, placing great demands on the gymnast's coordination as well as mental composure. If any one of those components is under or overplayed, this will have a detrimental effect on the integrity of the move. It is for this reason that the contact twist is employed sparingly by the higher-level gymnasts. However, it is likely that many top performers will have initially made extensive use of the contact twist technique before developing aerial initiation.

2. COUNTER-ROTATION TWIST

The coach can assist the gymnast's understanding of this technique by referring to it as the "hip swivel" that the performer will have encountered when executing seat drop half twist to seat drop ... "swivel hips." Syd Aaron used to describe it as "pike/extension/hip rotation"; a form of words that helpfully takes the performer through the physical process involved. Although this is probably the first method of aerial twist the gymnast will learn, it has its limitations. It is only practicable for increments of a half twist and although it is **technically possible** to execute the hip swivel more than once in the air before making bed contact, this is a cumbersome process which does nothing to enhance either aesthetics or efficiency. Try to imagine performing the one-and-a-half twists in the second somersault of a rudi out fliff by undertaking three consecutive hip swivels. I recall attempting to do exactly that during my self-taught period. In short, this technique is for performing single half twists only. The technique should be introduced through fundamental skills, such as the aforementioned swivel hips and late half twist to back drop before developing it through front somersault with half twist (embryonic barani), ball out barani and all the half-out type fliffs.

Over & Above

3. TILT TWIST

Although biomechanists have analyzed and described this process for creating aerial twist, the gymnast only needs to understand what action to make and when to make it. The performer **does not feel the tilt taking place** nor do they want to try and **make** a tilt happen. As I have already highlighted, the body will tilt sideways in the process of twisting within a somersault, whatever method is used, so the gymnast only has to know what action will start and finish the twisting process, then be aware of the outcome … hopefully a successful twist.

This technique, like the other two, depends on the gymnast creating the right amount of somersault rotation to enable the twist to work. It is a mistake to fill the performer's head with thoughts of trying to **create** tilt as this will only confuse and inhibit progress. The gymnast needs to know that by assuming an asymmetric shape during the somersault(s), they will start to twist. When body symmetry is regained then the twist will stop. The asymmetry can be achieved in a variety of ways that can be as simple as turning the head to one side during flight.

A useful and fun exercise is to ask the gymnast to perform a three-quarter back somersault in the straight position to a push-on mat. On the next attempt, ask them to clearly see the mat before landing on the front. Then ask the gymnast, when they see the mat, to simply turn their head to one side and hold it there. As the three-quarter somersault drops to the mat, the body will turn resulting in a flat back landing. The same outcome can be achieved by an asymmetric action of the arms, and if both head and arms are used asymmetrically, the twist effect (due to the greater tilt) can be dramatic.

This technique comes into its own during the performance of multiple twists in the second or third somersault of doubles and triples respectively. Increasingly, because of the extra height (time) available from modern trampolines, top performers use the tilt technique for the majority of their twists.

In order to prevent the gymnast's mistaken but understandable perception regarding the amount of twist required in advanced somersault skills, it is important to address the issue in the early stages of the gymnast's development. Rather than wait for the problem to emerge when skills such as full twisting back somersault are being tackled, I would recommend two courses of action.

1. Introduce **subtlety** of twist action as early as possible.

2. Apart from the half twist jump, full twist jump and half twist to front drop where contact twist is unavoidable, introduce only aerial twist techniques.

In the past, I would have recommended the use of contact twist for straight baranis and back somersault with full twist, but the vast improvement in modern apparatus that enables so much more flight time, even for very young gymnasts, strongly supports the use of aerial twisting within single somersaults. However, this approach only makes sense in the context of a young gymnast being developed through the performance chimney process and who has sufficient control during bed contact to make the best use of the additional airtime provided.

Here are my guidelines for the development of twisting technique with the aspiring World Class trampoline gymnast.

1. Ensure that twist direction is consistent in all basic twisting skills before combining somersault and twist.

2. Condition the gymnast's thinking from the earliest possible stage that "the twist is the easy bit."

3. Reinforce this with the way the first contact twists are introduced (e.g., show how a half twist jump requires only about one-eighth of a twist input, while the body shape is held straight during bed contact. It is this straight body shape and the airtime that allow the half twist to be completed).

4. Introduce the full twist jump using the same principle. (e.g., only apply a one-quarter twist input during contact and encourage the use of an arm drop or wrap to accelerate the twist to completion).

5. During the twisting jumps, make sure the gymnast always sees the trampoline bed.

6. Progress to inserting twist into a somersault only when the quality of somersault is consistently high with sufficient airtime to enable the straight exit during which the twist occurs.

Over & Above

7. Make a point of alternating early attempts at a twisting somersault with a reinforcing performance of the core somersault (i.e., without twist). I would even recommend a ratio of two core somersaults to one somersault with an attempt to add twist. If, during attempts at the core somersault, the quality deteriorates then avoid further attempts at twisting until the original quality is regained.

8. When the gymnast performs the complete skill with twist for the first time, always follow that with at least one quality performance of the core somersault before the next twisting attempt.

9. If the gymnast unexpectedly performs the complete twisting skill, particularly during an early attempt, don't assume they knew what they were doing. Return to reinforcing the core skill and postpone further work on developing the twisting somersault. Inexperienced coaches may be delighted by this unexpected "success" and fail to realize that this kind of beginner's luck is actually a cause for concern.

10. Question the gymnast about what they felt and saw with a focus on enabling an understanding and enjoyment of the skill.

11. If the whole twisting skill is achieved by the end of a particular session, on no account go straight into the whole skill on the next session without first confirming the quality of the core somersault. Build gradually on the previous day's achievement.

The Twist is the Easy Bit!

JACK KELLY: "In any twisting skill, with or without somersault...the twist is the easy bit."

CHAPTER 22

DEVELOPING A TRAINING "GPS" TO IMPROVE COMPETITION PERFORMANCE

SECTION THREE
TECHNICAL APPLICATION

The story so far has taken us from an appreciation of balance and imbalance, through the nature of locomotion and travel, to the benefits of height and the performance chimney. I have tried to take the reader from one principle to the next in a logically progressive fashion, so now let us consider the application of these principles to the training of competition routines.

The criteria for assessing a routine are well known but worth revisiting. The gymnast must demonstrate stylish execution (as defined by the FIG Code of Points), the ability to perform within the two-meter box and maintain height throughout (now measured by time of flight). In my experience, coaches and gymnasts have tended to focus on two main areas — form and control of travel — but may not have a clear plan for how these goals are to be achieved without destructive height loss. The gymnast, too, will certainly be trying to remain near the center of the bed and exhibit the best possible shaping within each skill, but may only have a vague notion about how this will be achieved. It is particularly helpful to have a model against which the gymnast can visualize exactly how they are progressing at each stage of the routine. A clear plan needs to be established, which the gymnast can apply and adapt, depending on their progress throughout the performance.

Over & Above

The GPS ('satnav') we use in our cars provides a brilliant analogy for negotiating a route from the preliminary jumps through to the end of a competition routine. Our GPS takes the starting point and destination we input at the beginning of the journey and guides us between the two points, stage by stage. If we accidentally take a wrong turn, it responds with an admonishing "recalculating" before redirecting us back onto the intended route. I want to look at how we can use the technical principles already established in this book to create a trampoline gymnastics version of the GPS.

For this we once again make use of the performance chimney, that 3D projection based on the center cross that not only gives the gymnast a central **bed position** but also a target **above the trampoline** for each skill in the routine. It is very demanding to perform a routine on the cross, but to do so **and** fully utilize the airspace above is, after all, the true goal. On at least two occasions, 2012 Olympic Champion Dong Dong (CHN) has delivered a final voluntary where he performed inside the chimney and reached the top on practically every skill. He is undoubtedly a great competitor, but I would also expect a young developing gymnast to work within the performance chimney, certainly during the execution of single somersault combinations and compulsory routines.

There is a concern however that once the difficulty level starts to rise, the young gymnast may perceive the need to perform the routine with zero travel and start to perform some skills with a "gaining" or "contra" action. This movement characteristic generally has the appearance of a "mistake," which can affect the execution score and the gymnast may be unsettled by how the action feels. I frequently see gymnasts reacting disproportionately to a "gaining" skill resulting in further and more costly errors of judgment as the routine progresses. A **slightly traveled** skill, on the other hand, has a much more controlled appearance and generally feels more comfortable to the gymnast. It makes sense to modify the performance plan to accommodate this by creating a slightly more generous base for the chimney and corresponding airspace. This more flexible approach nonetheless remains true to the performance chimney concept.

If the base of the performance chimney was expanded to encompass the entire two-meter travel zone as permitted by the code of points, we would have a 3D box as shown in the following illustration.

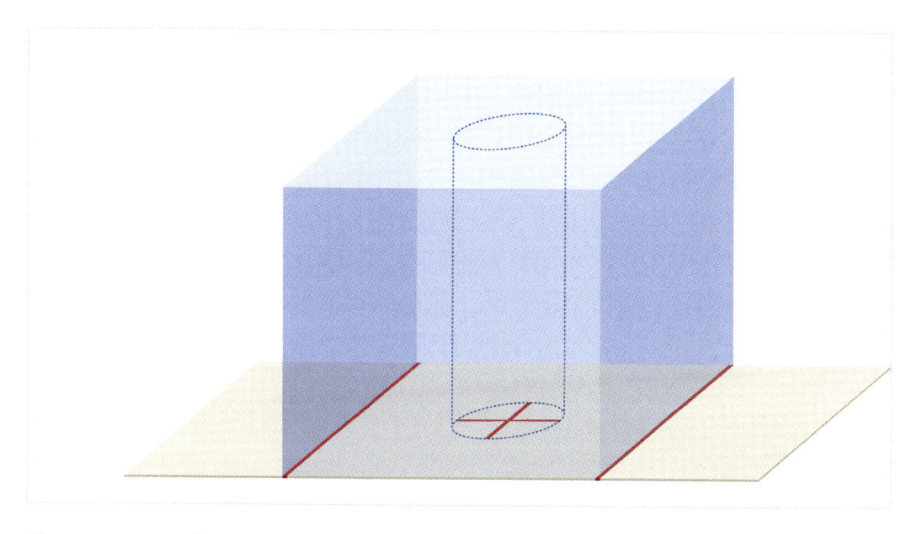

The two-meter performance box with the strict performance chimney indicated.

Although a gymnast should avoid deductions for travel while remaining within this expanded performance box, there is bound to be some height loss when travelling back and forth within such a generous space. That loss of height not only damages the Time of Flight but creates control problems that lead to breaks in form. It is therefore ill-advised to allow the gymnast to be satisfied with performing within such wide parameters.

So, if the strict performance chimney is a little too demanding for the execution of a voluntary routine and the expanded zone just described is too generous, we need a compromise. This is shown in the following illustration.

Over & Above

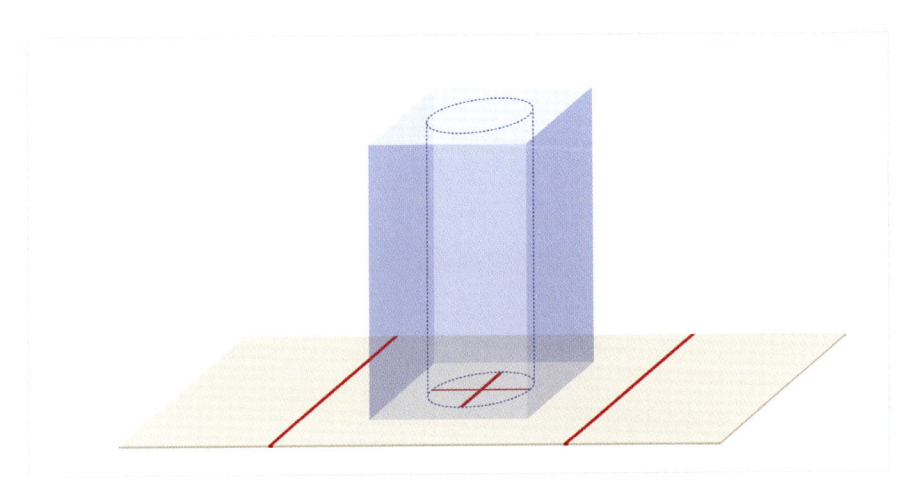

The modified performance box with strict performance chimney indicated.

If we expand the base of the strict performance chimney by half a meter in each direction, we create what I call the modified performance box within which the gymnast can still hit the top, travel and maintain height (and therefore time), as well as remaining well clear of the lines that incur a travel deduction. This less demanding zone and corresponding airspace allow for small errors and helps to ease the gymnast's anxiety during performance.

In Chapter 11, I pointed out that practically every substandard routine is the result of the gymnast's over-reaction to initial mistakes. If the gymnast becomes aware they are about to breach the two-meter zone and incur a travel deduction, their anxiety is likely to cause an over-reaction even before touchdown occurs; the correction causes height loss and a break in form. Compare that to a gymnast who is aware they are about to breach the limit of the *self-imposed* modified performance box with its built-in safety margin. They will be less likely to succumb to the damaging panic reaction that leads to over-correction. That may be sound enough in theory, but we need to put in place a training process that will equip the gymnast to perform with this level of confidence and composure.

Before describing how to develop the GPS, it is important to remind you that single somersaults and entire set routines should be initially trained to hit the top of the strict performance chimney on every skill. It is only when difficulty (DD) begins to rise, that the principle of the modified performance box comes into consideration.

The next illustration shows the **base** of the modified performance box, which is divided into three overlapping segments, A, B and C. To aid the gymnast's awareness during training, the limit of the segments can be marked on the frame pad with tape or chalk. An even greater visual aid can be constructed by weaving a length of colored fabric tape through the holes in the webbing of the bed. If video replay is being used, then a number of programs will enable demarcation lines to be placed on the screen for review purposes. Unfortunately this does not help the gymnast while **actually** performing.

Performance zone contained within the modified performance box showing overlapping segments.

The essence of this process is to allow the gymnast to use small amounts of "helpful" travel that aid the linking of elements within the routine. The degree of travel is small enough to free the gymnast from fears of height loss or travel deduction. The gymnast must study the routine they plan to perform and decide in which segment they would prefer to touchdown after each skill. The following familiar routine provides us with an initial example:

1. Back somersault (tucked)   B-B
2. Straddle jump   B-B
3. Seat drop   B-B
4. Half twist to seat   B-B
5. Half twist to feet   B-B
6. Piked jump   B-B
7. Back drop   B B
8. Half twist to feet   B-C
9. Tucked jump   C-C
10. Front somersault (tucked)   C-B

Over & Above

There is no need for the gymnast performing this routine to move from the base of the strict performance chimney and, apart from skills 4 and 5, they should be aiming to hit the top throughout. A small allowance is made for the half twist to feet from the back drop because if the gymnast attempts to keep this precisely in segment B, they are likely to overreact and create an undesirable gaining or "contra" effect. The tucked jump/front somersault finish, goes neatly from C to finish centrally in segment B. I stress that this is not encouraging travel but is making sensible use of permitted lateral movement while conforming to the principle of top. It is possible that different competitors, in consultation with the coach may create a different "route" but routines of this simplicity are unlikely to deviate much from the example given. The routine plan would initially undergo a period of trial and error to establish whether the original selections are realistic. After making appropriate adjustments, the coach and gymnast would then agree on the best plan.

As the difficulty of the routine increases, a slightly more flexible "route" may be needed, as in the following example, although I would still expect this routine to remain within the strict performance chimney rather than employing the modified performance box:

1. Back Somersault (straight)   B-A
2. Barani (straight)   A-B
3. Back Somersault (tucked)   B-B
4. Straddle Jump   B-B
5. Back Somersault (piked)   B-C
6. Barani (tucked)   C-B
7. Back Somersault to Seat   B-B
8. Half Twist to Feet   B-B
9. Tucked Jump   B-B
10. Front Somersault (piked)   B-B

The next example, because of the increased difficulty, may require the use of the modified performance box, but it still complies with the principles established earlier. The plan for the routine will be highly personalized for the particular performer, based on their strengths and preferences, although the placements shown are logical as a starting point.

1. Half out (piked)	A-B
2. Half in/half out (tucked)	B-C
3. Half out (tucked)	C-B
4. Double back (tucked)	B-A
5. Barani (straight)	A-B
6. Full twisting back	B-C
7. Rudi	C-B
8. Double full	B-A
9. One-and-three-quarter front (piked)	A-A
10. Ball out rudi	A-B

The danger with creating something that appears to be as prescriptive as these examples is that the performer becomes frustrated when the plan doesn't work out. But let me remind you that this is like any other drill or training exercise — it is simply a tool for the coach (craftsperson) to use in fashioning a quality product. Once the overall plan is agreed upon, the routine must be worked in sections with the gymnast becoming gradually more familiar with the placements before joining two or more sections together in the traditional way of practicing routines.

Remember that I called this a routine GPS and, as such, there will be "recalculation" required when the gymnast strays from the intended route. This is the real strength of the process, and the gymnast learns to make these recalculations with subtlety and precision rather than the reactive over-correction, which at best loses marks and at worst leads to a failure of the routine.

I am reminded of two apparently conflicting sayings, "If you fail to plan, you plan to fail," and conversely, "No battle plan ever survives the first contact with the enemy." These two statements are, of course, complementary and could be applied to the process covered in this chapter. Start with a clear plan but have the presence of mind and skill to make the right amount of changes when that becomes necessary in response to an error. On the other hand, many coaches and gymnasts may identify with the words of the late comic genius Spike Milligan who said:

"We haven't got a plan, so nothing can go wrong!"

CHAPTER 23

GETTING THE BIGGEST BANG FOR YOUR BUCK!

SECTION FOUR
MAXIMIZING POTENTIAL

Back in 1973, I discovered that a coach's technical knowledge of the sport, while important, is not enough to deliver World Class performance even if the athlete has all the necessary physical and mental attributes. Chapter 4, "A Radical Rethink," recounts the experiences that led me to consider how it was possible to compete with the full-time "professionals" of the Soviet Union. Most countries competing in trampoline gymnastics are now looking at the Chinese and asking themselves similar questions. It would be too easy to make assumptions that the Chinese have such unique social and genetic advantages that the rest of the world is competing for second place. There is plenty of evidence to support this negative view, and my experience with the British team in Kunshan at the 2007 World Cup did nothing to stimulate optimism. The Chinese men occupied the first four places after the preliminary routines, but their two guest competitors (permitted as the host nation) occupied fifth and sixth places! Even 2004 Olympic Champion Yuriy Nikitin and 2005 World Champion Alexander Rusakov found themselves almost a whole mark behind those six Chinese performers.

Thankfully, people in competitive sport, whether they be athletes, coaches or managers, will always strive to close the gap between themselves and the best, but it can be a mistake to try and copy what the

Over & Above

leading nations are doing without taking into account one's own particular culture. This was my view following defeat at the hands of the Soviets in 1973, and there are already indications that nations can find their own ways to compete with the Chinese. We caught up with the Soviets by 1980, and Rosie MacLennan's (CAN) victory at the 2012 Olympics suggests another gap is closing. Dave Ross's Sky Riders gym in Toronto operates within a society that could hardly be further away from the Chinese sporting production line, yet distills the essence of what is required to produce champions … very much within the Canadian culture (see Chapter 29: Introducing Dave Ross).

My approach was to look at time management and emphasize the most important aspects of trampoline training while eliminating the non-essentials. I still believe that this approach can work. Although a number of nations operate a residential centralized system (and there are great advantages in this), I have nonetheless observed significant levels of non-productive time within those systems. The opportunities presented can be squandered through a complacent attitude brought about by the luxury of time availability. Restricted time **can** become an asset if it helps to focus the minds of coach and athletes on making the most of every opportunity. I recall an Olympic gold medal winning oarsman saying, "You must constantly ask yourself – is what I am doing **now** helping the boat to go faster?"

HOW MUCH TIME IS NEEDED?

That obviously depends on what you want to achieve. Probably the best known study was carried out in 1991 by psychologist Anders Ericsson and his colleagues who looked into the causes of excellent performance. Readers may already be familiar with this much-quoted research, so I will summarize the work as a means of setting a context for my own experience.

Violin students at the Music Academy of West Berlin were divided into three categories based upon assessments by their professors. The first group consisted of those who were expected to become teachers of the instrument. The next group contained more accomplished players who were destined to be employed as professional musicians, while the third group was made up of the outstanding players who had the potential to become international soloists. Ericsson determined how many hours each student had invested in mastering their instrument, starting from the time they had committed themselves to the task of becoming a musician. The results revealed that the more accomplished the performer, the greater was the number of hours invested in striving for excellence. This raises many questions about the role of natural aptitude compared to the amount of time spent working to achieve excellence. My purpose for quoting this study is not to enter that particular debate but to provide a simple reality check for the coach and gymnast setting their sights on world class performance.

This is what Ericsson discovered:

Students aspiring to be teachers of the violin had undertaken around 4 thousand hours practicing their instrument.

Students destined to become orchestral musicians had practiced around 8 thousand hours.

Students likely to become international soloists had committed **at least** ten thousand hours to the enterprise.

Furthermore, Ericsson and his team determined that there were no exceptions. No one had found themselves in the "soloist" group who had done less than the ten thousand hours, and there was no one in the "teacher" group who had undertaken ten thousand hours of committed practice. Indeed, the psychologists stated:

> *"We argue that the differences between expert performers and normal adults reflect a life-long persistence of deliberate effort to improve performance."*

Following Ericsson's work, others have adopted what has been called "the ten year rule." It is said that an individual in any form of human activity will have spent at least ten years of committed, purposeful practice before attaining excellence. There are a number of high profile examples to support this assertion and here is one that is absolutely relevant to the subject of this book:

Over & Above

Stewart Matthews started trampolining at the Harlow Sportcentre Under Tens Club in 1970, and he became World Champion in 1980!

I have no intention of taking Ericsson's findings literally, but they cannot be ignored if one is striving for the goal of excellence in any activity. It must be remembered however, that the "ten thousand hour" findings related to musicians developing their expertise on a specific instrument, and it would be a mistake to assume that this automatically applied to the acquisition of sports expertise. Indeed David Epstein in his book, *The Sports Gene: What Makes the Perfect Athlete*, states:

> *"'In fact in absolutely every single study of sports expertise, there is a tremendous range of hours of practice logged by athletes who reach the same level, and very rarely do elite performers log ten thousand hours of sport specific practice prior to reaching the top competitive plane, often competing in a number of other sports and acquiring a range other athletic skills before zeroing in on one."*

There are many factors at work in this process apart from the hours. The aspiring athlete will require some natural aptitude, opportunity to participate, the right equipment, expert coaching, parental support, personal drive and an appropriate quality and quantity of work undertaken within each hour. For the moment, let us keep matters simple as we approach the reality check I promised.

Let me ask you, in terms of training for excellence in trampoline gymnastics ... when is an hour not an hour? I have worked with coaches and clubs who are proud to boast that their gymnasts train "twenty-four hours a week." They are also heard to denigrate opponents on the basis that they "only train eight hours a week." Those statements require some critical scrutiny and should not be taken at face value. The only verifiable truth is that the gymnasts may indeed spend twenty-four hours a week **in the gym** as opposed to those who spend only eight hours. Numbers quoted like that amounts to propaganda and doesn't necessarily relate to actual productive time. So when is an hour really an hour?

Getting the Biggest Bang for Your Buck!

Let us keep the ten thousand hour figure broadly in mind and examine how closely trampoline gymnasts are likely to adhere to it as they work toward World Class performance. I will examine the myth that is contained within a **declared** number of training hours.

The following scenarios are based simplistically on one trampoline for one hour with a given number of gymnasts. If we divide the sixty minutes by the number of gymnasts in the group, we get an idea of the amount of actual trampoline-specific technical work per hour.

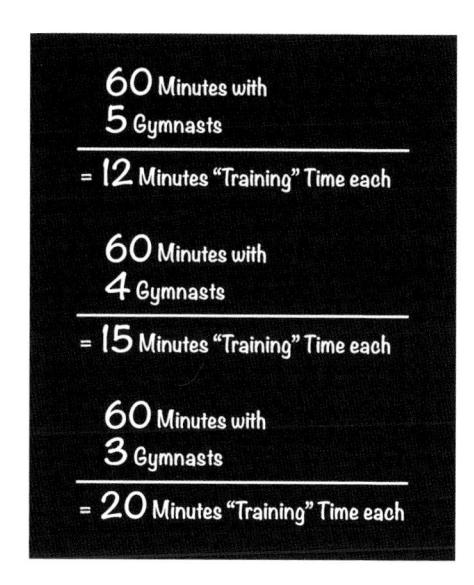

60 Minutes with 5 Gymnasts = 12 Minutes "Training" Time each

60 Minutes with 4 Gymnasts = 15 Minutes "Training" Time each

60 Minutes with 3 Gymnasts = 20 Minutes "Training" Time each

"Real" training time scenarios.

That little exercise is highly simplistic because it fails to consider the minimum of 20 seconds absorbed each time gymnasts change over on the trampoline. Furthermore it doesn't consider the wasted practice time on the trampoline due to a range of issues highlighted at the end of this chapter. These factors further erode the amount of time per hour that the gymnast actually performs on the equipment, effectively reducing the 60 minutes in scenario (a) by at least another four minutes. **A gymnast working in that environment with a daily two-hour session, seven days a week for fifty weeks a year would take over sixty years to complete the required ten thousand hours!**

On the other hand, a gymnast starting their trampoline career in that apparently unfavorable environment may still have their ambition ignited, leading them to seek more progressive opportunities elsewhere. This places an important responsibility on the coach to ensure sound fundamentals are instilled so that World Class development can take place when the conditions become more conducive. I have inherited numerous naturally gifted gymnasts who have required a total technical rebuild before the quest for excellence could begin. That is certainly not an example of overall good time management.

Over & Above

If we develop the three-gymnasts-to-one-hour scenario, which would appear more conducive to World Class aspiration, it will still take forty years to hit the ten thousand hour target! Maybe we have been kidding ourselves that we are really developing excellence with our performers or perhaps Ericsson should not have his findings quoted so literally in terms of attaining excellence in trampoline gymnastics. Who would argue that Stewart Matthews did not achieve excellence, but did he literally practice his art **on the equipment** for ten thousand hours before becoming the best in the world in 1980?

The following simplistic model shows that it may be possible to rack up ten thousand hours if we restrict our counting to hours spent as opposed to hours actually practicing.

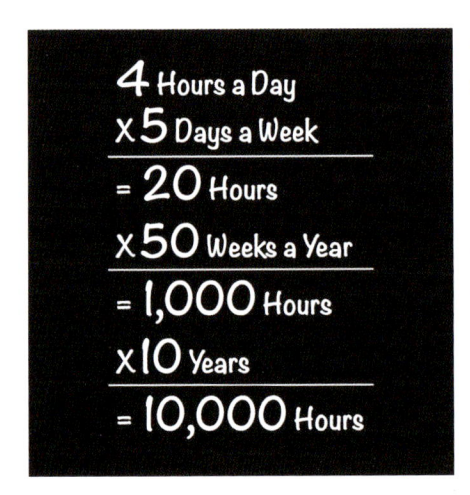

> 4 Hours a Day
> x 5 Days a Week
> = 20 Hours
> x 50 Weeks a Year
> = 1,000 Hours
> x 10 Years
> = 10,000 Hours

A possible "ten thousand hour" training time schedule.

At least that's only ten years instead of forty, so it might actually be achievable. However, there are very few opportunities that allow a trampoline gymnast to spend four hours a day actually on the trampoline (as the violinist has "contact time" with their instrument) or to find a facility that can accommodate twenty hours a week, five days a week, fifty weeks a year for ten years. Even if it were possible, how could it be financed? Lest you fear I am posing problems without solutions, let me assure you that the starting point for any successful project has to be an honest appraisal of the size of the challenge.

Now we can look at how to create an excellence-driven environment by maximizing the content of whatever hours are available. There is no doubt that the most important element in training to become a World Class trampolinist, is productive work directly on the trampoline itself. We have already seen how limited that time can be, which makes it all the more important to use this precious commodity wisely. But because an hour's trampolining can involve more "dead time" than "bed time," we should start by addressing that sizeable unproductive element. This was precisely the thinking that changed my way of working and created an environment from which two world champions emerged. The outlined structure of a training session with five gymnasts on one trampoline with one coach was as follows:

GYMNAST ONE: On trampoline working to prescribed program.

GYMNAST TWO: Just dismounted from the trampoline with recent work fresh in memory. Go to diary table and record work done and make pertinent comments.

GYMNAST THREE: Go to conditioning station (1) and perform set repetitions of appropriate prescribed exercise.

GYMNAST FOUR: Go to conditioning station (2) and perform set repetitions of **different** appropriate prescribed exercise.

GYMNAST FIVE: Waiting by the trampoline, mentally rehearsing the work about to be done on the trampoline.

I have written this as a simple one to five scenario, but it could be multiplied by the number of trampolines and coaches available and could certainly work with more than five per trampoline, although additional conditioning or activity stations would be required. The whole circuit is controlled on a timed basis by the performer on the trampoline, and no one moves to the next station until that gymnast has completed their allocated work. This is crucial, otherwise a "log jam" builds up around the trampoline thereby nullifying the effectiveness of the system.

As with all outline plans, there are a lot of details in this system that require managing in order to make it effective, but let's first look at the benefits.

1. Each gymnast can be positively **engaged in the process** of improving some element of their trampoline performance for the **entire sixty minutes of every hour**.

2. There is no longer any "dead time."

3. At no time are two gymnasts at the same point in the circuit. This prevents time-wasting conversations and distractions.

4. The need to balance work and active rest is catered for. (See Chapter 25: Principles of Fitness Training for Trampoline)

Over & Above

Having outlined the positives, it is important to consider the changes in attitude and culture that are needed to make this work. It **cannot be imposed**, and it will not manage itself! Here are the salient points for a successful operation:

- The gymnasts must agree to operate the system because they want to make the most of their training and any doubters need to be allocated to a less demanding group.
- The coach must be positioned where ALL members of the group can be seen and supervised.
- The conditioning exercises must be selected because they have a relevance to trampoline performance, yet not too demanding in energy terms so as to interfere with the next on-trampoline episode.
- The conditioning exercises must be taught thoroughly to the group as a whole before being inserted into the circuit.
- The coach needs to constantly deal with, and correct poor performance of the conditioning work.
- A small whiteboard is placed at each conditioning station listing the exercises to be performed on each circuit.
- The gymnasts must know exactly what their on-trampoline program will be for the session. This is particularly important for the gymnast waiting to go on, who should be mentally preparing for the work they are about to undertake.

In summary, this is one model for creating an excellence-driven training environment where each gymnast is **totally engaged** in the following positive cycle.

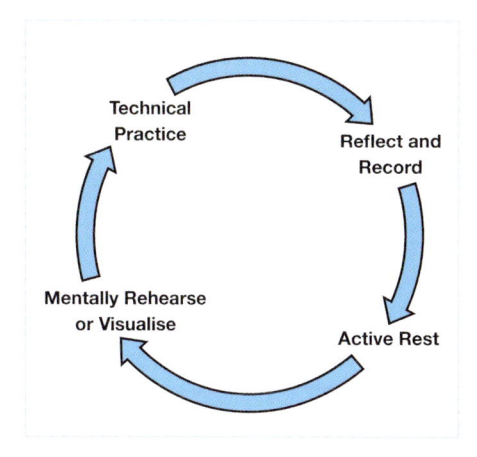

An "excellence driven" training cycle aimed at 100% gymnast engagement.

That process is only a **logistical** solution to try and address the hourly challenge. Ericsson's team reported that the necessary hours have to reflect "persistence of deliberate effort to improve performance." That has little to do with logistics and everything to do with attitude, character, commitment and leadership. Those qualities are required from both the gymnasts and the coach. (See Chapter 30: Introducing Dave Ross.)

It is not too difficult to assemble a group of gymnasts who will agree to comply with such a system, but there is a dramatic difference between *compliance* and *engagement*. The latter quality is the essential ingredient in the process of creating excellence. One often finds this quality in gymnasts with relatively modest natural gifts, while those with, what we would call "talent," **fail to engage** sufficiently to reach their physical potential. I have been fortunate to work with a wide range of young gymnasts who have demonstrated engagement to a high degree without having the greatest natural physical attributes. It could be said that they over-achieved, or as Mitch Fenner once told me, "You have become an expert in making silk purses out of sow's ears!" I am happy to say I also had the experience of making silk purses out of silk, but **engagement with the process** was always the decisive factor!

Over & Above

WHO IS THE MOST EFFECTIVE COACH?

It is revealing to divide an hour between the number of gymnasts in a group, but the same exercise can be undertaken by splitting the coach's time per hour between the gymnasts. You must expect a similar result. To begin addressing this additional challenge, I have transcribed a conversation with one of the Scottish National Squad gymnasts:

Gymnast: I don't see how I can reach World Class when I only see my coach four times a week.

Jack: Are those one-to-one sessions?

Gymnast: No, there are six in the group.

Jack: In that case, I would estimate you spend less than an hour a week directly working with your coach.

*Gymnast: I hadn't realized it was **that** bad! But now you can see what I mean.*

Jack: OK. Let's look at it another way. How many hours a week do you spend with yourself?

Gymnast: Obviously all the time!

Jack: Well you have to find a way to become your own coach, and then you have all the hours you'll ever need to help you reach World Class!

That apparently silly conversation opens up the way to achieving ten thousand hours of "deliberate effort to improve performance." I have long held the view that my gymnasts believed they coached themselves, and to a large extent they did. My role was to help them understand how to do that, as well as to guide the way they should be thinking and acting in relation to the sport and their goals. Of course my technical knowledge and inputs were valuable and indeed valued, but their **learning** actually took place within themselves. That could be taking place anywhere or at any time **after** my inputs had taken place – they were consciously and unconsciously assimilating what we had been working on.

It is reasonable to presume that we get better when we are actually physically practicing and carrying out the instructions of our teachers and coaches. My experience, on the other hand, is that our improvement often takes place in **the intervals between** practicing and then practicing again. That interval can be a matter of minutes or even weeks. A desired improvement in skill acquisition may be experienced at any time and does not follow a consistent pattern. It may occur during the gap between repetitions or during the period of rest between sets of attempts. It may even take a period of absence from training to show itself. I have a vivid recollection of some adolescent athletes returning from the summer break and showing progress simply as a result of the rest and change of environment.

Although I appear to be playing down the importance of physical practice, nothing could be further from the truth. It is crucial that the gymnast understands the importance of a positive mindset during repetitive practice and accepts that it is unreasonable to expect immediate dramatic improvement just because they have trained hard. A performer's negative attitude to frustrating attempts can be one of the greatest time wasters and subtracts from the productive hourly objective. I have had countless experiences both as coach and learner, when practice has been repetitive and frustrating with little visible improvement. Then, one day ... Wow! ... I can do that now!

It is essential that both coach and gymnast are aware of this dynamic, which has a remarkable potency if both parties are open to its possibilities. As a National Coach, I frequently encountered gymnasts who did not know how to get full value from the coaching they received, either from myself or indeed their personal coach. Equally, there are too few coaches who can see their role as anything other than a source of all technical advice and feedback. The requisite number of hours of "deliberate effort to improve performance" **are attainable**, firstly through logistical organization and secondly through the coach/performer relationship developing from a telling/doing partnership into enabler/learner team.

The purpose of this chapter was to stimulate thoughts on how to manage time productively and reduce waste in the drive toward World Class performance. I would urge those with such ambitions to consider their own environment and training behaviors with honesty. Start by listing the areas where valuable training time is currently being lost. This could be logistical, or it could relate to attitude, preparation, goal setting,

Over & Above

physical condition, health, nutrition, etc. Having made a list, how could these areas be addressed to create additional training time? Are the changes practicable, and when could they be made?

Here are some points to consider, each one of which has serious time-wasting implications. The list is far from comprehensive but several items refer to opinions expressed in earlier chapters. How many relate to your situation?

1. Logistical

- Inappropriate gymnast selection or group allocation
- Coach/equipment/gymnast balance
- Bed time and "dead time"
- Training frequency
- Session duration
- Tardiness – gymnasts and/or coach

2. Coaching

- "Telling" style coaching
- "Cosmetic" coaching
- Misleading words and phrases
- Myopic coaching (focusing on one gymnast while others are unsupervised)
- Lack of session planning
- Failure to outline session goals

3. Technical

- Brittle basics
- Unstable straight jumping
- Jumping without taking off/aborted attempts
- Losing sense of "top"
- Absence of "tempo" awareness

Getting the Biggest Bang for Your Buck!

4. Physical

- Injury
- Pain
- Dehydration
- Poor nutrition
- Work/rest balance

5. Mental

- Lack of engagement
- Frustration
- Loss of concentration
- External distraction
- Loss of confidence

> *JACK KELLY: "Effective coaches don't 'teach' the gymnasts, they enable them to 'learn.' Ultimately the gymnasts largely coach themselves."*

CHAPTER 24

THE TRAMPOLINE "TALENT PACKAGE"

SECTION FOUR
MAXIMIZING POTENTIAL

In Chapter One, I stressed that this book aims to pass on what I have learned from my 50 years in the sport and much of this, in modern academic terms, would be regarded as anecdotal rather than evidence based. Despite the absence of full academic rigor, I have been at pains to share only those ideas and processes that have worked for me on a consistent basis.

My thoughts on talent Identification began to form at a remarkably young age and are truly anecdotal. As a ten-year-old, I was the tallest boy in my class, which among other things, seemed to make my parents proud of me. Perhaps my father's height of 5 feet 7 inches (1m 70cm) had something to do with it. In his opinion, I was surely destined to be a "big man." My stature probably contributed to an ability to run and swim faster than my classmates, not to mention fight with older boys! When I moved up to the Aberdeen Grammar School, the Physical Education staff could be forgiven for playing me as lock forward in the rugby team and coaching me at shot putt and javelin throwing. By the time I was fifteen, I had grown a little more, but the acceleration in my classmates' growth had designated me as "average." So there I was, a small-to-average athlete still being expected to perform like a colossus! Lest you think I have told you this as some kind of catharsis, let me assure you it is simply to provide an example of talent identification gone wrong.

Over & Above

On becoming a Physical Education teacher myself, I found it was common practice, when selecting primary school soccer teams, to play the "best" player at center half (apologies for the dated parlance). The rationale being this was where the control of the whole team would come from. That may not sound too damaging in itself, but I observed an unusual number of senior teams with a skillful but vertically challenged center half. This reinforced my belief that drawing firm conclusions about a young person's talent at ten years of age based on their stature or *apparent* athletic ability is a serious mistake.

Some years ago at the National Sports Development Conference, I listened to a sports scientist explain how he had been involved in the physiological testing of athletes from the various national sports governing bodies to help assess each individual's training needs. Most of the athletes displayed clear evidence of physiological suitability for their chosen sport, but one female squash player caused amazement when her results were collated. She displayed all the characteristics of a World Class 800 meter runner. The sports scientists were so impressed with this talent indicator that they took time to make her aware of her exciting potential and recommended that she change sports. Her National Coach added weight to this by pointing out that, although she was part of the England Squad, she was not highly regarded as a future World Class squash player. Despite the discovery of her aptitude to become a world-renowned athlete, she was just not interested. Why? She said she just LOVED playing squash!

John Atkinson, former Performance Director with British Gymnastics once told me that when the Soviet Union was the supreme power in artistic gymnastics their numerous full-time professional coaches were asked about the qualities that characterized a future gymnastics champion. Many factors were listed but the top four were:

1. Love of the sport

2. Intelligence

3. Determination

4. Strength

Where are all the physical markers that would indicate gymnastic potential? Strength is there of course, but the top three qualities are non-physical. These experienced coaches were clearly aware that there are many young gymnasts who possess physical aptitude, but without the other qualities they would be unlikely to fulfill their potential. Nothing I have experienced in my coaching career has caused me to disagree with those priorities. I could name many trampoline gymnasts who demonstrated wonderful physical potential yet failed to reach World Class because they lacked the determination to work through issues that could not be quickly solved. In the end, perhaps they liked and enjoyed trampolining, but they didn't LOVE it. I recall the words of one World Class performer from a different sport:

"The way to high achievement is by turning up to train at the sport you love when you don't feel like doing it."

The highlighting of intelligence is interesting, but it would be too easy to assume this refers to academic ability. It must be remembered that this is a translation from Russian so I will try to clarify what I think is being referred to. The potential World Class performer must have an ability to interpret feedback and instruction both from the coach and by tapping into their own sensory experiences before making use of that information to effect improvement. I have known a number of National Team members who possessed fine intellectual capability (they were very intelligent) yet failed to harness it fully because of overriding emotional, attitudinal or personality limitations. Intelligence is undoubtedly a component in the talent package, but it must be realized how it relates to the other characteristics on the list. I have known athletes in a range of sports whose love of the sport was the most influential factor in their eventual achievements. They were intelligent enough to recognize their natural disadvantages and found ways to compensate, usually through hard work and determination, to succeed. Their passion for the activity and desire to succeed enabled them to excel beyond reasonable expectation. That sums up my own rugby playing career rather well!

Determination, intelligence and love of the sport can help the potential champion to recalibrate and refresh their motivation in the face of apparent failure or cope with months of rehabilitation and inactivity following injury. You may recall Stewart Matthews' demonstration of determination, intelligence *and* love of the sport following a long lay-off in 1972.

Over & Above

The process of selecting or identifying suitable individuals for high achievement in any activity is fraught with difficulties, but the first step is to identify the sport-specific characteristics that are known to be possessed by the most successful performers. That is only the beginning, because a reliable test is then required for each quality. As part of my work with the Singapore Gymnastics, I received an account of a course run by the Gymnastics Federation of Thailand conducted by Wang Ying from China. My informant reported:

> "On the first day, we were introduced to how to select the gymnast for trampoline according to their physical traits, such as size of head, wideness of shoulders, knees of gymnasts, feet of gymnasts, etc."

Jonathan McEvoy writing in "Mail Online" before the 2012 Olympics described the Chinese process for developing divers:

> "In China, children as young as six are tested for their size, skills and fitness as part of a talent identification strategy. They are monitored as they develop; the better ones moving seamlessly from their local schools to state, regional and national schools, in some cases until they reach their early twenties. Drawing on a population of 1.3 billion, it is a process rich in potential for world domination."

There can be no doubt that this works for the Chinese, but I have come to believe that in our culture the Self-Determination Theory holds sway. That theory was constructed by human behavior academics Richard Ryan and Edward Deci, stating that we have three innate psychological needs:

- Competence
- Autonomy
- Relatedness

In other words, we need to feel we are succeeding, that we are free from compulsion/coercion, and valued by our fellows for what we do and who we are. If these three needs are met, so the theory goes, we will be:

- Motivated
- Productive
- Happy

These are the kind of athletes I want to coach!

Every one of my gymnasts who followed their trampoline career to a successful conclusion arrived in my gym spontaneously, saw my club perform in a public demonstration, or responded to a suggestion they might want to come and try the sport. None were formally tested, although they all underwent a period of "try before you buy." Bearing in mind my own experience of being typecast on the basis of size at the age of ten, I confess I have always considered parental stature as one component in the sport-specific talent mix. No child who wanted to be a trampolinist was ever rejected, and following their introduction to the sport, they were allowed to find their own level. Rather than talent identification or selection, there was an invitation to be part of the journey toward excellence. It was their choice as to how far along that excellence road they travelled. Canada's amazing Dave Ross, whose gymnasts have stood on the podium at every Olympics since the sport's entry in 2000, told the *Toronto Observer* in September 2012:

> "You put in time with the little ones, hoping that you find some new stars, but at the same time the journey that kids go through is to try and get better. Any athlete that's willing to work hard, I'm really happy to work with. The journey is more important than the goal."

It sounds like Dave also buys into the Self-Determination Theory!

There are many sports where certain body types and proportions are essential for success at the upper levels. Some sports, like boxing and weightlifting, allow for differences by creating size categories. Rowing has introduced a lightweight category to bring Olympic achievement within reach of many smaller yet skillful athletes. The best trampoline gymnasts certainly fall within certain anthropometric parameters, but the range can be surprisingly wide. The most common physical characteristics are lightness and strength, both of which can be manipulated to some degree by training.

Over & Above

As trampolines become more powerful, enabling gymnasts to perform with increased airtime, it seems to me that the taller gymnasts are able to level the playing field to some extent, enabling them to compete with shorter athletes. Providing they are relatively slender, the taller performers can hold their own in the aesthetic department and perform world class difficulty. There have been a number of heavily built male gymnasts on the world scene, indeed no one could accuse Alexander Moskalenko (RUS) of being anorexic, yet he became the first Olympic Champion in addition to his five World Championship victories.

The FIG Code of Points for Trampoline Gymnastics may not be perfect, but it has a significant benefit for the gymnast who does not fit the artistic or even elegant stereotype. Providing the required shapes and straight exits are shown along with the compliance of straight arms close to the body, there is no reason why the execution judges should not make zero deductions. The word "deduction" sums it up however, because in our sport there is no credit given for adding creativity to the performance or for artistic merit. Comply with required shaping at the right time and deductions can be avoided. To some degree, this makes the sport defensive in nature. The gymnast starts with a "perfect ten" for execution and must perform in such a way as to prevent the judges from taking away points.

I raise this issue to counter the suggestion that the selection of gymnasts for World Class development should be based on their physical appearance. Of course the various body types can be more or less aesthetically appealing while on terra firma, but with sound technique, efficient power application and strict compliance with the Code of Points, bodily proportions may not play such a major part in scoring for execution.

I am reminded of watching penguins at the zoo, waddling around the pool with almost comic incompetence only to marvel at their grace, speed and agility once they enter the water. **That** is their **true** environment. I have seen international trampoline gymnasts walking to the apparatus with less than balletic grace only to amaze us with a penguin-like transformation as they metamorphose into elegant, powerful aerial athletes the moment they take to the air.

Some young gymnasts will display an affinity with the trampoline bed as if it is *their* natural medium, and coaches should encourage and develop this quality. The great aquatic athlete Ian Thorpe writes in his autobiography *This is Me:*

"As I begin to swim, I allow myself to feel where the water is moving around me, how it flows off my body. I listen for any erratic movement which means I'm not relating to the water, and I have to modify my stroke, change it until I feel the water moving smoothly past me."

He continues:

"It's really rewarding because I receive constant feedback without stopping. I don't need someone to tell me that my stroke looks great or that it looks terrible because I have an inner sense of the water, and the environment is already communicating with me."

Thorpe was not **taught** how to do this, and there are gymnasts with a similar feel for the action of the bed that needs to be recognized and nurtured through sensitive coaching.

Outside the nations whose culture enables a national screening and selection process to be undertaken, talent generally self-selects through the simple mechanism of walking through the gym door. Only after a period of trying the sport, does true potential begin to emerge. It is during this time that the beginner gets hooked and shows whether their attitude and aptitude are compatible with World Class aspiration. I take no satisfaction from my part in the following 1970 scenario that turned out to be a significant learning experience.

Jan Kelly, then Jan Allen, was still competing at international level but spent time coaching within the Apex-Harlow development program. Our conversation went as follows:

Jan: Jack, the boy who lives across the road from me is a member of the Sportscentre Under Tens Club, and he likes playing all the sports we do on a Saturday morning, but he only **really** wants to do trampolining.

Jack: That's why we do a different sport each week at the Under Tens, so his chance to do trampolining will come round again soon.

Jan: Yes, I know, but he's always talking to me about trampolining, and I think he could be **really** good.

Over & Above

Jack: Now I know the boy you're talking about. He's bigger than most of the other Under Tens and he throws his weight around when he plays football with them. He doesn't look like a future trampolinist to me!

*Jan: But can he join Apex because he's **so** keen?*

Jack: You know we don't take new kids in until they've gone through the whole process. I'm not making an exception just because he lives across the road from you.

Jan: Go on! Please! What if I take personal responsibility for him and he does a four-week trial, then you'll see I'm right. But if you disagree after that, I won't say any more about it.

*Jack: Well, OK, but this is **your** responsibility. I don't want to be involved! By the way, what's his name?*

Jan: He's called Stewart ... Stewart Matthews!

I feel like the investment banker who told the inventor of Velcro to take his silly idea somewhere else!

Talent transfer has been successful for many years with individuals like long jumper Alan Wells discovering his true event to become Olympic 100 meters champion and several of the 2012 GBR Olympic Team winning medals in the sport that was not their original choice. Some of the best examples come from cycling and Triathlon, while bobsled has benefitted from many former athletes like Ed Moses.

I am inclined to believe that talent identification in Western society is more of an art than a science, where luck, as well as good judgment, plays a significant part. Many young people have shown mild interest in an activity only to have it ignited into burning ambition by the passion of a coach or the presence of an inspiring role model. Daniel Coyle in *The Talent Code* uses the word "ignition" to describe one of the essential ingredients in the process leading to excellence. He writes:

"Ignition and deep practice work together to produce skill in exactly the same way that a gas tank combines with an engine to produce velocity in an automobile. Ignition supplies the energy, while deep practice translates that energy over time into forward progress."

So the beautifully proportioned, well-coordinated, strong young athlete who appears to epitomize the future champion trampoline gymnast may turn out to be seriously lacking in the essential non-physical components that complete the "talent package." Daniel Epstein in *The Sports Gene* relates natural aptitude to the hardware in a computer with the software being the acquired skills and techniques required for a specific activity. He states:

"The truth is, even at the most basic level, it is always a hardware and software story. The hardware is useless without the software, just as the reverse is true. Sport skill acquisition does not happen without both specific genes and specific environment, and often the genes and the environment must coincide at the same time."

CHAPTER 25

PRINCIPLES OF FITNESS TRAINING FOR TRAMPOLINE

SECTION FOUR
MAXIMIZING POTENTIAL

Principles of Fitness Training for Trampoline

In addressing this topic, I want to look at the principles involved rather than prescribing specific exercises for each required body part or energy system. These can be accessed through other publications on sports conditioning and the British Gymnastics Common Core resource material. I will restrict myself to an overall appraisal of the conditioning needs of the trampoline gymnast and what my experience has taught me about the effective application of relevant conditioning work.

In designing a conditioning program for any sport, the starting point must be to assess the specific demands of performing that activity to the level required. I pick those words carefully, because if the goal is simply to take part for enjoyment and recreation, the activity itself may be quite sufficient to satisfy the requirements of the participant. Indeed, the vast majority of those who play sport, including trampoline gymnastics, do so for fun and to maintain a healthy level of physical conditioning. It is possible to enjoy trampolining at a surprisingly high standard without any specific conditioning other than performing on trampoline itself. Chapter11: Trampolining Is Too Easy! looked at this phenomenon from a skill-acquisition point of view but there is a risk of similar complacency with regard to physical conditioning for our sport.

Over & Above

My former colleague, Simon Breivik, Sports Scientist to British Gymnastics, wrote:

> *"I have had to come to terms with the fact that physical training will take a back seat to technical training. This is to be expected; it is a technical sport that demands hours of practicing skills in the gym. But I frequently hear suggestions that gymnasts receive adequate conditioning from their technical training. Although gymnasts certainly receive **some** conditioning from technical training, I do not feel we should settle for that as adequate."*

Absolutely! But as Simon acknowledges, the first priority must be technical excellence, and I would go so far as to state that the best form of conditioning for the developing performer is — jumping with correct technique right from day one!

As Simon says:

> *"A runner should run, a swimmer should swim, a cyclist should cycle so a trampolinist should trampoline!"*

Nonetheless, faulty technique and mis-timing of physical actions in relation to the movement of the bed can have career-ending consequences due to traumatic or overuse injury. I recall one particular example of a gifted performer earning a place on the World Class Programme only to discover, during a medical appraisal, that what had been regarded as a minor back problem could be traced to poor foot placement during straight jumping. Incorrect use of the feet during the previous five years had set up a chain of compensating distortions through the knees and hips to the lower back where the injury finally manifested.

Consider how much accumulated stress will act on a particular body part over a period of time as a result of some technical misalignment. A gymnast training as little as three two-hour sessions a week could be striking the bed with the feet over two thousand times. That's two thousand times a week when the body is being subjected to a force of around ten times body weight (more or less, depending on the standard of gymnast).

Those repetitions could be multiplied by a period of years as in the example just quoted. It is hardly surprising when a weakness, technical or physical, eventually finds the most vulnerable part of the chain, causing malfunction and injury.

The main theme of this book has been the development of technical excellence, and I want to ensure that my observations on conditioning are set against that background. I have learned the importance of introducing conditioning at the right time, commensurate with the gymnast's level of commitment to their particular goals within the sport. It must be appreciated that a high percentage of young people is attracted to trampolining simply because it looks like fun. Unlike more high-profile sports, there is an absence of readily available role models through the media so beginners rarely have World Class ambitions from the outset. They (and their parents) may have little idea they are entering a sport that requires the highest levels of physical and technical preparation. I have found it to be desirable that the pupils are first hooked on the idea of becoming a World Class performer before a full program of physical conditioning is introduced. The coach needs to exercise sound judgment to make sure the developing gymnast is ready (physically and mentally) to engage with the conditioning program. I have misjudged this on occasion, resulting in "turning off" a promising individual who was still in the "isn't trampolining fun" mode.

This is where gymnastics clubs who cater to the full range of disciplines have a significant advantage, because their young members will have grown up with televised role models and a background of conditioning from day one. It is interesting to note that many outstanding trampoline gymnasts have come from a background of artistic gymnastics where it has been discovered that, while having strength and acrobatic ability, they could not tick all the flexibility boxes. This gave rise to Mitch Fenner's comment that "the best trampolinists are failed gymnasts!" A generalization perhaps but not without an element of truth as epitomized by Paul Luxon, Stewart Matthews and Carl Furrer, three World Champions whose backgrounds are well known to me.

Here is part of a conversation with 2011 World Champion He Wenna (CHN) (through an interpreter, of course):

Jack: *How old were you when you started trampoline gymnastics?*

He Wenna: *I started training in 1999.*

Over & Above

Jack: *That means you have taken twelve years to go from beginner to World Champion. Had you never been on a trampoline before?*

He Wenna: *I had done artistic gymnastics for nine years before becoming a trampoline gymnast. The gymnastic training was very helpful in learning to perform on trampoline.*

This twenty-two-year-old had started artistic gymnastics with its strength, flexibility and body management training as soon as she could walk and was selected to enter the National Trampoline Programme at the age of ten! I discovered that she and a number of the Chinese trampolinists would have preferred to remain as artistic gymnasts, but trampolining gave them a way to continue toward World Class performance in a related field after they had failed to make the national standard in their original discipline. This little insight into the background of a modern World Champion adds weight to Ericsson's "ten thousand hour" findings and indeed He Wenna's twelve years as a trampolinist is totally consistent with the "ten year rule."

The conditioning categories I wish to discuss are Flexibility, Strength, and endurance (what Simon Breivik calls "Engine Fitness").

FLEXIBILITY

While the comprehensive flexibility of the artistic gymnast may have some advantages to the trampolinist in terms of protection against injury, the specific demands of our sport focus on a few joint complexes only. Indeed too great a range of movement in certain areas can actually increase the technical challenge. Excessive spinal flexibility, for example, can cause difficulty with maintaining strong posture when the bed is delivering full power, resulting in a diffusion of the forces required to produce top (an example of conditioning having a negative impact on technique). There may also be a tendency to display exaggerated arched shapes causing execution deductions during required aerial straight positions. Excessive shoulder flexibility can cause similar problems, and the gymnast may experience difficulty in restricting their arm reach to directly overhead, particularly during the take-off phase for backward rotating skills.

The gymnast with a wide range of shoulder and spinal mobility may experience difficulties in maintaining upright posture during bed recoil, as well as showing excessive arched aerial shapes.

In case you think I am writing off the need for spinal and shoulder flexibility, let me stress that the opposite is equally undesirable. The trampolinist with poor spinal mobility may be risking injury when adjusting to ill-directed forces during bed contact following an error, while a more flexible spine may be better able to absorb some of the undue stress on the back.

The ambitious trampoline gymnast should undergo expert assessment with a physiotherapist to ascertain physical limitations and recommend remedial exercises or other appropriate treatment.

It is not unusual to find performers transferring from artistic to trampoline gymnastics because of their inability to meet flexibility norms, rather than any problem with acrobatic aptitude. The inability to perform splits or poor shoulder mobility have been particular difficulties that guided gymnasts to my trampoline programs. Limited shoulder mobility however can continue to be a disadvantage due to the accompanying rounding of the dorsal spine, rendering it impossible for the performer to stretch their arms vertically overhead or achieve an aesthetically pleasing aerial straight line.

The trampoline gymnast should undergo expert assessment to ascertain what remedial exercises would be appropriate and, if possible, have their movement range measured against norms before regular monitoring to evaluate resultant improvement. When coaching a trampoline gymnast with poor shoulder range, watch what happens when they are asked to raise their arms directly overhead. Frequently, in order to raise the

Over & Above

arms at 90 degrees to the floor, the upper body will have to lean back to keep the arms vertical. Imagine the repeated stress on the gymnast's back if they spend any time in contact with the bed while displaying that posture.

A gymnast with excessive shoulder stiffness will bend backwards in order to raise their arms to right angles with the bed.

If expert remedial attention fails to effect a significant improvement in shoulder mobility then a modified arm reach must be adopted with some consequential technical shortcomings. In such a case, it is better to compromise on the arm reach than risk continual repetitive stress on the lower back. I know of several performers who have competed successfully at international level when handicapped by a limited shoulder range (all male incidentally), but I fear they probably failed to reach their full potential as a result.

The two joint complexes requiring a full range of movement for excellence in trampoline gymnastics are the ankle and hip. The ankle mobility range requires more than the ability to show an aesthetic pointed toe (plantar flexion) during the aerial phase; the opposite range (dorsi flexion) is equally important. Both ends of the range have a part to play in order to maximize the outcome of efficient work during the bed-contact period. Chapter 15 dealt with the bed being driven down using leg and hip power while the feet remain flat, resulting in a gravity-driven dorsi flexion, e.g., the toes may be higher than the heel due to the curvature of the depressed bed. This will have the effect of stretching the Achilles tendon at the back of the ankle, making it important for the gymnast to perform regular Achilles and calf stretches as part of their flexibility program and to incorporate dynamic ankle work during the regular warm-up. As the bed returns with force to send the gymnast upward, the feet must maintain their flatness until the last few centimeters before delivery. It is during the final part of the take-off phase that the ankles should forcibly plantar flex to (a) deliver a final thrust and (b) demonstrate an aesthetically pleasing ankle extension or toe point.

While the form of the foot and ankle are important in execution terms, the range of movement in the ankle from maximum dorsi flexion to maximum plantar flexion has a bearing on the eventual power delivery. This is based on the principle that force applied over a greater distance will produce more power. We see this in the track sprinter's stride length and the swimmer's stroke length. The greater the range of ankle movement, the longer the force can be applied to the bed resulting in greater power potential.

The ability to fold the upper body close to the thighs while keeping the legs straight is essential for the developing World Class trampolinist, and as such hip mobility has always been a prime target in my conditioning work. There are two obvious reasons for giving this range of movement priority: it has a key biomechanical function in speeding up rotation, and the execution judges will require amplitude in piked shapes. If we have coached our gymnast to hit the top of the Performance Chimney on a piked somersault, their height/rotation balance will demand a close pike in order to achieve a straight exit. I prefer to describe the piked shape as a "body-fold." Any performer who hits the chimney top will feel the necessity to fold deeply at the hip to accelerate rotation. Ideally, we want the gymnast to be able to achieve a total fold while sitting on the floor but don't despair if the floor-based pike is less than complete. Providing the take-off is near vertical, and it is possible to achieve a significantly greater range of movement in the air than when seated on the floor. That is not to say the lack of complete hip mobility should be accepted, but while it is being worked on, a very acceptable aerial piked shape can be fashioned **as a result of a well-directed take-off**. Consider this: a performer with limited hip mobility can produce a reasonable piked somersault if they have the technical ability to hit the top. On the other hand, a gymnast with **total hip flexibility** may fail to reproduce it in the aerial pike if their take-off direction is technically incorrect. This is yet another example of technical excellence being more important than conditioning, but for the aspiring World Class trampolinist, both qualities must be maximized. Remember Nigel Rendell's neat little saying, "If you take-off steep, your pike will be deep!"

Over & Above

STRENGTH

I recall a performance review with one of Great Britain's senior women and her personal coach. She was a trampolinist of outstanding potential who had been under-achieving despite several years on the national team, and I was trying to discover why this was not being realized. The conversation turned to conditioning.

Jack: I believe you haven't been attending the conditioning sessions which were arranged for you at the Institute of Sport. Why not?

Gymnast: Every time I get stronger, I just over-rotate all my moves, and I lose confidence and then I can't even take-off!

Personal Coach: That's right Jack, she was getting too strong for trampolining, and it was making her lose her moves.

Jack: OK, I appreciate what you are saying, but you both need to understand, this is not the fault of the strength training. You have developed faults during take-off due to years of attempting skills with too high difficulty before you were technically competent. In your anxiety to maximize rotational force, you have been reducing your airtime, making it very difficult to retain a calm understanding of each move. I accept that getting stronger has exaggerated the problem, but we need to address the technical issues first.

Personal Coach: Do you mean she's "snatching" her take-offs?

Jack: Yes, that's a simplistic way of putting it.

Personal Coach: So what can we do about it?

Jack: First, I agree we must stop the leg power training for the moment until the technical issues are under control. The rest of the conditioning program must continue, and you need to liaise with the S & C coach to make sure he understands why we are doing this. In the meantime, I will help you design a remedial program to build an understanding of 'tempo' and 'top,' starting with the simplest of skills until she learns to appreciate how to reduce rotational input during bed contact. The Degree of Difficulty (DD) should only be increased when she feels the she can control (and *enjoy) the additional flight time. She'll certainly enjoy the increase in her execution marks!*

This process took two years of belief and commitment from coach and gymnast to gradually transform technique, execution and time of flight to the point where impressive international results started to be delivered on a consistent basis. I received a text from the coach following one successful international performance. It read:

"Thanks for your insight Jack!"

Strength is not a simple quality and comes in several forms, so it is important to focus on the specific types of strength that will enhance the trampoline gymnast's performance. The focus must be on three areas: 1) explosive strength; 2) static strength; and 3) strength endurance.

1. **Explosive strength** is required for two main purposes. First, leg strength will enable the gymnast to drive the bed down powerfully in order to create sufficient stored energy for height delivery. Second, to develop the fast contraction of the muscle groups in the abdomen, hips and back that are responsible for the closing and opening of piked and tucked shapes during the airborne phase.

2. **Static strength** enables the gymnast to maintain a strong posture during the process of delivering and receiving high levels of force during bed contact. There is little point in developing leg power without efficient transmission capability. Furthermore, the gymnast must have the ability to hold strong bodylines during the airborne phase, notably in straight somersault shapes and straight exits. I make no apology for once again stressing that most form breaks are not the result of the gymnast's lack of static strength but rather stem from their failure to harness the power of the bed to produce the right balance of vertical and rotational force. That is a technical failing not, as many coaches claim, a lack of core conditioning.

3. **Strength endurance** has a large part to play in the performer's ability to maintain ten consecutive take-offs of high quality and to deliver the same number of strong stylish shapes and exits throughout a high difficulty voluntary. The gymnast's entire musculature will be involved in this process; much of the strength endurance will be developed as a by-product of explosive and static strength training, linked to

high repetitions of complete routines on the trampoline. This quality of strength endurance relates closely to "engine fitness," underpinning the gymnast's ability to perform with quality while under severe physiological stress.

ENDURANCE

In 2002, physiologist Simon Breivik undertook some research with the Great Britain National Trampoline Squad to determine the dominant energy systems driving a trampoline routine. The research brought up a number of interesting points that questioned the way trampoline coaches had been approaching "engine fitness." This quality had generally been trained through high repetitions of routines and was almost regarded as a by-product to be acquired through the technical work of executing ten skills with competition form. By taking blood lactate recordings and heart rate measurements, Simon discovered that when performing a trampoline routine, seventy percent of the energy supply came from the long-term anaerobic system, twenty five percent from the aerobic system and a mere five percent was short term anaerobic.

It is important to differentiate between a gymnast training full competition routines and simply performing a few attempts at a single skill with some respite and coach feedback between efforts. Everything that follows relates to performing continuously on trampoline for between 30 and 45 seconds, which approximates to ten preliminary jumps followed by a ten-bounce routine. This relates to the promising junior right up to a senior international. (Note this is actual performance time and not time of flight.) Incidentally, Dong Dong (CHN) exceeded 50 seconds when performing his stunning final voluntary at the 2010 World Championships. This exceptional duration of effort was due to his need to take fifteen preliminary jumps before the arm-set. The height, difficulty, placement and sheer quality of shaping exhibited during the eventual performance of the routine epitomized **total physical conditioning**.

The interaction of the energy sources when performing physical activity is as follows:

SHORT-TERM ANAEROBIC	0 to 8 seconds
SHORT-TERM ANAEROBIC & LONG-TERM ANAEROBIC	8 to 45 seconds
LONG-TERM ANAEROBIC & AEROBIC	45 to 180 seconds
AEROBIC	180 seconds+

The body switches between the three energy systems depending on the intensity and duration of the activity being performed. The short-term anaerobic system will produce an immediate and powerful energy supply such as that required to perform a single skill from approximately six preliminary jumps. Once the effort increases in duration, such as performing a segment or indeed a whole routine, the long-term anaerobic system begins to take over. The disadvantage of this energy system, however, is the production of lactic acid, which accumulates in the blood and eventually causes fatigue. High levels of lactate are also associated with impaired concentration that must have a significant bearing on the gymnast's ability to continue delivering quality work toward the end of a routine. In fact, a study of judges' deductions will reveal that they increase in the second half of most voluntary routines. My experience suggests that the breakdown in skill and escalating deductions is most likely connected to the accumulation of lactic acid. While this hypothesis requires formal research, I would urge coaches to pay more attention to conditioning in this area rather than focus on form and technical execution during the latter half of routines. If the premise is accepted, then serious trampoline gymnasts must train in a way that will increase "engine fitness" so they can increase both height and execution marks.

The physical effort of the top class 400-meter runner can be reasonably compared to that of the high level trampoline gymnast where (for a male athlete) 45 seconds of sustained speed is required. Athletes preparing for this event undertake interval training with flat out efforts of varying durations. The work is interspersed with rest intervals that are progressively reduced to prevent complete recovery. This training can improve the tolerance of lactate and aid the athlete's ability to re-process it into energy. Bearing in mind Simon Breivik's findings, a similar training effect must be highly desirable for the competitive trampolinist, where the ability to produce energy at a

Over & Above

high rate while tolerating high levels of lactic acid can enhance the gymnast's ability to maintain both height and technique toward the end of a competition routine.

The athletes call it *speed* endurance, but I am suggesting that competing trampolinists need *skill* endurance. This is the ability to continue delivering highly skilled work in the face of mounting fatigue. The delivery of high quality work right to the end of a ten-contact routine can only be achieved either by reducing difficulty to a level that ceases to be competitive or through specific scientifically based conditioning.

In my many discussions with Simon Breivik, we have concluded that while the runner can perform speed drills of increasing duration and reducing rest, this presents different challenges to the trampolinist. The prime consideration must be safety and while it may be painful to run fast, over-distance repetitions with a three-minute rest interval, it is hardly life threatening! If, in order to condition the trampolinist in skill-endurance terms, we were to attempt "overload" repetitions of say, a voluntary routine plus half as much again at full difficulty (the equivalent of 600m for the 400m runner), the potential for serious skill breakdown and injury would make the risk too high.

We must therefore look at other ways of building the "engine fitness" required, without including the skill-endurance element, but doesn't that miss the point? Effective training of the long-term anaerobic system works through repetitions of 45 to 60 second bouts of near-maximal exercise punctuated by 3 to 5 minutes recovery. The work-to-rest ratio and the number of repetitions and sets is adapted to the individual and manipulated as they get fitter. That type of work can be done outside or in the conditioning gym using running, cycling or rowing and the gymnast can certainly condition their long-term anaerobic efficiency in a non-sport-specific way. But we simply don't know if this has a measurable transfer to trampoline-specific skill endurance. With this dilemma in mind, Simon experimented with a type of trampoline-based interval training that (with safety as a prime consideration) involved the gymnasts jumping sets of back somersaults and baranis lasting between 45 and 60 seconds with a 3 to 5-minute rest interval. This was fine in theory, but the skill of the gymnasts was such that it could hardly be categorized as a near-maximal exercise. In discussion, we agreed that if performed with sufficient frequency, some endurance benefit would be likely, but the process did not simulate, let alone overload, the stress of performing voluntary routines.

I have concluded that to train the long-term anaerobic system, the gymnast must consider a dual approach. Regrettably, the main work must be undertaken in a non-trampoline-specific way using running, cycling or rowing where the sets, repetitions, and rest intervals can be accurately controlled. It should be appreciated that this work is adding to the ten thousand hours. A sports scientist once put it to me this way, "your energy system doesn't know whether you are trampolining, running or cycling!" A good point perhaps, but we still need to find ways to translate the developing "engine fitness" into skilled performance particularly in the second half of high difficulty voluntaries. The second part of this dual approach needs to be based on the voluntary routine.

The simplest method is to apply the interval training protocol to repetitions of the full routine. This means controlling the rest interval by stopwatch, starting with a five-minute recovery period and gradually reducing it by 10 or 20-second increments to as little as three minutes. It must be obvious that this type of training depends on the gymnast having achieved a level of competence to guarantee, say, five repetitions of the exercise without failure. This raises the question of 'periodization,' where interval training would occupy the later part of the pre-season build-up, ideally with a six-week window during which they would allow the physiological adaptations to take effect.

In order to assist with technical excellence early in the preparation phase and to ease the gymnast toward adequate physical condition for effective interval training to start, repetitions of the planned voluntary can be performed with substitutions. The best example is where every backward skill is substituted by a straight back somersault or every forward take-off is replaced by a tucked half-out fliffis. This process can be flexible with the substitutions inserted at alternate take-offs or limited to one or two skills only, depending on the status of the gymnast in relation to their training cycle.

A common practice is for gymnasts to perform routines in segments, a totally appropriate method of focusing on specific skills and links. But this will not train the skill endurance I have referred to. Once the performer can competently deliver the full routine, coaches frequently go back to segments that have particularly troublesome links. This will have technical benefits, but the skill endurance isn't being worked on. In order to achieve a skill endurance effect, even before the final pre-competition phase begins, I would recommend that the second half of the voluntary should be started with a series of single somersaults rather than a controlled arm set. If we bear in mind that

Over & Above

when the gymnast enters the second half of a routine in competition, they will dealing with the build-up of lactate, as well as high heart and respiration rates. Work needs to be started on this while the gymnast gradually builds toward the final training phase.

There are several ways to do this, and I offer a few suggestions:

1. Perform five back and barani combinations to set up skill five of the voluntary and continue to the end.

2. As above, using half-outs and straight backs to set up the last five skills.

3. Perform thirty straight jumps before arm setting and delivering the last five skills.

4. From an arm set, perform the last five skills, finishing with a controlled straight jump then continue jumping before executing the last five again.

From those few basic ideas, the creative coach can develop variations of their own to overload any segment of the routine thereby getting closer to the development of skill endurance.

It must be appreciated that the process of interval training is extremely demanding and the gymnast needs to be highly motivated to undertake the work. Not only is the performer taken out of their physical comfort zone, but high motivation and a tough mental approach is required for the training to be effective. That is why exercise physiologists recommend that this type of training be limited to two sessions per week separated by two easier days. Furthermore, if the conditioning is to be performed away from the trampoline, it must be undertaken *after* technical training or on a different day.

A potential breakthrough in terms of training method for trampolining emerged as a by-product of Simon Breivik's 2002 research into lactate levels within the Great Britain squad. Although the gymnasts were undertaking a technical session involving the performance of complete and part routines, Simon noted that, as the session proceeded, the blood lactate levels in each trampolinist rose throughout the session. After less than an hour, the levels had become worryingly elevated to the point where performance, concentration and orientation were likely to be threatened. This was "lactate stacking," a familiar phenomenon to the physiologist, where the blood lactate increases with each successive bout of activity to levels far higher than the level after a single effort. Recovery from sessions where this occurs takes considerable time and sheds some light on what I call the good session/bad session syndrome.

Many coaches will have experienced training sessions where their gymnast worked extremely well and made significant progress but the next day's session turned out to be disappointing, with the performer failing to deliver even an adequate standard of work. Of course, this can be psychological where the coach and gymnast have been duped into unreasonable expectations following the euphoria of the previous day, but Simon's research indicated that their may be a physiological contribution. I will let Simon Breivik speak for himself:

> "During my research with the squad, I also discovered that there was a lactate stacking effect taking place during technical training. Unlike during a fitness training session where this is the desired outcome, during technical training this accumulation of lactate will simply add to fatigue and cause the demise of both performance and concentration levels."

But he offered an explanation and a solution that is the training breakthrough I hinted at earlier. He noted that the gymnasts habitually sat down after each performance to await the call for their next effort. He reported:

> "So instead of sitting down between efforts on the trampoline, gymnasts should perform light aerobic exercise to assist in the removal of blood lactate from the trampoline-specific muscles. The mode of exercise could be gentle cycling on a stationary bike, very light bouncing on an adjacent trampoline or walking around the gym."

I would refer you to Chapter 23, Getting the Biggest Bang for Your Buck! where I offered what amounted to a perpetual motion training session with an emphasis on work, active rest and mental engagement. In the 1970s, I evolved this process at Apex-Harlow to improve time management. Little did I know that my gymnasts were largely complying with a recommendation that would come from a sports scientist in 2002. The message is clear. Active rest between efforts and a methodical cool-down

Over & Above

or recovery session involving continuous gentle activity following repetitive competition routine training should become the norm. Sports science has not shone many insights onto trampolining, but here is a small glimmer that has the potential to deliver massive long-term rewards. The performance benefits of this simple piece of training discipline can be remarkable and conversely, failure to tap into this information can inhibit progress and lead to many of the frustrations that perplex coaches and trampolinists on a regular basis.

As a footnote to this chapter, Simon Brievik now operates fitness training and testing programs with football league referees. In a recent conversation, he stated that his focus is on making sure the referee has the "engine fitness" to be able to arrive at any place in the field at any time during 90 minutes so that he is able to see and think clearly for the purpose of sound decision making. That sounds exactly what I want the trampoline athlete to be capable of throughout their routine! It's just all speeded up and instead of two halves of 45 minutes, the task is 45 seconds long!

Principles of Fitness Training for Trampoline

Early experience of Artistic gymnastics can confer significant conditioning advantages.

CHAPTER 26

COACH LIKE A COACH, NOT LIKE A JUDGE

SECTION FOUR
MAXIMIZING POTENTIAL

Baron de Coubertin's idealistic *"citius, altius, fortius"* ... "faster, higher, stronger" is somewhat inappropriate for several of the sports that make up the modern Olympic pantheon. Gymnastic disciplines, although characterizing "higher" and "stronger" have no reason to measure "faster." Our victors are determined principally by five execution judges using a set of predetermined aesthetic standards. I believe the Olympic authorities are uncomfortable with "judged" sports, and this may account for the introduction of time of flight, which provides at least one measurable score, easily understood by the uninitiated spectator. Ironically, this timing process does not fit all that well with the concept of "faster." Our best athletes are the slowest! *"Tardius, altius, fortius*! (My apologies to any Latin scholars reading this text.)

As early as 1970, I started developing airtime with my young gymnasts as the prime objective, not as a measurable component to add to the score, but as a means of providing time for the gymnast to demonstrate high difficulty with elegant form. Time of flight has yet to be introduced to all junior competitions, but coaches should nonetheless be working on this component for the underlying benefits it brings.

By far the greatest proportion of marks making up the voluntary routine score come from execution. Loosely speaking, time of flight

Over & Above

and difficulty each contribute around ten less points. In a set routine, the relative value of the execution becomes even more significant due to the zero difficulty for juniors and the "no repeat" rule for seniors. The emphasis on execution marks naturally brings the coach's focus to bear on the Code of Points, with its required aerial shapes and exit lines. However, I see many coaches being so distracted by this aesthetic component that they evaluate their gymnasts' work in training with a judge's eye instead of a coach's insight. We must resist this distraction and concentrate our observation, analysis, and feedback on the technical and psychological aspects of performance, which in the end lead to those desired zero execution deductions. Does the chicken come before the egg?

It is clear that the effective coach must always bear in mind the ultimate evaluation of their gymnast will be undertaken against a set of visual criteria, just as the football coach knows his team must put the ball in the opposing net. Too often, however, the means by which the gymnast becomes airborne to create those aesthetic qualities is ignored in favor of "polishing" aerial shapes. I have called this type of coaching "cosmetic" for it is lipstick and eye shadow rather than the natural technical beauty of the sport. Although the true origin of the following expression is vague, it first made an impact on me when the late Bert Scales said, "Jack, you can't polish shit!"

Following the 2000 Olympics, a more demanding set of aerial criteria was introduced in order to merit a zero deduction. Deep and precise shapes had always been expected but now somersault exits were required to show a straight body line between 12 o'clock and 1 o'clock, held until 3 o'clock before preparing for landing. If we take the example of a tucked back somersault, there are two ways to match the exit criteria. The gymnast must have a lot of airtime in which to show a deep tuck on the way up to the top enabling the exit to take place within the required segment before being held until 3 o'clock. Alternatively, height and direction can be compromised in order to somersault faster, thereby allowing the required straight exit. Too often in junior events, I see the latter method being employed because coaches have the misguided belief that straight exits are the priority. This is a seriously short-term strategy because the young performer is learning poor take-off direction, which will have to be changed radically if they hope to succeed as seniors. Furthermore, their routines suffer from loss of height through this "spin-and-kick-out" approach. (See Chapter 16: The Performance Chimney — "Beware the self-destructive chain.")

It must be realized that the FIG Code of Points is designed for international competition and has no modifications for juniors or developing performers who cannot yet be expected to meet the full criteria without developing bad technical habits. It is unreasonable to use international criteria for assessing the best juniors, let alone young "development grade" trampolinists at the local level. Most sports with a constructive approach to development have created modifications in equipment, pitch size and competition rules to encourage future high achievers to acquire correct technique and fitness as they grow. Although there is much talk of long-term athlete development in our sport, this is not reflected in the rules and criteria for competition.

An attempt to create a development-orientated form of scoring in the UK for graded competitions was proposed in 2007, where each judge would assess one specific element of the routine. Height was to be measured by two judges with stopwatches and the average time recorded. Another judge was to assess travel, while two judges would be responsible for specific form requirements. Each quality was to have an equal weighting with the aim of developing all the technical requirements for long-term success. Not only would this have focused coaches' minds on the technical areas that lead to high performance, it would also have greatly assisted the judges' development by training their observation skills. At the moment, judges are expected to assess a routine using the full FIG criteria, immediately on completing their initial training, which simply adds to the problem. Sadly, the proposal failed to receive enough support and a progressive development opportunity was missed.

The crucial difference between a coach and a judge is that the judge assesses outcomes while the coach is the architect of the inputs that in turn produce those outcomes. Many excellent coaches are also international judges, but they know how to separate the two roles and use each area of expertise for the benefit of their gymnasts. Judges at the lower end of the sport who also coach trampolinists will undoubtedly find the separation of roles more challenging, and I hope the insights provided in this book will increase technical knowledge to the point where they learn to coach like a coach and judge like a judge.

Over & Above

Let us consider what the execution judges deduct marks for. Bearing in mind that time of flight is now a measurable component, the judge is still concerned with: 1) loss of height; 2) travel; and 3) form breaks. I have listed these in order of priority from a coaching perspective. First, the gymnast must establish height and remain at that level throughout all ten skills in the routine. Second, there should be a minimum of travel/cast/gain on every element within the routine.

It is important to recognize the crucial link between these two requirements. If the gymnast travels significantly from the central area he/she is bound to suffer a consequential loss of height. Simplistically, some of the force that should have sent the gymnast toward the top of the chimney has been redeployed into lateral displacement. The third area for potential loss of execution marks, form breaks, is also closely linked to the first two requirements. If height is lost on any skill then the time to perform it is reduced. Not only is this likely to induce a form break on the move itself, it immediately applies pressure on the next skill, increasing the possibility of a further form break. The National Technical Priorities that I presented to senior British coaches in 2005 stated:

> *"Trampolining is a game of consequences where each skill performed leaves the gymnast with either a reward or a penalty. We must ensure that the linear direction of each move results in a vertical descent, providing the 'reward' of a perfect first contact as the starting point for the production of the next skill."*

It should be clear, therefore, that the most likely cause of aerial form breaks will be poor technique during the bed contact phase rather than any lack of aesthetic appreciation or the much-quoted core stability. Travel and you **lose height**, lose height and you **lose time**, lose time and you are made to rush, hence **the break of form**. That sounds like a "lose-lose-lose" situation to me! And don't forget the time of flight score. That makes it "lose" times four!

If the FIG Code of Points is correctly interpreted, it is totally in line with the technical focus we, as coaches, should be working with. If from day one we enable our gymnasts to achieve top, this will give the young performer the airtime to create well-defined shapes, as well as clean straight finishes, **but** do not expect exits to be shown at 12 o'clock until physical maturity makes it possible to perform with sufficient airtime. Coaches must think of somersault shaping and exit in biomechanical terms rather than the aesthetic. The close shaping within any move is designed to accelerate the somersault and the straight exit is for decelerating. Yes, it's that simple, but the key to applying the "accelerator" and the "brake" (a favorite analogy of Bert Scales) is the amount and direction of the initial input. That should bring our focus right back to the "business end" ... first contact to full depression (landing phase) and full depression to last contact (take-off phase).

When we watch accomplished athletes in any sport, whether it is track and field, swimming or any of the ball sports, they perform with a style and elegance that belies the complexity of the skills they are employing. This quality of movement is not motivated by the desire to score high execution marks but is a by-product of the balance, timing, power and precise decision-making required by their specific event. It is time that coaches of trampoline gymnastics became more aware that aesthetic excellence is simply the logical outcome of that same balance, timing, power and decision-making. Any coach who can fully appreciate the implications of that paradox will be well on the way to developing World Class performance.

CHAPTER 27

READINESS

SECTION FOUR

MAXIMIZING POTENTIAL

Readness

Much of my writing has emphasized the need to develop basic technique, working within a framework of principles to create a physical and perceptual foundation enabling progress toward World Class performance. There is nothing new about stressing the importance of fundamental skills for development toward high achievement in any area of life. Many coaches I meet and work with, acknowledge this and profess to believe in it, but few are prepared to confront it with the regularity and commitment it requires. I have already expressed the view that complex skill usually breaks down when a basic element within it malfunctions. That is why high-level performers **in any** field regularly revisit, practice, and improve basic skill.

I see the process of learning a skill like a mechanical drill boring into solid rock. The tip of the drill has to be strong and abrasive enough to make the initial penetration, just as the beginner must confront those uncomfortable, challenging, and even scary early attempts. Like the tip of the drill, which gradually becomes overheated, the beginner can only tolerate a relatively small amount of this pressure before resting or changing to another focus. The next time the drill bores into the rock, its initial passage is easier because of the work done on the previous session, but soon the tip meets the resistance of the virgin rock once more. The effort of

Over & Above

penetrating the rock continues until the tip becomes blunt or overheated and a cooling down period again becomes necessary. Each time the drill is inserted, it progresses further and more easily into the hole before confronting the resistance once again. The pupil and the coach must be aware of, and understand, how this process relates to skill learning. This is where the quality of determination from the Talent Package (Chapter 25) is required to harden the tip of the drill.

Daniel Coyle, writing in *The Talent Code* describes this uncomfortable, challenging process of confronting a new skill, technique, combination or routine as "deep practice." The coach and gymnast must work with vision, determination, and frequency to eventually break through while appreciating that the mistakes being made are essential to the gymnast "getting it." The coach must also recognize when the sharp point of the pupil's learning capacity has become overheated and allow it to cool down.

How does the coach and/or the gymnast recognize when a technique or skill element has been sufficiently mastered to permit progress to the next stage? I am often asked this by student coaches at all levels and would love to be able to supply a formula to fit every occasion. Coaches are often disappointed when I don't have a simple answer. What I *can* do is use my experience to outline what I call the signs of readiness. These will vary depending on what skill or progressive stage is being learned.

Happily, there are many generic signs that we can use to guide us in making the decision to advance the learning process. These signs are a blend of physical condition, technical competence, and psychological control. I would caution against placing too much reliance on how the execution of a skill or progressive stage looks, or even how confident the gymnast appears. These may simply be superficial indicators that mask reality. In order to give full consideration to the technical and psychological factors at work, I offer the following guidance for assessing any progressive stage on the journey to a new skill or combination.

Has the gymnast shown the following characteristics **consistently** over multiple repetitions?

1. Good vertical direction from take-off.
2. Height maintained relative to the arm-set.
3. For single somersaults – no travel.
4. For double or triple somersaults, minimal travel, definitely less than 30cm.
5. Absolutely **no gaining** action (contrary to the direction of rotation) whether single, double or triple somersault.
6. Clear and decisive shaping.
7. Clear and decisive exit phase.
8. Sufficient airtime to accommodate all aspects of the next progressive stage. In other words, total compliance with items 1 to 7.

Bearing in mind my warning about making judgments based simply on appearance, the above indicators are all visual in nature, but they are only the starting points for making the decision whether to move on. Next we must overlay these considerations by an ongoing dialogue with the gymnast.

1. Is the feedback you are giving in accordance with the gymnast's own feelings and understanding of the process? For example, are you *seeing* what the gymnast is *feeling*?
2. Is the gymnast "seeing" at key points in the process?
3. Is the gymnast happy "landing" the progression unaided?
4. Has the gymnast truly had the "ah-ha" moment?
5. Does the gymnast express a desire to move to the next stage?

Finally, as you watch each attempt do you:

1. Feel a *growing* confidence and *belief* that the gymnast is in control of the progression?
2. Recognize that the performance is "crying out" for the next stage to be added?

Over & Above

If you have doubts about *any* factor in the above lists then progress should be resisted. This may involve a dispute with a gymnast who has already declared confidence and a desire to progress. The gymnast's confidence is important, but that must be set against all the other factors listed. The coach must maintain an objective overview. The above method will help the coach assess a gymnast's state of readiness to move to the next progression or prep for a new skill, but judging when to apply some "jam" to the "bread" is not as straightforward.

There has to be a constant awareness of the developing pupil's need to have fun, to experience the joy of exploring the movement possibilities of this unique apparatus. We must guard against the "trampolining-is-too- easy" attitude where thrilling skills performed with poor technique begin to dominate each training session. On the other hand, it would be totally counter-productive to keep gifted young gymnasts working on basics throughout every training session. My advice when coaching younger gymnasts is to allocate 50% of each session to basic skills and techniques, and devote the second 50% **to applying those principles** in the acquisition of new skills or combinations. As young gymnasts develop, the balance can gradually change to 40/60 percent but even with international performers, I wouldn't drop below 20% for technical drills and 80% on skill development or the training of routines.

This balance will, of course, be affected by periodization when, at certain times of the year, whole sessions could be devoted exclusively to technical drills, routines, or new skill acquisition. It makes sense to weave technical drills into the regular trampoline-based warm-up, even if the session plan is to focus on a different theme. If my emphasis on basic techniques seems somewhat prescriptive, it must be remembered that the coach cannot **impose** a set of drills on the gymnast without their **total engagement** in the process. This is another reason for developing the young performer's **appreciation of why** sound technique is crucial to achieving the shared goals.

Another area where readiness must be assessed is the insertion of newly acquired skills into a routine for the purpose of raising the difficulty score. I always worked by the principle that, until the existing voluntary routine could score 24.00 for execution, I would resist an increase in difficulty. Since the routine total is the most important factor, it would be folly to increase difficulty if the resultant execution mark produced a lower total score. This policy can sometimes have a negative effect on a gymnast's morale because no matter how much one tries to change attitudes, performers want to be able tell opponents they are using an increased DD on competition day. Although bragging rights can be important before the competition, there is no better feeling than ending up with a higher total score than the opposition.

I always introduced routines of increased difficulty by using subsidiary competitions rather than pitching the gymnast into one of their "target" events with an untested routine. This process would start with simulated competition pressure during training and perhaps an entry in a local "open" event where the new skill or skills would form part of the voluntary. I might even reduce the routine tariff by the use of substitutions for the express purpose of exposing just one new skill to the competition environment. Whatever method is employed, it must be part of a gradual process of acclimatizing the gymnast to cope with new work under escalating pressure.

CHAPTER 28

PREPARING TO COMPETE

SECTION FOUR
MAXIMIZING POTENTIAL

Preparing to Compete

There is a great deal of literature about the psychology of achieving peak performance at the right time, and I have no wish to repeat what has already been written. Neither do I intend to stray outside my area of expertise, but I believe the reader can benefit from what I have learned through my experience and the opportunity to work with a number of sports psychologists.

Different gymnasts will display widely differing behaviors in the run-up to a competition, and the coach must tune in to the mind-set of each performer. There are many aspects of competition preparation that are beyond the control of gymnast or coach, consequently all preparation should be targeted at the factors that **can** be controlled.

My approach to the "uncontrollable" is first to work on building the gymnast's appreciation that trampolining is a sport in which the opposition can have no direct effect on one's performance. This should be seen as a reassuring characteristic of the sport. There is no need to fear the opposition! In tennis, it might be embarrassing to lose to an opponent without winning a game and a boxing opponent may be physically intimidating, but a trampolinist making their international debut can still deliver their best work against the World Champion, safe in the knowledge that not even the world's best can do anything to prevent it. In other

Over & Above

words, there is no **extrinsic** threat and the only way opponents may be allowed to exert an influence is within the gymnast's own mind. Once the competitor understands this, work can begin to control the controllable and develop the confidence to rely on one's own performance capability. This is not something to be left until the week before an event and must be a continuous process of building the performer's belief in their ability to deliver good work, despite the impressive presence of "star" performers.

There is bound to be pre-competition anxiety, bringing with it the familiar unpleasant physical symptoms of nervousness. The inevitable feeling of butterflies in the stomach must be recognized by the gymnast for what it is—indications that the body is preparing to compete. The gymnast has to understand that they are not expected to **enjoy** or even **ignore** these feelings, but rather to **recognize** their role in the process of delivering high quality work when it matters. It is ironic that this natural process for creating the physical state to maximize performance should generate uncomfortable feelings that can induce negative thoughts and undermine confidence to the point of failure. As someone who is not a psychologist, I venture to suggest that when the unpleasant "fight or flight" symptoms arise, the competitor must learn to choose fight rather than flight. Again this must be addressed as an issue during regular training rather than trying to apply an emotional "Band-aid" at the event.

There is no substitute for long-term technical and physical preparation as a means of building the gymnast's confidence in their ability to deliver. I have found that, ironically, the most important mental training is thorough physical preparation because any doubts about the ability to deliver competent routines in training will become exaggerated when the pressure of competition kicks in. Technical and physical preparation is the key "controllable" element and as such must underpin everything else. My former colleague Mitch Fenner, now doing a great job with Dutch gymnastics, has said:

"Too many gymnasts are afraid of their routines!"

Once the gymnast can guarantee their routine in training, they can be helped to build strategies to deal with unexpected and uncontrollable conditions that may arise in the lead-up to the event or at the competition itself.

Simulated competition pressure can be introduced to training sessions but should not be left until the week before an event. Failure to deliver under this simulated pressure without time to adjust can be even more damaging than avoiding that type of training altogether. The simulations should start at least six weeks before an event, giving both coach and gymnast time to develop strategies for dealing with issues that may arise from those simulations.

The fundamental aim of training is to create positive adaptations within the gymnast. The gymnast's movement patterns, strength levels and physiological capabilities all require a sustained level of work in order to create the necessary adaptations. I believe mental training must also be given sufficient time to modify the gymnast's thinking, and it is likely to take even longer than physical or technical conditioning to become effective. I have seen too many situations when a sports psychologist has been brought in to give emergency help to a gymnast with deep-seated competition "issues." On occasion, a final reassuring word from a specialist may indeed be all that is required, but it is unreasonable to expect long-term benefit from this approach.

SIMULATIONS

It is impossible to train for all eventualities, but to get the full benefit from competitive simulations, the "event" should be announced well in advance, with all the details normally available, e.g., time table, warm-up arrangements, jump order, etc. This will create sufficient status for the simulation to induce feelings in the gymnast similar to those that will be experienced before an actual event. If the simulation is to be held at the normal training venue, when possible, the trampolines should be turned into an unfamiliar orientation so as to disturb the comfort zone of regular training. The coach should find ways to increase the perceived pressure in the mind of each gymnast using a variety of devices. I recall running one simulation with my Apex-Harlow squad where I decided to formally introduce each gymnast using a microphone and also played the role as chair of judges, instructing each gymnast to "begin please." In the debrief after the simulation, Alan Green, one of my senior internationals said:

"I hate it when you do all that announcing stuff. It makes me REALLY nervous!"

I think he got the point!

Over & Above

It is important that simulations don't become predictable in themselves, otherwise the impact is lost and the learning experience is largely negated. If the timings and jump order have been announced in advance, this opens up the possibility of changing arrangements at the last moment, thereby introducing a surprise element to enrich the learning opportunity. Numerous distractions can be introduced, including asking the competitor to "begin please" then calling "stop" as they begin their preliminary jumps. The gymnast is then kept waiting before being asked to restart. With a little imagination, coaches can turn simulations into a realistic mental training exercise. The effectiveness of distractions or interruptions will of course be lost if every gymnast is subjected to the same process, so it is important that the coach targets the vulnerabilities of particular performers for the purpose of improving their robustness on competition day.

While a simulation with various unexpected variations can be a valuable exercise, the real benefit comes when conducting a debriefing to ascertain how each gymnast felt during the exercise. Did they feel nervous as they might in a real event? How did they react to the distractions? How did they overcome the unpleasant feelings of nervousness? If they performed badly, what reason do they give? Clearly there could be many questions for stimulating discussion, helping to identify individual issues that may need to be addressed.

One of the biggest threats to a gymnast delivering their best work is unreasonable expectation. Each gymnast must learn what I call a "range of acceptability" with regard to routine performance, both in training and in competition. No athlete in any sport will deliver their personal best performance on every occasion, but the expectation or hope of doing so, when unfulfilled, can act as a negative drain on the gymnast's confidence and self-belief. There was a 1967 pop song by The Tremeloes called "Even the Bad Times Are Good," and that is what I would want from my performers — to be so well prepared that on a "bad day" they are still good enough to register a high score. We are familiar with outstanding soccer and rugby teams that know how to "win ugly" when they are not on top form, but this is a difficult mental challenge for the gymnast who is a perfectionist. Of course the coach must work **toward** perfection but also help the gymnast to understand their range of acceptability. When I worked with the Dutch senior team, several gymnasts had a tendency to approach a routine in training with the hopeful attitude that "this is going to be an outstanding routine."

When they encountered the first minor error and the routine ceased to match those expectations, one could immediately detect negative body language, often leading to an aborted routine. These unreasonable expectations can seriously damage a training session and worse still can lead to long-term damage in a number of areas.

Consider the following:

1. Routines that are not completed in training constitute a lost technical learning opportunity.

2. Routines that are not completed in training lose the potential fitness benefit.

3. Failed routines can lead to frustration in both the gymnast and coach with the potential for creating disharmony and damage to the relationship.

4. Failure to deliver up to the level of an unreasonable expectation begins to undermine self-confidence.

5. Not only is training time wasted in relation to the aborted routine, but there are many consequences that detract from efficient use of training time in the future.

It was clear to me that the group behavior experienced by these Dutch squad members was contributing little to the overall aim of achieving excellence.

Following one damaging session, I devised a training episode in consultation with National Coach Lennard Villafuerte and the team psychologist, to try and combat the issue of unreasonable expectation. Each gymnast's name was placed on a flip chart with space to record the outcome of each of five voluntary routines. The gymnasts were required to self-assess each routine and place their score on the flip chart. The following categories are of course very approximate and designed simply to create a meaningful training experience.

Over & Above

Routine voluntarily aborted. (No fitness benefit. Confidence damaged.)	Score 0 points
Routine completed with substitutions. Untidy execution. (Some fitness benefit obtained. Confidence in ability to "survive.")	Score 1 point
Routine completed with full DD. Untidy execution. (Fitness benefit obtained. Optimism that quality can be improved.)	Score 2 points
Routine completed with substitutions. Clean execution. (Fitness benefit obtained. Confidence that quality can be delivered.)	Score 3 points
Routine completed with full DD. Adequate execution. (Fitness benefit obtained. Confidence that total routine score will be competitive.)	Score 4 points
Routine completed with full DD. Clean execution. (Fitness benefit obtained. Confidence that a margin for error now exists.)	Score 5 points

Obviously it is impossible to cover every possible category of routine but the aim was to make the gymnasts appreciate that even the poor performance of a complete routine can have a fitness benefit and a potential confidence boost in performing all ten skills. The exercise certainly had a short-term benefit in changing the gymnasts' attitudes about the performance of routines in training. Those who had been starting the routine with a goal of perfection were now approaching it in the knowledge that a range of benefits was available aside from simply completing. Those gymnasts with a tendency to stop at the first mistake started reacting positively when an error became apparent. The "strike rate" for routine completion increased significantly, which was the prime objective. This exercise succeeded for a number of reasons:

- It focused the gymnasts' minds on a simple, clear objective.
- It relied on self-assessment, which raised their sense of personal responsibility.
- It refreshed the somewhat monotonous process of simply repeating routines.
- It highlighted the damaging negative effect of routine abortion.
- It highlighted the positive benefits of completion.
- Each gymnast posted their score for all to see.

An exercise such as this can only be used periodically as a stimulus and will become ineffective if used too frequently. I have quoted this example, with all its imperfections, to encourage coaches to invent exercises to address particular issues and to use creativity to break into the humdrum process of routine repetitions without a clear goal other than a vague hope that "this is going to be a great routine!"

When I was responsible for teams at World Cup events, World Championships and European Championships as well as stand-alone internationals, the team would be made up of gymnasts from a variety of clubs. It was important to establish rapport with each performer and ascertain what their individual goals were for the event. Thus, it was important to set up discussions with each gymnast at the individual post-event debrief where valuable lessons were often learned. Meaningful post-event dialogue with the personal coach on returning home was also made easier.

In order facilitate this process, I designed the following form, which made it clear, among other things, how the gymnast intended to use pre-competition training (a great assistance to the team coaches in the absence of the personal coach). Normally the form would be completed by each gymnast on the aircraft as we travelled to the event and the content discussed with the team coaches before the first training sessions. I recommend coaches consider a similar process with club gymnasts before and after competition in order to get the greatest long-term benefit from taking part in the event.

Over & Above

OUTLINE OF PERSONAL GOALS

Gymnast Name:

Name of Event:

Date:

This form has been designed to help you assess the effectiveness of your preparation and also to act as a basis for the post-competition debrief with your team coaches. You will, no doubt, have a more in-depth debrief with your personal coach on returning home, but the information you give on the form will also be shared with your coach.

Please use the following headings to clarify the way you think about your goals. **Whatever you state on the form will be confidential between yourself, the team coaches and your personal coach unless you choose to share the goals with your teammates.**

1. PROCESS GOALS: Think about the period between leaving GB and stepping on the trampoline to compete. For example: How will you prepare for the first training session? What will you do on each training day? What will you do in each pre-competition warm-up? How many sets? How many vols? What routine parts? Any other things you will do that have a bearing on the event.

2. PERFORMANCE GOALS: Think about the training days, pre-competition warm-up and the actual competition. How do you aim to perform technically? For example: Number of pre-routine jumps, placement of the first skill, any particular execution or technical focus you and your coach have been working on.

3. OUTCOME GOALS: The first two types of goal are controllable by you and as such are the most important, but the "outcome" can be greatly influenced by the opposition and the judges. However, it is likely that if you can control the "process" and the "performance," you will stand a greater chance of influencing the "outcome." Think in terms of place, score in each round, qualification for the final, placing within the British Team, ranking in each routine, etc.

Process Goals:

Performance Goals:

Outcome Goals:

Outline of Pre-Competition Personal Goals Form

CHAPTER 29

USING SWOT ANALYSIS AS A PLANNING TOOL

SECTION FOUR
MAXIMIZING POTENTIAL

Goal setting and then planning a program that aims to reach those goals is an essential part of any coach's job, but it can be challenging to find a starting point. Using a SWOT analysis generally gives me a sense of perspective when approaching a new challenge. The method is credited to Albert Humphrey who introduced it during business conventions at Stamford Research Institute in the 1960s and 1970s. Professor Humphrey has my gratitude, although my applications may be a little less weighty than his original intentions. The essence is in the words making up the acronym.

Strengths: The characteristics that tend to give an advantage.

Weaknesses (or limitations): The characteristics indicating a disadvantage.

Opportunities: External chances to improve performance.

Threats: External elements that could cause trouble.

I have found the process useful in the following scenarios:

1. To assess a current situation.
2. To create an agenda for discussion.
3. To help with goal setting.
4. To create an action plan.

Over & Above

For the sake of illustration, here are two examples from our sport. First is the SWOT I used to remodel a national Trampoline Gymnastics Programme in more than one country and then a SWOT applied to an actual gymnast on that elite program. Although I have made a few minor changes to safeguard confidentiality, the process took place exactly as outlined.

EXAMPLE 1: A NATIONAL HIGH PERFORMANCE TRAMPOLINE PROGRAM

Strengths

- Tradition of high national achievement at international level since 1967
- Existing successful role models
- Senior coaches with experience of developing gymnasts to international success
- Numerous well-qualified, energetic, ambitious young coaches

Weaknesses

- Lack of a clearly stated vision
- No National Technical Policy
- No technical performance monitoring
- Serious technical shortcoming arising from the "tariff culture"
- Time management issues
- Lack of a dedicated national training facility

Opportunities

- New Olympic cycle
- Well-funded support for the program
- Coach development opportunities between experienced and younger coaches
- Outstanding club facilities throughout the country

Threats

- Constant improvement of other nations
- The disproportionate focus on the Olympics, which involves so few potential qualifiers
- Disharmony between coaches and the governing body
- Disharmony between experienced and younger coaches
- Coach education at odds with World Class direction

I should point out that each of these lists was considerably longer, and I have only itemized the prime factors as a means of illustrating the process. The following action plan has also been abbreviated for the same illustrative purpose.

Action Plan

- Use the most recent World Championships performances by national gymnasts as a benchmark
- Compare nation's performances with those of leading nations
- Identify the size of the gap
- Design a National Technical Policy
- Obtain agreement from lead coaches to buy into the policy
- Enable those coaches to communicate the policy to their gymnasts and younger coaches
- Delegate coaching responsibility for leading gymnasts from the National Coach to personal coaches
- National Coach to work with gymnasts and personal coaches as individual units

That illustrates the application of the SWOT to a national program. The second example relates to a specific gymnast who was experiencing various life challenges, including uncertainty about who would be the best personal coach to take them forward. I created the SWOT to provide an agenda for a meeting with the gymnast and the coaches involved. The main objective was to create an effective action plan.

Over & Above

EXAMPLE 2: GYMNAST "A"

Strengths

- Natural spatial awareness
- Athleticism
- Gymnastics background
- Competitive robustness
- Support service availability

Weaknesses

- Poor basic technique resulting in low execution scores
- Too much DD before attaining technical competence
- Poor goal focus
- History of recurring minor injury
- Social uncertainty

Opportunities

- Support service resources (medical, rehab, strength & conditioning, dietary, lifestyle counseling)
- Possibility of World Cup experience
- Time to develop and repair technical weaknesses because of age (15 years)
- Selection process for World and European Championships
- Olympic selection process

Threats

- Possible loss of national elite program support
- Progress of rival trampoline gymnasts
- Complacency due to previous international success
- Recurring injury
- Coach uncertainty

With the agreement of the gymnast and coaches, I drew up the following action plan.

ACTION PLAN FOR GYMNAST "A"

- Personal decision about commitment by (date agreed and noted)
- Decision on personal coach situation (date agreed and noted)
- Rationalize social issues (employment, year out, college, university, etc.)
- Goal setting meeting with National Coach and personal coach (date agreed and noted)
- Technical drill program to start immediately

I commend this process as the first step in assessing a situation before making decisions that will be acted upon. The range of applications is extensive and can include a review of the coach's own situation, the state of a particular club, existing facilities, etc. Indeed, I believe many of us intuitively perform a SWOT-like form of thinking before making many of our life decisions, but it is remarkable how the mind becomes more concentrated when applying the formal discipline provided by this framework. I would even recommend teaching the gymnasts how to use SWOT analysis prior conducting goal setting and review meetings.

CHAPTER 30

INTRODUCING DAVE ROSS

SECTION FOUR
MAXIMIZING POTENTIAL

I have introduced this chapter because of my admiration for what this great Canadian coach has achieved but also to give readers a different "flavor" in terms of philosophy and approach from the one I have been promoting throughout this book. Although the "flavor" is different the "food" is the same. It's just cooked up by two different chefs using their own blend of ingredients.

When Rosannagh MacLennan became Olympic champion in 2012, Dave Ross confirmed his status as the world's most successful coach. Since trampolining made its Olympic debut in Sydney 2000, gymnasts from Skyriders gym in Toronto have never failed to occupy a podium step. It all started with Karen Cockburn and Matt Turgeon taking the bronze medals in 2000, before Karen went one better in Athens 2004. I was convinced that Jason Burnett's great final routine in Beijing 2008 had upset the Chinese applecart, but the judges scored him a mere three tenths behind Olympic Champion Lu Chunlong.

In London 2012, Rosie finally clinched the deal for Canada, Skyriders, and Dave Ross!

Over & Above

Dave Ross with two of his "warriors" — 2003 World Champion Karen Cockburn and 2012 Olympic Champion Rosie MacLennan.

The international successes of Dave's athletes are too numerous to mention and because of the Olympics' high public profile, it would be easy to forget that Karen Cockburn was World Champion in 2003 and World Synchro Champion with Rosie MacLennan in 2007. These achievements could be seen as the pinnacle of Dave's coaching career, but as I write, I ponder whether this is simply a very high plateau with the "pinnacle" yet to be scaled. Certainly, the passion and devotion to his athletes is undimmed, while his knowledge, experience, and wisdom increase with the years. That is a potent mixture! As Dave himself said of Matt Turgeon's competitive attitude, "It is difficult to compete against obsession." Dave, it takes one to know one!

Dave Ross and I had known about each other for many years but had never actually met until we both accepted invitations to speak at the British Gymnastics Conference in 2005. Both our presentations featured the development of trampoline gymnasts toward World Class, yet they **appeared** to differ widely. If you have read up to this point, you will not be surprised that my presentation focused on a technical and methodical approach. It soon became clear that we were two coaches coming from different directions but with the same destination in mind.

In his presentation, Dave barely alluded to the process of working for technical excellence. Was that because he didn't think it was important? Of course not! His emphasis was on the commitment of the coach and the essential "warrior" quality of the athlete, which no amount of technical excellence can replace. He developed the theme of commitment and athlete selection through the building of relationships where both parties worked to get the best out of each other. This was beautifully expressed in one of his favorite quotes:

"They won't care how much you know until they know how much you care."

In my presentation, I barely touched on such matters. Was that because I didn't think they were important? Of course not! Certainly, many of my gymnasts had exceeded expectations, largely due to technical competence, but those who **did** make a World Class impact also displayed Dave's "warrior" outlook. Neither could one doubt the technical competence of Dave's gymnasts, but the Skyriders gym also has its share of technically competent "non-warriors." Their names just don't happen to be Turgeon, Cockburn, Burnett, or MacLennan!

In conversation, it emerged that both he and I had been instantly captivated by the potential of the trampoline and pursed the sport with the same exploratory zeal. We were both self-taught, and as I commented at the time:

"We might have been better jumpers if we hadn't had such lousy coaches!"

Although Dave went on to compete in eleven Canadian Nationals and was constantly motivated by a love of "throwing myself in the air, challenging myself and learning," he always thought he could have accomplished more. That simply made him want to become the coach he never had.

We discussed our formative years in coaching, when we pursued every source of information that could help us improve the work of our athletes. We loved to study the skills of current top performers and amusingly, the generation gap revealed itself when Dave spoke of "watching tapes of international meets." I pointed out that tapes were not available when I was at that stage. I used 8mm film that had to be sent away for developing. That meant a two-week delay before I could start analyzing what I had filmed!

Over & Above

Jack Kelly with cine camera. It used to take two weeks to have 8mm film processed before performances could be analyzed by projecting the images onto a screen in a darkened room.

We both learned a great deal from our first star athletes. In my case, it was during the 1970s, Simon Rees, World Age, European Youth and British Senior Champion at 15 years of age. John Ross (no relation) and Alison Pester who both made the 1980 World Championship Finals enabled Dave to obtain a fascinating insight into his own personality.

"Both these athletes had 'attitude,' and over the years I have realized that I too, have attitude!"

Dave loves George Bernard Shaw's words:

"The reasonable man adapts himself to the world; the unreasonable man persists in trying to adapt the world to himself. Therefore all progress depends on the unreasonable man."

"I figure it gives me the right to be unreasonable!"

Nonetheless Dave Ross has a sensitivity to the needs of his gymnasts and a realization that no two athletes are the same. He balances this skillfully alongside a fierce competitive focus. He says:

"Whatever the style or personality, coaches should be more like gardeners than drill sergeants! As a young coach, I tried to get athletes to accomplish **my** goals. If you want great results, both you **and** your athletes have to want it."

He quotes the late Jack Donohue (Coach to the Canadian National Basketball Team):

"Don't try to get a pig to sing. It doesn't work, and it annoys the pig!"

Dave is generous in his desire to "get my ideas out there," and I am pleased to be able to act as a conduit for some of them. As coaches, it has become evident that we have more similarities than differences and the following list highlights some of the key points upon which we agree.

- Love the sport to the point of obsession.
- Energy, passion, commitment and reliability come before knowledge.
- Pursue sport-specific knowledge but keep an open mind to what could be adapted from the wider world.
- Study the current world's best but look beyond and try to identify trends.
- Learn from recognized experts but develop your own style.
- Be prepared to move if you're present venue isn't conducive to matching your goals.
- Create an excellence-focused environment.
- Ensure your goals and those of the gymnasts are the same.
- Don't rely on apparent physical talent.
- Learn to recognize gymnasts with the character to go the extra mile.
- Make the development of your gymnasts' confidence a priority.
- Train often and use your time efficiently.
- By your commitment, support and understanding, show the gymnasts that you care.
- When things go badly, stay calm but show concern.
- Learn from your gymnasts.
- See it through with all your gymnasts before getting over excited by the new generation.

CHAPTER 31
LOST AND FOUND!

SECTION FOUR
MAXIMIZING POTENTIAL

All coaches and athletes enjoy the sudden enlightenment that comes from a particular incident in their career — that wonderful "ah-ha" moment. There are other times however, when it can be more like an "oh-no" moment!

In 1969, as an inexperienced coach, I was working with the outstanding 11-year-old Simon Rees, later to become a double World Age, European Youth and British Senior Champion.

At that time in Great Britain, it was permissible for age group gymnasts to compete in senior events if they could perform the appropriate compulsory routine. This was generally the World Set used at European and World Championships. Simon was already performing the routine, with the exception of skill ten — a back somersault with double twist. He used a full twisting back in his voluntary, so I judged he was ready to take on the double full. To my delight, after six attempts, he was performing a double full with apparent ease ... job done! Well, not quite!

The next day, when he took off for the full in his voluntary, it came out as a double full! I now realize this was entirely predictable. That was my first trampoline "oh-no" experience!

Over & Above

Naively, I concluded that the gymnast had simply experienced a momentary loss of concentration. The remedy seemed obvious — perform the full back in isolation to remind him of the particular move pattern. However, each attempt at the full still came out as a double twist! I felt my initial relaxed response turn to panic, but although puzzled, I remained outwardly calm and had enough sense to consider how the gymnast must be feeling. With each attempt it was becoming clear that his confidence and self-belief (never previously in doubt) were becoming seriously undermined.

Simon Rees gave the author his first experience of having to manage a performer going through a period of skill confusion.

I have recounted this experience only as a means of introducing one of the most challenging and frustrating areas confronting many (but by no means all) trampoline gymnasts and their coaches. To complete this anecdote, let me quickly explain how we overcame the problem. Bear in mind that this was nearly forty-five years ago, and this coach and gymnast were encountering an unknown and unseen enemy for the first time.

Paul Luxon, who three years later would become the first ever non-American World Champion, was a regular visitor to our club, and I watched his coach, Brian Moore, experiment with straight arm twisting (later to become the Luxon trademark and now commonplace). I resolved to rebuild Simon's full twisting back using straight arms in order to differentiate it from the double full where we would use the more conventional arm wrap. That sounds like a neat solution and indeed it was, but it glosses over the many hours of practice, regression, anxiety, and frustration involved in the rehabilitation.

I can't recall when I first came to know this lurking menace as "Lost Move Syndrome" (LMS), but in discussion with my contemporaries, I soon discovered that many coaches had experienced similar episodes with their pupils. Regrettably, the phrase Lost

Move Syndrome creates a sense of finality that can fill both coach and gymnast with foreboding. It is used in academic papers, so I must accept that the description is a valid one, but it does little to encourage optimism and the possibility of a return to normality.

A syndrome is "a group of things or events that form a recognizable pattern, especially something undesirable." However the more well-known medical definition highlights "a group of signs or symptoms that together are characteristic of a specific disease or disorder." This medical connection can add significantly to the negative feelings already being experienced by an affected gymnast.

Dave Ross recognized that not only does the gymnast experience a blow to their self-confidence when the first signs of the problem arise, but using a phrase like LMS places a further obstacle in the way of recovery. In his dealings with a gymnast exhibiting the characteristic signs, Dave will use the phrase "Temporary Skill Confusion" (TSC) as they start the remedial journey. This is a smart piece of coaching from an intelligent and creative trampoline gymnastics thinker.

TSC acknowledges there is a problem but also indicates that it can be resolved — it is "temporary" and is the result of "confusion" that can be unraveled once the gymnast clarifies the way they perceive the skill in question.

Of course, no number of euphemistic words will act as "faith healing," but they do create a more positive starting point for resolution, and I wholeheartedly commend the approach.

There have been very few serious studies of TSC in trampolining although numerous related papers do exist, and the reader would do well to delve into the literature on the psychology of skill learning. However, one notable trampoline-specific paper has come to my attention: "The Causes of and Psychological Responses to Lost Move Syndrome in National Level Trampolinists" by M. C. Day and Joanne Thatcher from the University of Wales. This gives some worthwhile insights into the reaction of national standard gymnasts, coaches, and parents when the syndrome begins to take hold.

I intend to look at examples of this phenomenon, try to explain what causes the confusion and offer various strategies for recovery. I will continue to refer to Lost Move

Over & Above

Syndrome in a general sense or when quoting the words of other authors, but when specifically referring to trampoline gymnastics, I will adopt Temporary Skill Confusion.

THE "YIPS" AND OTHER MANIFESTATIONS

Trampolining is by no means the only sport where expert performers suddenly discover, to their horror, that they can no longer perform what was once a well-established skill. High-ranking professional golfers have found themselves suffering the "yips," rendering them unable to make a smooth putting stroke, despite being able to drive the ball 300 meters! Test match bowlers in cricket, notably slow pace, spin bowlers, have found themselves frustrated by an unexplained failure to release the ball at the right moment in their action. Darts players can be affected by what they call "dartitis," involving a sudden inability to let the dart leave the hand. Former World Snooker Champion Stephen Hendry has told of his struggle to overcome a difficulty in following through the ball with his cueing action, despite being previously renowned for the accuracy and fluency of his technique.

Pittsburgh Pirates star pitcher Steve Blass suddenly found he could no longer rely on his ability to release a standard delivery, and when other pitchers had similar experiences this became known as the "Steve Blass Disease." Another baseball star, Steve Sax, experienced an unexplained loss of ability to make routine throws to first base and when other players had similar problems this became the "Steve Sax Syndrome."

Perhaps this desire to give a name to what appears to be a generic sporting problem simply underlines the mystery and lack of understanding that accompanies it. The lack of real understanding among otherwise able coaches makes it all the more difficult for a trampolinist to deal with. Furthermore, consider the difference between a golfer, afraid of missing a short putt worth many thousands of dollars and a trampoline gymnast afraid of a double somersault with twist. Both athletes have "done the business" hundreds of times before, but something paralyzes their normal actions. A two-foot putt is hardly life threatening, but launching oneself skyward without a firm understanding of what one's body will do is likely to present a more serious mental challenge.

But the golfer and the trampolinist have one thing in common — pressure to perform. When under control, this pressure is essential for delivering high-level performance, but when the athlete becomes over aroused, it has the potential to become debilitating and even disabling.

Matthew Syed, in his fascinating book *Bounce: How Champions Are Made* (the title does **not** relate to trampolining), describes his experience at the 2000 Olympics when he had a real chance of a medal in table tennis. He was in good form, his preparation had gone well, and there were many of his supporters in the crowd as he faced a beatable first round opponent. He writes:

"This was the match I had saved for a career, a contest that could be life-transforming.

And then it happened.

Franz (the opponent) stroked the ball into play — a light and gentle forehand topspin. It was not a difficult stroke to return, not a stroke I would have any trouble pouncing upon, and yet I was strangely late on it, my feet stuck in their original position, my racket jabbing at the ball in a way that was totally unfamiliar. My return missed the table by more than two feet."

As the match progressed he sensed something was wrong but things got worse:

"I found my body doing things that bore no relation to anything I had learned over the last twenty years of playing table tennis: my feet were sluggish, my movements alien, my touch barely existent. I was trying as hard as I could; I yearned for victory more intensely than in any match I had ever played; and yet it was as if I had regressed to the time when I was a beginner."

This disconcerting experience is what is known as "choking," and Syed goes on to describe other examples in sport, but is this the same thing as TSC in trampolining? I have never known a performer have an issue suddenly arise at a competition resulting in a Syed-like "choke." Nonetheless the symptoms are too similar not to be connected.

Over & Above

It can be helpful in trying to understanding both choking and TSC by revisiting the three stages of learning.

1. COGNITIVE: The novice broadly understands what the outcome of the skill should be. Concentration and attention are necessarily high, and there are many errors. The learner needs help to correct those errors.

During this stage, there are huge advantages to using a high level of conscious control as the novice explores the movement and tries to make sure every body part moves in the right order and at the right time.

2. ASSOCIATIVE: By now the basic technique is becoming established and the athlete begins to refine some of the parts. Less concentration is required, and the number of errors decreases. Although there is evidence of self-correction, some outside correction is still needed.

During stage two, it benefits the learner to let the parts of the movement they are comfortable with simply happen. Attention can then be directed at the parts still requiring practice.

3. AUTONOMOUS: This stage is reached only after much repetitive practice and the movement can be performed with little or no conscious control. The athlete can now focus more on form and accuracy rather than the separate moving parts of the skill.

When stage three is reached, it is a disadvantage to apply the level of conscious control used in Stage One. Instead, the focus can turn to the quality or placement of the skill and its role within the routine, rather than the individual parts. There are many sporting and everyday life examples of this skill autonomy. When the tennis player's strokes have become autonomous it becomes possible to make judgments about which stroke to use in the context of a rally. As we learn to drive, the skills of steering, braking and changing gear became autonomous thereby enabling us to focus on traffic conditions and the route directions.

It must be appreciated that these stages of learning represent a simplistic model because learning does not move smoothly from one stage to the next. There are many overlaps where skills and their individual parts regress as well as progress and this can have a bearing on TSC and the remedial process.

When symptoms of TSC begin, the gymnast, who has been performing a skill without conscious control (they are now "expert" and the skill has autonomy), starts to increase their attention to small parts of the skill as if they were back in stage one. This can be highly disconcerting because they are now in unfamiliar mental territory, having left that level of awareness many repetitions ago.

WHAT CAUSES TEMPORARY SKILL CONFUSION?

Returning to choking for a moment, Matthew Syed describes it as "a neural glitch that occurs when individuals are under pressure." There are numerous examples of sports performers who have successfully addressed this issue with and without the help of sports psychologists. It must be appreciated that there is no miracle cure. In every case, overcoming the tendency to choke has required a great deal of mental training before returning the athlete to a state where they can compete in a carefree manner while still understanding the importance of peak performance. This is a delicate balance to achieve.

M.C. Day, et al., state "related research suggests that LMS is the result of increased conscious control (Collins, et al., 1999) or fear, anxiety and loss of control (Silva, 1994)."

I think it is reasonable to conclude that a trampoline gymnast succumbing to TSC is responding to some form of stress, anxiety or pressure. Most coaches who have had to deal with TSC already understand this. But what kind of pressure is at work? What is causing the anxiety? Why does the athlete perceive a loss of control?

The need to perform well in competition provides a constant pressure, and this can be increased with the requirement to achieve qualifying scores or even having to use an unfamiliar skill in a compulsory routine. Furthermore, the gymnast may experience unacceptable levels of pressure from parents and/or coaches, as well as the pressure they put on themselves. Many of these pressures can be linked to uncontrollable outcome goals. Coaches need to be wary of too much focus on the athlete's outcome aspirations. The focus should be directed toward the process and performance goals over which the competitor has more control by undertaking appropriate technical training.

Over & Above

If the gymnast suddenly reverts to a conscious control of a skill that has become autonomous, thereby disturbing the way the skill is being performed, I must ask:

"Was the skill in question **actually being performed autonomously** in the first place, or did it just look that way?"

Remember my warning that it is unwise to consider a skill ready based on appearances alone (see Chapter 27: Readiness). There are many performers who are fast learners, and the nature of the trampoline can beguile such an athlete and their coach into a **false belief that solid learning has actually taken place** (see Chapter 11: Trampolining Is Too Easy).

In Day's study, a number of the gymnasts questioned reported that having to learn a specific skill for a compulsory routine had a damaging effect on their confidence. Some reported that the skill in question did not come naturally and the learning process was difficult. Others said they picked up the skill quickly because it was easy to learn. Paradoxically, both of those extremes should ring warning bells. Those who found the learning process difficult probably never attained the status of autonomy for the skill in the first place, rendering it vulnerable to TSC. Those who found it easy to pick up probably didn't go through the learning stages with enough repetitions to reach autonomy. (This is typified by my experience with Simon Rees and the double full.)

The problem is, how do we know when a skill has reached the autonomous stage? It is not like boiling a kettle where the power switches off as soon as the required temperature is reached; no green warning light appears on the gymnast's head to tell us the desired level of learning has been achieved. The coach's experience and judgment are the only indicators available and that places a great responsibility on us to get it right. Part of this responsibility is making sure the skill has been learned by means of progressive practices (preps) and that **each prep is, in itself, autonomous** before moving on. This process of progressive practice not only builds solid skill but enables the coach and gymnast to retrace their steps if difficulties with the whole skill arise later. In other words, **prevention is better than cure** (see Chapter 27: Readiness).

POTENTIAL SKILL TRAPS

There are a number of classic TSC traps lying in wait, but if the coach is sufficiently aware, they can be largely avoided. I hope I can increase that awareness and understanding without creating a sense of paranoia. As with choking, TSC seems to occur most often when everything is going well for the athlete, raising expectations and possibly stimulating faster progress. This can sometimes disrupt the focus on progressing methodically through all the stages of learning.

Most of the following examples are from experiences with my own gymnasts so I know they are real, but I am aware they also occur on a widespread basis. I have tried to indicate possible causes, although the underlying culprit will almost certainly be some form of stress or anxiety, perhaps even unrelated to trampolining.

- A novice jumper having "learned" a tucked back somersault can no longer take-off and simply "freezes." (Insufficient safe, supported repetitions before gradual weaning from support. Uncontrolled head during take-off leading to disorientation and anxiety. Pupil wasn't made aware to look at the bed on coming in to touchdown.)
- An improving novice can no longer jump without performing an involuntary back somersault. (Normally associated with most of the above but also linked to being introduced to the somersault too soon and without sufficient attention being paid to straight jump technique and the process of creating small controllable amounts of backward rotation without travel, through seat and back drops.)
- Similar to the above but most likely to occur with a developing competitive gymnast. The gymnast can't straight jump to any height without doing an involuntary back or front somersault. (Coaches should be able to see this coming because as competitors become confident, they often "flip" a low back or front somersault when they have finished a sequence of skills instead of making a controlled stop. It is essential that the coach adopts zero tolerance to this undesirable habit that can turn into a learned behavior. Insist on a controlled stop every time the required piece of work has been done.)
- A young gymnast, having been taught a barani, can no longer perform a front somersault without twisting. This is a frequent occurrence! (The pupil has been allowed to perform too many consecutive attempts at a half twisting front somersault

without interspersing those attempts with a non-twisting front somersault. Because the front somersault has a blind landing, the gymnast begins to enjoy seeing the bed before touching down from their newly acquired barani. Again, the vigilant coach can see this coming if the gymnast is gradually becoming careless about the tucked or piked shaping of the front somersault. If involuntary twisting does start to occur, the gymnast should be made aware that "if you're actually holding your knees in the tuck, you cannot twist!" The implications of this "lost" front somersault are far reaching and if untreated can stall progress toward half outs, triffs, etc. The problem can be headed off by making sure each barani is alternated with a plain front somersault until autonomy has been achieved in both skills.)

- The gymnast, having "learned" any twisting single somersault can no longer perform the core skill, e.g., can do a full but can no longer do a back somersault without automatically twisting. (The cause of this is likely to be similar to the barani/front somersault confusion. There have been too many reps at the full, without regular reinforcement of the core somersault. The full/ double full confusion tends to occur the same way, although a failure to ensure the gymnast has strong visual control in the full can stimulate a blind head turn, which triggers an accidental double twist. Different mental and physical cues should be built into the learning process to clarify differentiation.)

- Twisting in the first somersault of an intended half out fliff. (Insufficient reps of one and three quarter front, with conscious vision of the bed during the exit to create a reliable checkpoint. Inadequate mental prep of the twist timing, through practices of ballout barani. Failure during basic training to establish that "the twist is the easy bit" and the concept of "learn the move then add the twist." The gymnast can be reassured by knowing that holding the tuck or pike with the hands will prevent accidental early twisting.)

- "Ducking under" when performing double rotations with twist, resulting in an unplanned two-and-three-quarter somersault. (According to Dave Ross, one of the triggers for this confusion can be performing repetitive double porpoises during casual warm-up, linked to a tendency to take-off for a warm up skill, without due attention then turning it under to back landing. As Dave points out, "it is essential during warm up for the gymnast to pay attention and only deliver the intended skill." Also bear in mind that as soon as the performer feels insecurity during flight, they will tend to adopt a protective fetal position. This is equivalent to tucking and causes a sudden acceleration of somersault speed, which the gymnast can't control. It is crucial therefore that the gymnast is encouraged to see at key points in the move as a means of judging when to exit or twist. (This is a significant "banana peel" lying in wait for the advanced performer!)

Those are some classic scenarios, although it doesn't cover all the moves that are TSC-vulnerable. However, any one of those episodes can develop into a progressively damaging chain of events where the performer becomes incapable of committing themselves to take-off for **anything**, regardless of the intended skill.

Let us consider the gymnast's initial reaction when, during a successful training session, they suddenly can't perform a skill that was previously straightforward. This may arise because they took off for the intended move only to find that it turned into something else or they noticed a different sensation during its execution. The full/double full and front somersault/barani confusions are good examples.

The initial response may simply be "oops!" However, the next time they take-off for the move, there is likely to be a small element of doubt. This can be the start of the gymnast revisiting "stage one" of the learning process where concentration and compartmental thinking are employed to try and recover the familiar feeling. As we have seen earlier, this increased level of attention can be disruptive when trying to perform a skill that has already become autonomous. If, after repeated attempts, there isn't a high level of success with performing the planned move, the seed of doubt is likely to germinate and take root.

An episode such as described above can appear relatively innocuous, but we have to consider what happens when the gymnast leaves the training hall and spends time alone. It is here that more damage can be done through what practitioners of Cognitive Behavioral Therapy (CBT) call "ruminating." This is the process of thinking and re-thinking about an issue that is causing concern to the point where the negative aspect looms progressively larger and more real.

Trampoline gymnasts who have reached the level of performance where they can become exposed to TSC will certainly be serious about their sport to the point where memories of the recent training session will remain with them while away from the gym.

Over & Above

They are likely to worry that the confusion will damage their immediate competition plans and, despite trying to remain positive, a corrosive mental process can take place. Of course they will think about many other things away from the gym, but the level of commitment necessary for high achievement guarantees that there will be much mental rehearsal between trainings.

This can be a positive force in the athlete's upward path and should be encouraged (Chapter 23: Getting a Bigger Bang for Your Buck), but when the gymnast ruminates about the strange onset of this relatively minor skill confusion, the level of anxiety can build to uncontrollable levels. This is simply because the sport **really matters** to the gymnast, and I urge coaches to be aware that this process will be taking place within the mind of their gymnast. M.C. Day, et al., stated that:

> *"Self-doubt and negative self-talk were noted as the main reasons for the athlete's inability to perform or attempt the lost move."*

One of the performers interviewed for the study said:

> *"I'd wake up in the morning knowing I had a training session and think I can't do this, I'm not going to do it."*

This repeated negative thinking and perceived failure in subsequent training sessions can very quickly lead to damaged self-esteem where the gymnast's belief in their ability to perform other skills (or indeed to take-off for any skill) becomes undermined.

In my experience, the actual skill-confusion incident is less damaging than its aftermath, which involves rumination and a lack of understanding about what is really going on.

Day states:

> *"A lack of understanding was attributed by 14 participants (out of 15) as being partly responsible for the worsening of LMS. Participants presented two main issues; the first was a general lack of understanding of the syndrome. This lack of understanding of LMS was demonstrated*

> *by participants themselves, friends, family, and even their coach. Secondly, participants also described an inability to explain how they were feeling during this time."*

Here is Day again:

> *"As the syndrome developed, participants noted negative reactions from their coach. These included annoyance, frustration, anger and they felt the coach was ignoring them."*

In the discussion section of her paper, M.C. Day tells us:

> *"It had become apparent in pursuing this study that lost move syndrome is currently an unexplainable and perplexing syndrome for those who suffer from it and their coaches."*

So where does that leave us when faced with managing such a perplexing challenge? I have always believed that in order to succeed in anything, one must understand the challenges ahead so as to construct an effective winning strategy. In other words, we need to know the enemy!

According to Day, we don't understand everything about this particular enemy, but experience tells me that we know enough to construct an effective battle plan. Many coaches and trampoline gymnasts have confronted this foe and triumphed. Dave Ross quotes Bo Turbey, National Coach of Denmark.

> *"Everybody I know who worked at it has solved this problem. The desire to do the skill must be stronger than the fear of failing it."*

Over & Above

BUILD A SOLID DEFENSIVE STRATEGY

Here are my recommendations for defending against the onset of TSC based on what we **do** understand.

1. Progressively develop the gymnast's technique and understanding, including high levels of awareness (visual, kinesthetic, auditory) to arm them against TSC and provide a pathway that can easily be retraced if confusion issues arise.

2. During the learning process, do not be satisfied with a skill looking "right" or even allow the gymnast's confidence to convince you that the learning has actually reached the autonomous stage. Follow the readiness checks from Chapter 27.

3. When developing a skill through the three learning stages, be aware that each stage is not defined by a specific boundary, and the overlaps require constant regression to consolidate previously "learned" components.

4. Take great care when inserting new skills into a competition routine, as the additional pressure can plant self-doubt in the mind of the gymnast even though they may appear to handle the new addition with confidence.

5. Dave Ross warns of two particular areas where the coach must apply strict discipline in order to defend against the onset of TSC.

    a) During casual "freestyle" warm-ups, make sure the gymnast completes the skill intended at take-off because as confidence in aerial awareness increases, there is a risk of a mind-change in flight to "invent" an alternative landing.

    b) Beware athletes who warm up with consecutive double porpoises because they are programming their bodies to duck moves under, creating the potential for an 'accidental' two and three quarter front instead of an intended double somersault with twist.

These "defensive" strategies fit comfortably into the development philosophy promoted throughout this book, but there can be no guarantees that a problem won't arise at some stage.

REHABILITATION OF A GYMNAST WITH TEMPORARY SKILL CONFUSION ISSUES

When dealing with a gymnast who is already affected by TSC, there are a number of different approaches depending on the nature of the issue, e.g., twist confusion, ducking under, inability to take-off, etc. No two gymnasts will react the same way to the problem and, indeed, different gymnasts may be more "far gone" than others. I know from experience, and this is confirmed by Day's research, that the gymnast will feel fearful, frustrated, stupid, anxious and puzzled. We know they won't understand what is happening and will experience a range of negative emotions and plummeting self-esteem. It is crucial therefore that the coach appreciates this and takes steps to demystify the problem and confirm that it is solvable with the right approach.

Here are my recommendations.

1. Treat the occurrence as a "normal" training glitch. If the gymnast has heard of Lost Move Syndrome, discourage the use of the phrase and explain why Temporary Skill Confusion is the appropriate description.

2. Take time away from the trampoline to sit with the gymnast and outline the stages of skill learning and how self-doubt can cause a reversion to the early learning stage where the gymnast thinks their way through the skill like a beginner rather than like the expert who can perform automatically.

3. Explain how this can affect top performers in other sports and can be remedied.

4. Emphasize that you and the gymnast will work together to re-establish normality and give an assurance that you understand the problem.

5. Where possible, try to avoid the gymnast working remedially during sessions where their colleagues are performing normally with ease. This can make matters worse, seriously undermining the affected gymnast's perception of their status within the training group. There is also anecdotal evidence of unaffected gymnasts beginning to doubt their own skill robustness when witnessing a respected teammate having difficulty.

6. Discourage the gymnast from ruminating about the issue when away from the training hall. This is easier said than done, but if the gymnast can be taught a

Over & Above

whole-body relaxation technique to use whenever thoughts of the problem pop into their head, some of the subsequent damage can be limited.

There is no way to make the gymnast feel good about the situation, but the reassurance of being able to rely on an understanding and supportive coach can ensure damage limitation. Those initial six steps should form the basis for remedial work to begin in the gym.

Dave Ross offers much valuable advice:

"Firm control and a one-to-one coaching ratio are best at this point because **the athlete is likely to be his own worst enemy**.*"*

"A positive approach is recommended. All progress should be praised. Write down every time the skill was done correctly. Don't count the total number of tries or the number of mistakes. Keep things positive. The athlete is likely to be lamenting that they can't do today what was easy before. The athlete can only view these small improvements as positive, once he has **fully accepted** *the hole he is in. Then with a commitment to do whatever is needed to climb out, real progress can begin."*

When a range of moves is affected by TSC, an additional strategy can be employed.

Dave Ross again:

> "The basis for this approach is to define the 'circle of confidence.' Find out which skills the athlete can still do with complete confidence. **Spend most of the workout time in the circle of confidence**. Make up drills and routines which allow the athlete complete success. This will help the athlete to regain self-confidence. Then venture outside the circle of confidence and try to capture a skill from outside and slowly bring it inside."

I have even suggested to Dave that this imaginative concept could be represented graphically by the gymnast in their training diary as a further means of enlisting their engagement with the solution.

Until now, everything I have written has been directed at the positive process of developing excellence. It was with some reluctance that I included a dissertation on what could hardly be considered a creative part of trampoline gymnastics. However, to avoid the subject would have been like denying the presence of yet another elephant in the room. It is likely that every coach will have to deal with such issues as they and their gymnasts aim for world class performance. Intelligent, empathetic coaching can do much to prevent the onset of TSC and, should it arise, an understanding of the issues involved can significantly assist rehabilitation and the fulfillment of long-term goals.

CHAPTER 32

THE THIRTY ESSENTIAL PRINCIPLES

SECTION FOUR
MAXIMIZING POTENTIAL

The Thirty Essential Principles

This thirty-point practical guide distils the essence of knowledge gained from fifty years coaching trampoline gymnastics where my ideas and methods have continually responded to developments in equipment, advances in athlete preparation, and the changing demands of the FIG Code of Points.

There is no fast track to excellence. There is no magic formula. These principles will only deliver high-quality performance if they are applied with intelligence, consistency, and commitment. This is a **framework** allowing coaches to use individual creativity and initiative as they strive to develop World Class Trampoline Gymnasts.

THE PRINCIPLES

1. All trampoline take-offs are simply straight jumps with various modifications.

In a straight jump, the force applied by the gymnast depresses the bed, and the resultant recoil is transmitted through an upright posture to produce flight without rotation. When this process is repeated with varying degrees of force redirected around either of the main axes, somersault and/or twist rotation is created. The skill of modifying the straight jump to the right degree, at the right time during bed recoil, is crucial to the performance of complex moves with height and control.

Over & Above

2. **Straight jumping is an example of a "closed skill."**

Many sports skills are classed as "open skills" because they require the performer to respond to a range of changing and unexpected situations. Games-playing skills typify this and the trampoline gymnast in mid routine will also be in an "open-skill" situation when mistakes occur that require instantaneous and unplanned reactions. Straight jumping, however, takes place in a closed environment and, as such, should be treated as a "closed" skill. A characteristic of a closed skill is the ability to practice it to the point of perfection. The aspiring World Class trampolinist must practice straight jumping to the point where no amount of competition stress can interfere with its height, accuracy and control.

3. **Straight jumping drills should form part of every training session.**

Following Principles 1 and 2, straight jumping must become the core of every training session until the gymnast gains total command over balance, posture, placement and height. Drill variations are required to sustain interest and should be capable of measurement in order to identify whether the gymnast has indeed acquired straight jumping as a "closed skill."

4. **The gymnast must become consistently aware of the moment when the "top" of a straight jump has been reached.**

It must not be assumed that the gymnast is intuitively aware of that "magic moment" when they have stopped going up but have not yet started to come down. This is the vertex of the flight parabola but should be referred to as "top." This is the constant reference point against which both coach and gymnast assesses height maintenance.

5. **All shaped and twisting jumps must hit the top. Seen by the coach and felt or perceived by the gymnast.**

*This process highlights the gymnast's need to begin shaping before the top is reached in order to show the shape at the "top." This has a strong relationship to the eventual shaping of somersaults that exit **at** the top. When performing twisting jumps, the gymnast must be encouraged to develop delicacy during the twisting action during bed contact to minimize any loss of top.*

6. The flight phase leading to all body landings (seat, back, and front) should hit the TOP, STOP then DROP!

These body landings have a greater importance than simple control of the body part that contacts the bed (a key safety factor of course). In the context of developing World Class execution, the flight phase from feet to the top is crucial because each of these skills is a microcosm of all backward and forward somersault take-offs.

7. Coaches should adopt a "zero tolerance" standard to all basic take-offs. This can be described as "beam routine accuracy."

*The artistic gymnast performing a beam routine does so with unerring accuracy. Why? Because she has to! Trampoline gymnasts, even at the highest levels, perform most routines with a wide margin of tolerance. Why? Because they **can**! During the development process, all jumps, body landings and single somersaults should be performed with the accuracy of the artistic gymnast performing on the beam **before progressing to more complex work**! Lack of "beam routine accuracy" in early development inevitably leads to control problems during the performance of more challenging work.*

8. "Checkpoints" or "sighting points" must be emphasized in the learning of all skills.

From the beginner's first jump, the coach should emphasize the importance of seeing the bed at key points in a movement. This becomes even more important when a specific action like an exit or a twist has to be activated in flight. It should never be assumed that, just because the gymnast is performing the movement with apparent skill, they can actually see or know where they are. Only by asking can the coach be sure that the performer is seeing. The answer may well be, "My eyes are closed!"

9. The other senses, notably feeling and hearing, should be used in conjunction with vision to enhance the gymnast's developing awareness.

Gifted gymnasts often have an innate ability to sense body position or aerial orientation. It is unwise to allow the gymnast to rely solely on this ability, and it is necessary to reinforce awareness through the employment of all the senses. Kinesthetic awareness is indeed a gift, but if totally relied upon, the gymnast can become unsettled when a familiar skill "feels" different from the norm. The inappropriately named "lost move" problem can be avoided and even rehabilitated by ensuring that the gymnast has a range of sensory cues or references available.

Over & Above

10. The principles listed so far make exacting demands on coach and gymnast so it is important to balance disciplined work with fun and challenge during training.

Coaches should not be afraid to demand high levels of accuracy and control during the development years and may be surprised how well their pupils respond to exacting standards. The nature of trampolining does however appeal to many beginners as a fun activity, and it is important to create a balance between work and play. Sound judgment is required when striking this balance.

11. Coaches must learn to focus their attention on the application and direction of forces as they are applied through correct body posture during the period of bed contact rather than being distracted by what is seen in the air.

This focus can be challenging for many coaches because the aerial phase attracts most attention and is visible for much longer than the period of bed contact. Furthermore, the bed contact phase is largely out of sight due to the masking effect of the frame and bed. This contrasts with the focus of a diving coach who can stand on the pool deck to get a complete view of the depression and rise of the springboard in response to the performer's actions. Coaches should consider using different viewpoints to aid their focus on the "business end" of the gymnast's work.

12. Aerial aesthetics must be regarded as less important than timing and technique during bed contact.

Good form or execution as assessed by the judges is only achieved as a result of technical efficiency during bed contact. Attempting to polish aerial form in order to improve the judges' scores is counterproductive when developing excellence. This is a short-term policy. It is cosmetic and as such masks the technical faults that will inhibit long-term progress. Height, direction, and accuracy must be given priority even if, in the short term, form marks may be lost.

13. Following the application of principles 4, 5 and 6, single somersaults must be taught with the emphasis on top rather than speed of rotation.

Potential World Class trampolinists must be comfortable with spending time in the air, and coaches must facilitate this. During the teaching of somersaults there is a risk that the priority will be speed of rotation rather than height. There is, of course, a need to ensure that early attempts are performed with a safe amount of surplus rotation, but gradually the vertical direction should take precedence. "High and slow is the way to go!"

14. Before allowing a developing gymnast to link somersaults (including somersaults linked with jumps) the coach must ensure the individual somersaults are performed with top. In other words, *"direction must precede connection."*

The linking of somersaults should be discouraged when the direction of the initial somersault is poor. If a somersault has travelled or lost height, the gymnast has created a problem to solve, in addition to the challenge of linking to another skill. Trampolining is a game of consequences wherein each element performed leaves the gymnast with a reward or a penalty. Coaches must insist that the linear direction of each somersault results in a near-vertical descent to the bed thus providing the reward of a perfect first contact with the bed. The touchdown (first contact) from a somersault should replicate the outcome of an "arm set" from straight jumping.

15. The coach must enable the gymnast to become comfortable with somersault landings that may at first feel "short."

When approaching first contact with the bed following a somersault, the gymnast's instinct will be to "land" upright. This comes from the misconception that when the bed comes into view, it is like the floor. The coach needs to help the gymnast appreciate that as the feet contact the bed, the bed moves downward dropping the performer into a "hole." The objective must be to make first contact slightly "short" and arrive in an upright posture when the bed has become fully depressed.

16. The coach and gymnast must understand and adopt the principle of First Contact (F/C) ... Full Depression (F/D) ... Last Contact (L/C).

The first contact or "touchdown" is NOT the landing but simply the first point in the **landing phase** that continues until full depression is reached. The **landing phase** is then complete and the **take-off phase** begins. The **take-off phase** continues as the bed rises and is only completed when the gymnast is propelled into the air at **last contact**.

Over & Above

17. The landing and take-off phases should be referred to by coach and gymnast in relation to the gymnast's bodily actions rather than using the simplistic and misleading references to "landing" and "take-off."

*This follows from Principles 11 and 12, which emphasized the need to focus on bed action rather than aerial outcome. By referring to the different phases of bed action, the coach starts to help the gymnast appreciate not only **what** action to perform but **when** to perform it. It must be stressed that the F/C, F/D, L/C concept is simplistic because there are numerous intermediate points in the bed's fall and rise between those three staging points. Sophisticated coaching begins to address the challenge of the gymnast matching body and limb action to the particular timing of the bed's movement.*

18. Once this concept is adopted, the coach should eliminate misleading words and phrases from the vocabulary.

To say "at take-off" now becomes nonsensical because there is no "instant" of take-off. It is a process that starts at F/D and finishes at L/C. The specific point in the process should now be referred to using language such as "when you approached last contact." The statement "when you landed" is equally nonsensical because the landing phase is also a process and not an instant. If the coach is referring to the moment of first contact then that is precisely what should be said, e.g., "As you made first contact with the bed." Equally accurate and helpful is to say, "when your feet first touched the bed" or "at touchdown." Conversely, the coach should encourage the gymnast to refer to the various points in the landing and take-off phases with similar accuracy. The value of mutual communication like this cannot be over emphasized in the drive toward excellence.

19. As young gymnasts begin to develop their jumping height, the coach should highlight the regular tempo created through the depression and rise of the bed. The gymnast can be helped to appreciate this with the analogy of a musical beat.

The lead-in jumps before a routine set the tempo, just as a drum beat might set the tempo for a piece of music. The tempo is created by the feet contacting the bed ... "DOWN" followed immediately by the recoil. ... "UP." So a series of straight jumps creates the music-like tempo DOWN/UP ... DOWN/UP ... DOWN/UP. This sets the tempo for the routine, combination or individual skill that follows, and the aim should be to maintain the DOWN/UP rhythm throughout that work.

20. The awareness of tempo should be linked to the pre-existing understanding of top, thereby differentiating between the bed contact period and the longer aerial phase. The extended tempo concept now has three beats. DOWN ——— UP ————————————— TOP.

Depending on the gymnast's stage of development, attention can be focused on any one of the points in the three-beat tempo. Reminders of top awareness or the down/up beat should be frequent, and it should not be assumed that, following initial practice, the gymnast has mastered these reference points.

21. The gymnast must learn to perform "bed down ... body up" as the means of completing one skill prior to the start of the next.

*Coaches frequently urge their gymnasts to raise their arms vertically in the transition between the landing and take-off phases. It is absolutely right to stress this, but ironically the best way to achieve it is **not** to emphasize the arm swing/reach. Frequently, the gymnast will focus on swinging the arms up but omit the most important action ... raising the torso until it is at a right angle to the floor. If the arms are raised but the body remains in the forward inclining posture of first contact then a flawed take-off phase is likely. Conversely, if the coach focuses the gymnast's attention on "bed down ... body up," the arms are likely to swing through and reach vertically, achieving the desired result.*

22. The gymnast must acquire the ability to regard the "finish" of each somersault as the moment full depression has been reached following first contact.

*One of the most frequent causes of routine failure is when the gymnast anticipates the end of one skill and starts preparing prematurely for the next take-off. This is usually the result of the gymnast interpreting the touchdown or first contact as the "landing." This is a unique difficulty in trampolining because of the bed's non-floor-like behavior. The gymnast's vision and body awareness has to be retrained to become patient following first contact and to apply "bed down ... body up" before arriving at the **true finish of the skill**.*

Over & Above

23. The shaping and straightening of somersaults should be treated as biomechanical requirements, not as an aesthetic exercise. Shaping is designed to accelerate, while straightening slows rotation. Somersault exits must be *appropriate* to the height, speed, direction and time available in each *specific* instance.

The take-off quality should determine the point at which the gymnast exits the somersault. Often a gymnast will "pike down" because spatial awareness informs them that producing a straight-body exit would result in a dangerously short landing. They have sensed that the somersault is too low or too slow. Coaches may attribute the lack of a straight exit to the gymnast's poor aesthetic sense or even laziness. Quality coaching looks beyond the obvious to trace the root cause, which will almost certainly be related to the bed contact phase.

24. With developing gymnasts it is a mistake to demand adult aerial form in terms of somersault exits until the quality of work during the bed contact phase delivers sufficient height and direction. *Allow* the gymnast to develop earlier, straighter and longer exits *gradually* as strength and technique improve.

It is folly to attempt spectacular "zero deduction" exits before the gymnast has mastered the principle of "every take-off is a modified straight jump." Indeed, many promising juniors have failed to make the transition to successful seniors due to this misguided approach.

25. In all twisting skills, whether somersault rotation is involved or not, *the twist is the easy bit!*

*When a gymnast is learning to insert a twist into a jump or somersault, there is an understandable desire to focus on the new additional element. Not only does this present a conceptual dilemma but the physical challenge of performing two contrasting actions with different power inputs can cause further confusion. In a half in, half out fliffus for example, the somersault requires a different power input in terms of height and rotation compared to the twist (if executed during contact). In this case, three different directions of force with three different amounts of power input applied simultaneously! These mental and technical factors are not helped by the way many twisting skills are annotated. The words "half in - half out" only refer to the twist element. The skill is in fact a double somersault with full twist. **That** use of words prioritizes the somersault element.*

A "full twisting back" also highlights twist in its wording, whereas "back somersault with full twist" makes the somersault the technical priority. I am not advocating an official change of wording for such skills but would advise coaches to consider ways of communicating the nature of twisting skills in a way that is more conducive to the gymnast understanding the power balance

26. In all twisting skills, the priority is the *right* amount of height, somersault speed, and airtime to enable the right body shape to be achieved for a long enough time to allow the twist to work.

*That statement holds true for twisting jumps, as well as twisting somersaults. The **right** amount of somersault rotation in a jump is, of course, none! Frequently, poor twisting is the result of poor body alignment at the right time to enable twisting to be initiated, or indeed to be allowed to continue. A gymnast failing to learn a twisting skill often runs out of airtime before the twisting action can take effect. Coaches encountering twisting difficulties should first address the power and directional inputs during the bed contact phase before tinkering with twisting technique. This should be addressed through the core skill upon which the twisting skill is based. For example, barani difficulties should be addressed through revision of the tucked and piked front somersaults.*

27. Tariff or routine difficulty (DD) should only be increased when a minimum agreed score can be consistently achieved with the existing routine.

*Execution and technique are far more important than DD in terms of total score and **long-term development**. The scoring system supports this. A competitor increasing DD by 0.9 can have that "advantage" wiped out by a resulting 0.1 execution deduction from three single elements! The introduction of time of flight shines the spotlight even more brightly on technical execution over difficulty. The world's best performers of course, score highly on all three counts.*

28. Difficulty should be easy!

New and more difficult combinations should be developed as a result of a sound basic technique. It is coaching folly to expect that basic technique can be improved at the same time as working on challenging, complex skills and combinations. This can only be achieved by working basic drills and combinations of reduced difficulty before a gradual transfer to more complex situations.

Over & Above

29. Simplify and simulate, don't complicate!

Find ways to simulate complex combinations using the generic technical factor. A combination such as piked half out, double back, tucked half out, could be simulated in a variety of ways, for example, replacing the double back with a straight back somersault or substituting a piked barani for the piked half out. All that is required is an appreciation of the generic quality to be practiced and a little imagination. This process of simulation can deliver results even when the difficulty score is in the high teens.

30. New routines and combinations should be trialed and practiced in controlled events before exposure to major combination.

Working on the principle that "difficulty should be easy," developing gymnasts need time to assimilate new and more demanding skills into competition routines. Several exposures (in full or in part) should be undertaken until the gymnast has complete confidence in the new work. If insufficient low-level competitions are available then internal simulations should be arranged. "Too many gymnasts are afraid of their routines!" The gymnast must be able to approach the voluntary routine at a major event with total confidence in their ability to execute, their only concern being the quality of performance.

FINALLY: The most effective coach is the one who progressively manages to become redundant!

The skillful coach will work to improve the gymnast's decision-making ability to the point where they can perform independently in competition. An aspiring World Class gymnast must be prepared to deal with unusual training and competition conditions when representing their country. They may even find themselves in an unfriendly team environment with a team coach who is unfamiliar with their work. Personal coaches should have conducted a gradual weaning process over a period of years to enable their pupil to perform robustly, regardless of the circumstances.

The Thirty Essential Principles

The author during the 1980s.

CHAPTER 33
CONCLUSION

SECTION FOUR
MAXIMIZING POTENTIAL

Conclusion

In writing this book, I have shared many of my coaching experiences and provided advice and information "over and above" anything previously written about trampoline gymnastics. This volume captures the essential ingredients for high achievement in a sport that is constantly evolving, but I believe my words will transcend all future developments. The basic formula for achieving excellence does not change!

It is my sincere wish that coaches and gymnasts will have been informed and inspired by some (if not all) of my writing. My current knowledge and skills owe a great deal to the many trampoline pioneers, and I have simply tried to contribute my own experience to the development of our wonderful sport.

Our goal has always been a simple one ... to fly with style and complexity "over and above" George Nissen's amazing creation!

Over & Above

REFERENCES

1. *This is Trampolining: Two Seconds of Freedom.* Frank La Due and Jim Norman. Nissen Trampoline Company, Cedar Rapids, Iowa.

2. *Trampoline Tumbling.* Larry Griswold. Fred Medart Manufacturing Company, St Louis, Mo. Kessinger Publishing. www.kessinger.net

3. *The Talent Code.* Daniel Coyle. Arrow Books. ISBN 9780099519850.

4. *The Sports Gene: What Makes the Perfect Athlete.* David Epstein. Yellow Jersey Press, London. ISBN 9780224092081. www.vintage-books.co.uk

5. "The Causes of and Psychological Responses to Lost Move Syndrome in National Level Trampolinists." M.C. Day and Joanne Thatcher. University of Wales, Bangor.

6. *Bounce: How Champions Are Made.* Matthew Syed. Fourth Estate. Harper Collins Publishers. ISBN 978-0-00-735052. www.4thestate.co.uk

7. *Fitness Training for Trampoline.* Simon Breivik MSc. BSc (Hons) Gymcraft, December 2006. British Gymnastics, Ford Hall, Lilleshall National Sports Centre, Newport, Shropshire. TF10 9NB.

ACKNOWLEDGEMENTS

Although this book outlines my experience and current coaching philosophy, it is by no means the end of that journey as I continue to keep my eyes and mind open. I owe much of my current practice to all the coaches and gymnasts I have had the pleasure of working with over the last fifty years. Many believed that I was the one doing the teaching, and they didn't realize just how much I was learning from them. Thank you, all!

I am particularly indebted to Graham Parker for his determination and commitment to enable my philosophy and method to reach the whole trampoline community. Graham joined my club in the 1980s as a raw but athletic 21-year-old trampoline fanatic. Together we transformed his technique to the point where he was scoring 27.00 plus for compulsory routines and competing at the highest national level. If only he had walked into my gym as a 12-year-old!

While I banged away at the laptop keys, Graham was taking care of all the logistics that would turn my manuscript into a published volume. Yes, he has been like my "agent" but that doesn't fully cover the role he has played in encouraging my efforts, offering critiques, and taking care of business. He also introduced me to the distinguished graphics artist who produced the illustrations and cover designs. Despite being Graham's older brother, Peter Parker knew nothing about trampoline gymnastics and spent many hours trying to understand what I wanted from each illustration. He is a man of infinite patience and consummate skill.

I was delighted that my long-time friend Mitch Fenner agreed to write the foreword, taking time out from his current role in transforming men and boys' gymnastics in Holland. We have had an association lasting over forty years, and I am proud that this innovative and passionate coaching celebrity was prepared to provide the springboard for my literary efforts.

It is doubtful whether I would have committed myself to this work had it not been for one of Mitch Fenner's former gymnasts, Olympian Jeff Davies. Jeff was keen to launch a technical magazine on behalf of British Gymnastics and persuaded me to write a few articles for *Gymcraft*. The "few" articles soon became "many," with Jeff assuring me that they would provide the ideal platform for writing a book. He was right!

Over & Above

However, it was only when Dave Kingaby and Paul Kitchen of Brentwood Trampoline Club asked my permission to publish the articles on their website that I realized how many people were interested in what I had to say. I started receiving emails from across the world seeking advice and guidance, as well as permission to reproduce some of my ideas in club coaching manuals.

It was gratifying to know that Dave Ross was prepared to let me pass on some of his ideas, and he was generous enough to endorse my writing as a means of getting his ideas out there. Have you noticed how truly great practitioners have no fear of people "stealing" their ideas? They just want to share the passion that made them great in the first place.

My former colleague at British Gymnastics, Sports Physiologist Simon Breivik displayed a similar willingness to share his expertise, and I thank him for our many conversations and his contribution to chapter 24.

If any of this work makes sense and is written in passable English, it is due to the red pen of Sarah Burson. It would be true to say that Sarah was my first reader. Thank you, Sarah!

The process of writing has been a formidable task but the costs and logistics involved with creating the finished volume have been equally challenging. I am grateful for the invaluable support of Eurotramp's Denis Hack along with the cooperation of Claire Greenstreet and the directors of Gymaid Ltd.

Finally, the task of converting my manuscript into a finished volume has been coordinated by Sabine Carduck of Meyer and Meyer Sport. She has my sincere thanks for the professional and tolerant way she has dealt with my many pedantic requests.

CREDITS

Coverdesign: Sabine Groten

Cover graphic: Peter Parker

Graphics: Peter Parker

Typesetting and layout: Claudia Sakyi

Copy editing: Michelle Demeter

Photos:

Mitch Fenner personal archive: pp.9, 31
Jan de Koning Fotografie: p.10
Fédération Internationale de Gymnastique: pp.11, 69, 80/81, 91, 97, 139, 147, 181, 303
Jack Kelly personal archive: pp.15, 18, 23, 47, 51, 58/59, 264
Nissen Trampoline Company: pp.25, 36, 78
Harlow Gazette: pp.26, 33, 38, 45, 52, 53
Herts and Essex Newspapers: p.27
Aubrey E. Smith: p.30
British Amateur Gymnastics Association: p.32
BTF News: p.54
Scottish Amateur Swimming Association: p.62
David Lewis: p.65
Graham Parker: p.122
Bo Tureby: p.231
Dave Ross personal archive: p.262
R.C. Walker: p.269
Gymaid Ltd.: p.295

There are instances where we have been unable to trace or contact the copyright holder. If notified the publisher will be pleased to rectify any errors or omissions at the earliest opportunity.

„It is a pleasure and honour for us to support and congratulate Jack Kelly on this great book!"

EUROTRAMP®
TRAMPOLINE

🏠 eurotramp.com   f EurotrampTrampoline

Gym-aid

🏠 gymaid.com   f Gymaid